USSR

CHAHAR

A

Kueisui   Kalgan
Paotou   Pingsui
          Railway
SUIYUAN   Tatung   HOPEH
                              Pinghan Railway
         SHANSI
Yellow River   Taiyuan
Yenan   Grand
         Tungpu Railway   Canal
              Chengchou
    Sian   Lunghai Railway
SHENSI   HONAN

HUPEI
ECHUAN
              Wuhan
Yangtze
Chungking

         Changsha
         HUNAN
         Hengyang   KWANGSI   FUKIEN
KWEICHOU   Taipei
         Kweilin   **TAIWAN**
KIANGSI   Yung Chiang   KWANGTUNG
Hsi Chiang   Canton

Hanoi

NA

The Greatest Tumult

The Chinese Civil War 1936–49

The Greatest Tumult
The Chinese Civil War 1936–49

E. R. HOOTON

BRASSEY'S (UK)
Member of Maxwell Macmillan Pergamon Publishing Corporation
LONDON · OXFORD · WASHINGTON · NEW YORK · BEIJING
FRANKFURT · SÃO PAULO · SYDNEY · TOKYO · TORONTO

First edition 1991

UK editorial offices: Brassey's, 50 Fetter Lane, London EC4A 1AA
orders: Brassey's, Headington Hill Hall, Oxford OX3 0BW

USA editorial offices: Brassey's, 8000 Westpark Drive, Fourth Floor, McLean, Virginia 22102
orders: Macmillan, Front and Brown Streets, Riverside, New Jersey 08075

Distributed in North America to booksellers and wholesalers by the Macmillan Publishing Company, N.Y., N.Y.

Library of Congress Cataloging-in-Publication Data
Hooton, E. R.
The greatest tumult: the Chinese civil war, 1936–49 / by E. R. Hooton. — 1st ed.
p.   cm.
Includes index.
1. China—History—1937–1945.   2. China—History—Civil War, 1945–1949.   I. Title.
DS777.518.H66   1991
951.04'2—dc20   90–26363

British Library Cataloguing in Publication Data
Hooton, E. R.
The greatest tumult: the Chinese Civil War 1936–49
1. China. Wars. History 1927–49
I. Title
951.042

ISBN 0–08–036690–2

Printed in Great Britain by B.P.C.C. Wheatons Ltd. Exeter

Contents

List of Plates

List of Plates

List of Maps

Preface

DESPITE the importance of the Chinese Civil War there has been no detailed account of the conflict for some 25 years. At that time a translation was published of an account by the French General Chassin, written in the early 1950s! The prime purpose of this book is to fill that gap but it is no more than a pathfinding work, pending the complete opening of the archives of both sides. Yet I trust that scholars of modern Chinese history will find it of value for, while that great nation's political and social scenes have been examined in detail, its military history has been neglected.

A re-examination of the war suggests that many previous assumptions have been inaccurate. The brilliance of the Communist general Lin Piao's Manchurian campaigns has blinded observers to the fact that it was his colleagues Liu Po-cheng and Chen Yi in central China who really broke the backbone of the Nationalist régime. By wrecking the enemy army, they both shattered the régime's foundations and destroyed its political credibility in a region where it enjoyed its greatest apparent success.

The Communist victory is often portrayed as the triumph of guerillas but this too is a false assumption. Guerilla warfare is popularly portrayed as a conflict involving armed civilians but this is only the first stage. In China the guerilla quickly became a professional soldier operating in formations which engaged the enemy army in mobile warfare using light infantry tactics. Eventually these People's Liberation Army (PLA) formations could meet the enemy on equal terms, either in the field or in positional warfare. Guerilla warfare ('sparrow warfare' in Chinese Communist jargon) supported these later operations, harassing enemy communications and diluting Nationalist power. Whilst the philosophy of sparrow warfare exerted a profound influence at all levels, the PLA's senior commanders recognised that the only means of securing a decisive victory was to destroy the enemy army. For this reason, they preferred semi-conventional operations.

While guerilla warfare assisted the PLA in its military operations, it was fundamentally part of the political process by which the Communists mobilised the masses. By weakening the Nationalist security forces in the countryside, while eroding the political and social influence of the traditional rural leaders, guerilla operations supported the Party's political activity. By winning over the majority of the peasants, the Party created an infrastructure which provided the PLA with supplies, labour and recruits. I have tried to describe this relationship between guerilla warfare and the political process and how mobilisation was achieved and this has required some description of rural conditions. However, as there are numerous works on Chinese rural life and Communist mobilisation techniques, I have deliberately dealt with this subject in outline only. For the same reason, I have largely ignored the political and diplomatic aspects of the Civil War except where they were relevant to the military conflict.

I have paid greater attention to the two armies, especially the Nationalist's whose motivations might otherwise seem bizarre in Western eyes and which contemporary American observers from Stilwell onwards seemed unable to comprehend. PLA motivations were more understandable but the unusual triple-tiered organisation is worthy of closer examination, especially for those unfamiliar with revolutionary warfare. I have also tried to provide some information on the background of the leading military personalities in order to begin the process of characterisation and lift them above the level of the stereotype. A point worth making here is that, on both sides, generals who showed concern for their men's welfare (such as Fu Tso-yi) inspired a dog-like devotion among the soldiers and they could, in Ho Lung's words, '... lead them to the gates of Hell'.

Readers may well be surprised that Mao Tse-tung seems to figure so little in the text while Chiang Kai-shek is prominent. The reason is that Mao played little direct part in the military, as distinct from social–political events, as indeed the famed

Thoughts of Chairman Mao would appear to confirm. By contrast, Chiang was the key figure in Nationalist China, as he so cruelly demonstrated to Acting President Li in 1949.

For military readers, this work examines both the basics of revolutionary war and its application at the 'operational' rather than tactical level. Western military students have only recently become aware of warfare at the 'operational' level (see p. 189f/n9) and still conceive of it in mechanised warfare terms. Yet the Chinese Communists practised it with armies little different from those which fought in the Napoleonic and American Civil Wars and were capable of making such movements with crude communications in conditions of absolute enemy air superiority. This ability should, I suggest, inspire further study.

The Chinese Civil War is closely entwined with the First Indochina War (1945–54) and the Korean War (1950–53). The part played by both the Nationalists and the Communists in the Viet Minh's victory might also well be worthy of further study. It is interesting to note that the Yunnan troops who supplied the Viet Minh with weapons in 1945–46 were later transferred to Manchuria, defected in 1948 and in 1950 became part of the Chinese expeditionary force in Korea.

Purists may well quibble at my use of the Wade–Giles form of transliteration when the more accurate Pingyin form is now more commonly accepted. I have retained the older method because most English-language sources use this. I have used Pingyin only when referring to titles published in the People's Republic of China. Place names are based upon spellings in the Times Atlas of China.

Because their names are universally known I have often referred to Chiang Kai-shek and Mao Tse-tung as Chiang and Mao while with other names I have usually given both the family and personal names. Where a person appears frequently in a chapter, I have taken the liberty of simply referring to him by his family name e.g. Nieh Jung-chen becomes Nieh, Fu Tso-yi becomes Fu or, where appropriate, by his nickname either in full or abbreviated form e.g. 'One-eyed Dragon' (Liu Po-cheng), 'King of the Northwest' (Hu Tsung-nan). In describing the campaigns, I have adopted a geographic, rather than chrono-logical approach because of the distinctive styles of operation in each theatre and because it facilitates understanding by the reader.

Nationalist units are given numerical designations (e.g. 32nd Army) while Communist ones are given alphabetical ones (e.g. Fourth Army). Until 1949, Communist field armies had their own designations for subordinate armies (i.e. First, Second, etc.) and to avoid confusion where two field armies operated in conjunction, I have applied a simplified designation e.g. the First Army of the Central China Field Army becomes the First Central Army while the First Army of the East China Field Army becomes the First Eastern Army. With regard to formations, the Chinese system is extremely confusing for two or three divisions (*shih*) formed a *chun*, which is organisationally a corps, although strictly translated it is an 'army'. By describing a *chun* as a corps, conventional descriptions of larger concentrations may be given e.g. army rather than 'group army'.

In researching this book I have largely relied upon secondary sources, partly because full access to primary sources is not available and partly because these works represent a largely untapped seam of knowledge. I would like to express my appreciation to my friend Raymond Cheung and to the staffs of Langley Library, Berkshire and the library of the School of Oriental and African Studies (SOAS) for their courtesy, consideration and assistance. I must also express my gratitude to many individuals who provided data and comments. These include Gary Bjorge of the Combat Studies Institute of the US Army's Command and General Staff College, Mr Danny J. Crawford, head of the reference section of the US Marine Corps History and Museums Division, Major General Chang Chao-jen, Director of the Military History and Compilation Bureau, Ministry of National Defence, Taiwan, Mr Edward C. Ezell, Curator of the National Firearms Collection at the National Museum of American History, Smithsonian Institution, Mr Lee Ness, Will Fowler, Keith O'Callaghan, Lieutenant Colonel William Prince as well as my cartographers Nikki Benge and Tony Wright. I would also like to thank my researchers and translators Frank Dikkotter, Sue Whitfield, and Katherine Till.

I owe a special debt of thanks to Mr R. G. Tiedemann, Lecturer in the History of the Far East at SOAS who reviewed the original drafts and made many valuable suggestions. Thanks are also owed to Major General Tony Trythall, Executive Deputy Chairman of Brassey's and to Angela Clark, the General Manager, for their encouragement and advice.

Last, and by no means least, I must thank my wife Melinda for her patience during my mental departure to China and for all her support while I worked upon this project.

E. R. HOOTON

Chronology

1918

November   11:   End of the First World War

1919

May   4:   Protests by Peking students against China's treatment at the Paris Peace Conference leads to a political and cultural renaissance in China.

         7:   Treaty of Versailles

October   10:   Sun Yat-sen reorganises the China Revolutionary Party into the Chinese National People's Party (Kuomintang).

1920

May: Creation of the Chinese Communist Party

1921

July   23–31:   First Congress of the Chinese Communist Party in Shanghai. Attended by 15 delegates including Mao Tse-tung.

1923

January   26:   Sun Yat-sen and the Soviet Union sign an agreement by which the latter will assist the former to reunify China by providing arms and advisers.

1924

January   21:   Congress of the Kuomintang at Canton to prepare for national reunification

1925

March   12:   Sun Yat-sen dies

1926

June   5:   Chiang Kai-shek becomes Commander-in-Chief of the National Revolutionary Army (NRA)

July   1:   Northern Expedition, a military campaign to unify China under the Kuomintang, begins

1927

March   22:   NRA enters Shanghai

April   12:   Chiang Kai-shek begins purge of Communists

	18:	Chiang and the Right Wing Kuomintang establish government at Nanking
	27:	Communists and Left Wing Kuomintang create rival government to Chiang Kai-shek at Wuhan
May	5:	Chiang Kai-shek defeats the Wuhan government
August	1:	Communist uprising at Nanchang. This is regarded as the Red Army's birthday
	5:	Red Army abandons Nanchang
October	:	Mao Tse-tung establishes revolutionary base in Kiangsi. Other bases are established in central and southern China

1928

| June | 8: | NRA takes Peking which is renamed Peiping on June 28 |
| October | 10: | Chiang Kai-shek becomes Chairman of the Nationalist Government |

1930

| December | : | First of the 'Bandit Extermination Campaigns' against Chinese Communist bases. Others followed in April 1931, July 1931, the summer of 1932 and April 1933. None is successful |

1931

| September | 19: | The Mukden Incident leads to the Japanese occupation of Manchuria |

1933

| December | : | Opening of the Fifth Bandit Extermination Campaign. By September 1934 this is on the verge of crushing the Communist bases. |

1934

| October | 18: | The Communists abandon their bases and begin the Long March first westwards then northwards seeking secure new territory. |

1935

| September | 21: | The end of the Long March as the |

Communists reach Kansu. Later they move into Shensi establishing a new capital at Yenan

1936

December 12–25: Sian Mutiny

1937

July 7: Outbreak of the China Incident
December 13: Japanese take Nanking

1938

May 20: Japanese take Hsuchou
October 21: Japanese take Canton
  25: Japanese take Wuhan

1940

March 30: Japanese establish puppet government under Wang Ching-wei at Nanking

August 20–
November 30: The Hundred Regiments Offensive

1941

January 1–7 New Fourth Army Incident in Anhwei. Nationalist forces destroy headquarters of Communist New Fourth Army.

December 7: Japanese attack Pearl Harbour

1942

March 7: Rangoon, capital of Burma, falls
May 1: Fall of Mandalay in Burma completes isolation of Nationalist China

1944

May 7– Japanese Ichigo Offensive inflicts major
November 30: defeat upon Nationalist forces in central and southern China

1945

April 23: Communist Seventh National Congress (to June 11)

August 6: Atom bomb dropped on Hiroshima
  9: Atom bomb dropped on Nagasaki
USSR enters the war against Japan
  10: Japan orders ceasefire

	14:	Japan surrenders
		Sino-Soviet Treaty of Friendship and Alliance
	20:	Communists take Kalgan
	23:	Nationalists order Japanese to hold their positions until relieved by Chungking troops
	28:	Mao arrives in Chungking
	30:	Shangtang Mountains Campaign in Shensi (to October 8)
September	9:	Cannon Project (to September 28)
	30:	US marines begin to land in north China
October	10:	Adjournment of negotiations between Communists and Nationalists
	18:	Kueisui–Paotou Campaign in Suiyan (to December 7)
	24:	Chang River Battle on Hopeh–Honan border (to November 2)
November	1:	Liaoning Corridor Campaign in Manchuria (to November 29)
	26:	Hurley resigns
	27:	Marshall appointed as Truman's special representative
December	15:	Announcement of Marshall Mission
	23:	Marshall arrives in China

1946

January	10:	Ceasefire agreement (takes effect January 13)
	11:	PCC meets (until January 31)
February	25:	Military unification agreement
March	11:	Soviet withdrawal begins (completed May 3)
	17:	Kuomintang Central Executive Committee conditionally accepts PCC constitution
April	18:	Communists take Changchun
	28:	Ssuping campaign in Manchuria (to June 7)
May	4:	Communist Central Committee issues Directive on Liquidations, Rent Reductions and Land Problems

	5:	Nationalist government returns to Nanking
	19:	Nationalists capture Ssuping
	23:	Nationalists recapture Changchun
June	6:	Second ceasefire (takes effect June 7)
	25:	First Tsingtao–Tsinan Railway Campaign (to July 12)
	29:	Communist breakout from Tapieh Mountains (to August 28)
July	7:	South Shansi Campaign (to October 24)
	16:	South Kiangsu Campaign (to September 17)
	16:	East Anhwei Campaign (to July 30)
	18:	North Anhwei Campaign (to August 10)
	20:	Communist Central Committee alerts bureaux to prepare for 'a war of self defence'
	29:	US Marines ambushed at Anping, Hopeh
August	3:	Tatung besieged (to September 20)
	15:	Jehol Campaign (to October 13)
	19:	Communists formally ordered to mobilise
	20:	East PINGSUI Railway Campaign (to November 11)
	29:	Nationalists capture Chengte
	30:	United States sells war-surplus supplies to China
September	1:	West Shantung Campaign (to September 22)
	1:	West PINGSUI Railway Campaign (to September 20)
	11:	North Kiangsu Campaign (to September 22)
	30:	Second Tsingtao–Tsinan Railway Campaign in Shantung (to October 12)
October	10:	Nationalists take Kalgan
	20:	Tantung Campaign in Manchuria (to November 4)
November	4:	Sino-American Treaty of Friendship, Commerce and Navigation
	12:	Lin Piao's first raid across the Sungari (to January 6)
	19:	Chou En-lai leaves Nanking

December	18:	Truman confirms the United States will not become directly involved in the civil war

1947

January	1:	Nationalists promulgate new constitution
	2:	I-tsao Campaign in Shantung (to January 20)
	6:	Marshall recalled
	8:	Marshall departs and is nominated US Secretary of State
	5:	'First Sungari Battle' in Manchuria (to January 16)
	19:	Communist First Hopeh Offensive
	21:	Marshall sworn in as US Secretary of State
	30:	Laiwu Campaign in Shantung (to February 24)
February	16:	Nationalists introduce wage-price freeze
	21:	'Second Sungari Battle' in Manchuria (to March 5)
March	7:	'Third Sungari Battle' in Manchuria (to March 18e
	12:	Truman Doctrine presented to US Congress
	14:	Nationalist Offensive into North Shensi (to August 13)
	19:	Nationalists take Yenan
	29:	Liu Po-cheng's North Honan Campaign
April	8:	Communist Second Hopeh Offensive (to April 30)
	20:	First Siege of Yuncheng in Shansi (to May 12)
May	11:	Mengliangku Campaign in Shantung (to May 16)
	13:	'Fourth Sungari Battle' and siege of Ssuping (to June 30)
	14:	Communist Third Hopeh Offensive (to June 30)
	21:	Truman signs bill to provide military and economic aid for Greece and Turkey
	25:	Hsiangning Battle in Shansi (to May 25)
June	27:	Nanma Campaign in Shantung (to August 1)

	4:	Kuomintang State Council orders national mobilisation
	5:	Liu Po-cheng marches to Tapieh Mountains (to August 25)
	9:	Wedemeyer Mission visits China (to July 24)
September	1:	Chiaotung Peninsula Campaign in Shantung (to December 31)
	2:	Communist Fourth Hopeh Offensive (to September 15)
	13:	Communist National Land Conference opens
October	1:	'Fifth Sungari Battle' in Manchuria (to November 6)
	1:	Communist Fifth Hopeh Offensive (to November 12)
	10:	Communist Agrarian Law
	28:	Nationalists ban the Democratic League
November	12:	Communists take Shihchiachuang in Hopeh
	21:	Election for National Assembly (to November 23)
	27:	Nationalist Offensive into Tapieh Mountains (to January 1)
December	17:	Second Siege of Yuncheng in Shansi (to December 28)
	19:	Truman proposes European aid programme
	20:	PINGHAN Railway Offensive in Hopeh (to January 14)
	22:	Truman Administration requests four-year aid package for China

1948

January	16:	First Communist Offensive in Manchuria
February	15:	Ichuan Campaign in Shensi (to March 1)
	18:	Truman presents China Air programme to US Congress
	22:	Communist Central Committee demands protection of middle peasants
	25:	Communist coup in Czechoslovakia

March	8:	Loyang Campaign (to April 5)
	9:	Communist Offensive in central Shantung (to April 27)
	12:	Communists take Ssuping
	17:	Brussels Treaty lays foundation for NATO
	29:	National Assembly meets in Nanking
	30:	Communist PINGSUI Railway Offensive (to May 24)
April	2:	US Congress passes China Aid Act
	16:	Wei Valley Campaign in Shensi (to May 27)
	19:	Chiang elected president
May	23:	Second Communist Offensive in Manchuria
	26:	Kaifeng Campaign in Honan (to July 6)
June	10:	Communist Offensive along TSINPU Railway in Shantung (to July 16)
	24:	Berlin Blockade begins
August	19:	Nationalists' emergency economic reform programme
September	12:	Liao Shen Campaign in Manchuria (to November 2)
	14:	Siege of Tsinan (to September 24)
October	3:	Peiping–Tientsin Campaign (to January 21)
	9:	Communists take Chinchou
November	2:	Communists take Mukden
	2:	Truman elected as US president
	5:	Huai-hai Campaign (to January 11)

1949

January	1:	Nationalists offer to negotiate
	7:	Marshall resigns as US Secretary of State
	11:	Mao lays down terms for negotiation
	16:	Nationalist Cabinet discusses Communist terms
	21:	Chiang announces withdrawal from public life
	21:	Dean Acheson becomes US Secretary of State
February	14:	Nationalist delegation visits Peking to

		discuss peace terms
April	4:	North Atlantic Treaty signed
	21:	Yangtze River Crossing Campaign (to May 25)
	24:	Communists take Nanking and Taiyuan falls
May	9:	Wei Valley Campaign in Shensi (to June 20)
	12:	Berlin Blockade ends
	15:	Communists take Wuhan
	27:	Communists take Shanghai
June	20:	Nationalists announce blockade of Communist coast (takes effect on June 26)
July	3:	Communists take Changsha
	11:	Hengyang Campaign (to October 16)
	15:	Kiangsi Campaign (to September 30)
August	17:	US Embassy transferred from Nanking to Canton
	25:	Communists take Lanchou, capital of Kansu
	25:	Suiyuan Province surrenders to the Communists
September	20:	Ninghsia Province surrenders to the Communists
	23:	Soviet Union explodes first atomic bomb
October	1:	Mao proclaims the establishment of the People's Republic of China (PRC)
	11	Kwangtung Campaign (to October 26)
	14:	Communists take Canton
	17:	Communists take Amoy
	17:	Assault on Chinmen Island (Quemoy)
November	30:	Chungking falls
December	8:	Nationalists transfer capital to Taipei, Taiwan
	9:	Governor Lu Han of Yunnan defects
	16	Mao arrives in Moscow
	27:	Chengtu falls

1950

January	6:	The United Kingdom recognises PRC
	8:	PRC demands Republic of China's seat on

UN Security Council

	12:	Acheson's speech to National Press Club on United States' defensive perimeter excluding Korea and Taiwan)
	13:	Soviet boycott of United Nations (to August 15)
	14:	United States recalls all diplomatic personnel from northern China
	30:	Nationalist remnants driven into Indochina
February	14:	Sino–Soviet Treaty signed
	18:	PRC recognises Ho Chi-minh's Democratic Republic of Vietnam
	19:	Nationalist remnants driven into Burma
	20:	Truman authorises military aid for French in Indochina
March	1:	Chiang resumes position of president
	27:	Sikang Province defects
May	1:	Communists take Hainan Island
	17:	Nationalists abandon Choushan Islands
June	25:	Outbreak of Korean War
	27:	Truman orders US 7th Fleet to patrol the Straits of Formosa

Historical Note: The Background

COMPLEX though the political scene throughout the whole world has been since the Paris Peace Conference concluded its deliberations on 4 May 1919, nowhere has it been more convoluted than in mainland China.

This study of the Chinese Civil War starts at the end of 1936 at a time when China was divided between the Nationalist forces of Chiang Kai-shek's Kuomintang government and those of the Communists under the political leadership of Mao Tse-tung. The situation was complicated by growing pressure from Japan which violated Chinese territorial integrity in 1931 to seize Manchuria. In succeeding years the Japanese lived up to their Chinese nickname of 'bandit dwarfs' by encroaching across the Great Wall and attempting to dominate Hupeh Province.

To understand the events of the following years, we must first take a very brief look at the tangled skein of conflict which created the situation. To assist the reader a chronology covering the period from 1911 to 1950 will be found on pages xiv–xxiv.

After a century of exploitation by the industrialised world a rebellion at the triple city of Wuhan in 1911 ended a millennium of Imperial rule in China. The Chinese Republic was established with the great national leader Sun Yat-sen nominally at its head but his attempt to create a parliamentary democracy on European lines fell foul of the ambitions of former Imperial War Minister Yuan Shih-kai.

Increasingly military force dictated political action and this was symbolised by the growing importance of the provincial military governors. With Yuan's death in 1916 the frayed ties of

xxv

obedience to central authority were finally sheared and the military governors strove for mastery of China. Answerable to no one except themselves they were called 'warlords' by the foreign press and under this title they will be described in the following pages.

The warlords were essentially provincial leaders and their success depended upon complex and fragile alliances. All competed for supreme power in the devastating warlord wars which lasted into the mid 1920s but the quest for personal power meant that any who came near to achieving this goal were quickly neutralised by other warlords fearful for their own position. The only national political organisation of any regard belonged to Sun Yat-sen but it was militarily impotent in the face of anarchy.

China's political and cultural renaissance may be said to have originated from 4 May 1919 when students in Peking demonstrated against the terms of the Paris Peace Conference which gave Japan control of Shantung Province. The protests were quickly suppressed but led to the creation of the Kuomintang (an acronym for Chinese National People's Party) by Sun Yat-sen in October 1919 and the Chinese Communist Party in May 1920. Both sought profound political and social reforms but the Communists' solution was clearly the most radical.

In the early 1920s Sun Yat-sen concluded that the Kuomintang would need its own army to unify China and he sought aid from the young Soviet Union. This was provided but the price was an uneasy alliance between the Kuomintang and the Communists. Nevertheless the two sides laid the foundation for successful co-operation and created the National Revolutionary Army which was to strike the warlords in the Northern Expedition.

But on the eve of the campaign, in 1925, Sun died and tensions grew between the allies. The Northern Expedition was directed by Chiang Kai-shek and by 1927 all of China south of the Yangtze acknowledged Kuomintang rule. However, Chiang was a conservative and his growing power led to a split between the Kuomintang, who established the new national capital at Nanking, and the Communists whose power base was at Wuhan. Chiang's troops crushed this and other Communist rebellions and the battered remnants of the Communists fled to remote areas of central and southern China where they established bases. Meanwhile Chiang struck north of the Yangtze and by

1928 had taken Peking, the former Imperial and Republican capital.

For Chiang the victory proved hollow. The northern warlords had not been defeated, rather they were persuaded to become the Kuomintang's allies. In return they recognised the Kuomintang as China's rulers but they refused it absolute authority within their bailiwicks. When Chiang attempted to reduce their military power it provoked a series of rebellions which required considerable effort to suppress and left the warlords with considerable regional autonomy. Chiang was also under pressure from the Left within the Kuomintang under Wang Ching-wei and was unable to neutralise him until the mid-1930s.

With the Nationalists pre-occupied Communist power grew within their scattered mountain redoubts. The Communist Party began to implement Mao Tse-tung's proposals for a rural-based revolution and created sufficient support to expand their bases. However, in the early 1930s Stalin's Russian-based Comintern re-established control over the Chinese Communist Party and returned to the path of Marxist orthodoxy by seeking to create an urban-based revolution.

The Japanese attacks allowed the Communists to take a nationalist pose as well as further diverting Chiang Kai-shek's troops. However, in 1933 Chiang was able to focus upon the growing Communist menace and began to crush their bases in a vice-like grip. The Communists had no alternative but to break out of the encirclement and march westwards seeking new sanctuaries. The Long March saw the Communists brought to the verge of destruction yet it also proved a period of rebirth during which Mao Tse-tung deposed the Comintern leadership.

The Communists established a new base in Shensi Province with their capital at Yenan as Chiang Kai-shek concentrated forces around them, principally troops of the former Manchurian warlord Chang Hsueh-liang who had been driven from his home by the Japanese in 1931. The Communists beat off the first Manchurian probes and made great play of their anti-Japanese stance to the homesick warlord troops. An unofficial truce descended upon Shensi to Chiang Kai-shek's fury and he flew out to discover the reason.

Biographical Sketches of Important Civil War Figures

Nationalist

Chen Cheng (b. 1897)

Minister of War (December 1944 to June 1946). Chief of the General Staff (June 1946 to May 1948) and Director of the Northeastern General Headquarters (September 1947 to February 1948) (concurrent). Chairman of the Taiwan provincial government (December 1948 to December 1949) and Commissioner, Southeast Military and Political Administration (1949) (concurrent).

Educated at the Paoting Military Academy, where he qualified as a gunner, Chen joined the Kuomintang in 1920 and was the artillery instructor at Whampoa. Subsequently he held senior staff positions in the NRA as well as commanding Chiang Kai-shek's bodyguard.

In the 1930s he fought against both warlords and Communists but displayed greater ability against the former than the latter. Chiang's regard for him was shown in 1935 when he joined the Kuomintang Central Executive and directed the re-organisation of the army.

In the first year of the war against the Japanese he held various senior field positions including command of the 9th War Zone together with positions in organisations dealing with the air force, training and military administration. In November 1938 he resigned from all these positions but returned to command a minor war zone in 1940. From January 1943 he commanded the American-equipped expeditionary army (Y-force) and from June 1944 commanded the 1st War Zone.

A long feud with War Minister Ho Ying-chin saw Chen surplanting his rival in December 1944. Subsequently he held senior positions in the Nationalist Army and, with Marshall and Chou En-lai, he was one of the triumvirate of arbitrators to whom all disputes during the cease-fire were referred.

Chen Li-fu (b. 1900)

Head of the Kuomintang Organisation Department (1944 to 1948), Vice President of the Legislative Yuan and secretary general of the Kuomintang Central Political Committee (1948), Minister without Portfolio (from late 1948).

A nephew of Chiang Kai-shek's great friend Chen Chi-mei, Chen Li-fu was a mining engineer who had graduated in both China and the United States. However, when he returned to China in 1926 he joined the Kuomintang's investigation bureau and controlled Chiang Kai-shek's prime internal security organisation until 1938. Simultaneously he held high office in the Kuomintang and was three times head of the Organisation Department. This influence led to the creation of the famous CC Clique, named after the two Chen brothers Li-fu and Kuo-fu (see below), which was at the heart of the Renovationist Movement.

In the latter years of the civil war Chiang Kai-shek appears to have trusted Chen Li-fu less, partly because of the latter's political influence. He was given no role in the re-organisation of the Kuomintang (KMT) on Taiwan as Chiang prepared his island redoubt and subsequently Chen Li-fu went to live in the United States.

Li-fu's brother Kuo-fu (b. 1892) was also head of the Organisation Department from 1926 to 1932. From 1945 he was chairman of the Kuomintang Central Finance Committee but tuberculosis prevented him playing a major role in post-war political life. In December 1948 he departed the mainland for Taiwan where he died a few years later.

Chiang Kai-shek (b. 1887)

Chairman of the National Government of the Republic of China (ROC) and Chief of State (1943 to 1948) and President of the ROC (March 1948 to January 1949).

Chiang's early education was in Chinese and Japanese military schools and in the latter he met Chen Chi-mei a

KMT activist who became a close personal friend. When Chen was assassinated in 1916 Chiang adopted his two nephews Chen Kuo-fou and Chen Li-fu who were to become the heart of the CC Clique.

In 1921 Chiang became Sun Yat-sen's protege and rapidly rose in the KMT's military organisation becoming commandant of the Whampoa Military Academy in 1924 and commander in Chief of the National Revolutionary Army (NRA) in 1926. He faced much political opposition and in August 1927 withdrew from public life for four months until he was asked to return.

From 1929 to 1936 he had to suppress regional revolts in the north and in the south by a mixture of military force and diplomatic compromise. However from October 1928 he held various appointments which made him de facto head of state although it was not until March 1938 that he accepted the title of 'party leader' of the KMT.

It was not until August 1943 that he accepted the title of Chief of State and two months later he became Chairman of the National Government. Chiang retained the highest offices in the ROC until January 1949 when he nominally withdrew from public life although he continued to wield absolute power. It was not until March 1950 that he began to act openly when he 'returned' to public life but he was not re-elected President of the ROC until March 1954.

It should be noted that his name strictly was Chiang Chieh-shih and that the universally used Kai-shek was actually the southern pronunciation.

Fu Tso-yi (b. 1895)

Commander of the 12th War Zone/Changyuan Pacification Area (1945 to 1947), Director of the North China Rebellion Suppression Headquarters (1947 to 1949).

Born in Shansi, much of Fu's career was spent as a commander of warlord forces first under the patronage of Yen Hsi-shan (qv) and later under the 'Young Marshal', Chang Hsueh-liang. When his forces were briefly part of the NRA he distinguished himself at the three-month siege of Chochou (between Peking and Paoting).

From 1931 he was Governor of Suiyuan which put him at the forefront of operations against the Japanese and despite fighting against the KMT in the early 1930s he joined its Central

Executive Committee in 1935. In the war against Japan he was a theatre (War Zone) commander.

During the Civil War he distinguished himself by reopening PINGSUI Railway for which feat he became Governor of Chahar in November 1946 and de facto commander in chief of north China in August 1947. Following his surrender in 1949 he held various positions in the government of the PRC.

Hu Tsung-nan (b. 1895)

Commander of 1st War Zone/Sian Pacification Area/Sian Pacification Command (1945–1949). Director, Ministry of National Defence's Northwest Command Headquarters (1949).

After completing his education Hu became a primary school teacher but joined the Whampoa Military Academy in 1924. He distinguished himself in the NRA and then against rebels and the Communists. He first went to Northwest China in 1932 and he spent most of the succeeding years in that region earning the nickname 'King of the Northwest'. In 1943 he became commander of the 1st War Zone and he remained the senior Nationalist military commander in the region until his forces were driven out in 1949. With the destruction of his forces at Chengtu he escaped to Hainan in March 1950 and later went to Taiwan.

Ku Chu-tung (b. 1893)

3rd War Zone (to January 1946), Director of the Hsuchou Pacification Command (February to September 1946). Commander in Chief of the Chinese Army (May 1946 to May 1948 and from April 1949) and Director of the Chengchou Pacification Command (September 1946 to February 1947 concurrent). Director of the Hsuchou Pacification Command/ Hsuchou Command of the General Headquarters Army (February 1947 to July 1948) and Chief of General Staff (May 1948 to April 1949) (concurrent).

Born in Kiangsu, Ku had a military education then served with warlord forces until 1921 when he joined the KMT. He held commands in the NRA and in 1931 he joined the KMT Central Executive Committee then became commander of the German-trained Government Guards Army, later nicknamed the 'Generalissimo's Own'.

From 1933 he fought the Communists and in the aftermath of

the Long March became the Central Government's senior figure in southwest China. After the Sian Incident he reorganised the Northwestern forces before handing them over to Hu Tsung-nan (qv). In the war against Japan he was commander of the 3rd War Zone in eastern China and played a key role in the New Fourth Army Incident.

Li Tsung-jen (b. 1890)

Director of the Generalissimo's Headquarters in Peiping (1946 to 1948), Vice President of the ROC (April 1948), Acting President of the ROC (January 1949 to March 1954).

Born in Kwangsi Li had a military education, one of his school friends being Pai Chung-hsi (qv). He served in Kwangsi warlord forces and with Pai became one of the triumvirate controlling the province.

In 1926 his forces merged with the NRA and took part in the Northern Expedition. When Chiang withdrew from public life in 1927 Li was one of those who persuaded him to return. He rebelled against the imposition of central authority and with Pai created a rebel state in Kwangsi and Kwangtung which defied the KMT for several years.

The growing threat from the Japanese led to a reconciliation in 1936. In the war against the Japanese, Li held important war zone commands and was a key figure in the Japanese defeat at Taierchuang in 1938. At the end of the war he commanded the 5th War Zone shielding Chungking in the east.

After the war he was given a sinecure command in Peiping but real authority was in the hands of Fu Tso-yi (qv) and Sun Lien-chung (qv). His election as Vice President in April 1948 brought no significant change and his elevation to Acting President in January 1949 made public his impotence.

With the collapse in southern China in 1949 he went to Hong Kong and relinquished his duties, but not the title of President. In December 1949 he flew to the United States for medical treatment retaining the title of President until formally voted out of office in March 1954.

Tang En-po (b. 1903)

3rd Front Army (to April 1946), Commander of Nanking–Shanghai Garrison and 1st Pacification Area (April 1946 to 1948). Deputy Commander in Chief of the Chinese Army from

July 1946 (concurrent). Pacification Commissioner in Chuchou (1948). Commander Nanking–Shanghai Garrison General Headquarters (January to May 1949), Commissioner for Fuchou Pacification Administration (May to December 1949).

The son of a landowner, Tang served with Chekiang warlord forces. Between 1925 and 1927 he studied at a Japanese military academy, aided by funds provided by his patron Chen I, then became a staff officer in the NRA.

During the 1930s he fought warlords, the Communists and ultimately the Japanese winning China's first victory against the last at *Taierchuang* in 1938. With the Chinese defeat at *Hsuchou* a few months later he was responsible for breaking the Yellow River dikes to prevent the invader advancing westward.

He held various senior commands during the war and even the collapse of his forces during the Japanese *Ichigo Offensive* in 1944 did not see his star wane. On the contrary he was later given command of an army of American-equipped troops, a tribute more to his loyalty to the Generalissimo than his military talents. In 1949 this loyalty led him to channel men and material to *Taiwan* and to arrest his former patron *Chen I*.

Pai Chung-hsi (b. 1893)

Vice Chief of the General Staff (to June 1946), Minister of National Defence (June 1946 to March 1948), Commanding General, *Chiuchiang Command Ministry of National Defence* (November 1947 to July 1948) (concurrent). Director, *Central China Rebellion Suppression Headquarters* (July 1948 to April 1949). Director, Central China Military and Administrative Command (1949).

Pai's career largely paralleled that of his school friend *Li Tsung-jen (qv)*. A man of high military reputation, he received important positions in the *NRA* including commander of the Woosung–Shanghai garrison at the time of the purge of the Shanghai Left in 1927 and later was a member of the triumvirate, with Li and *Ho Ying-chin*, which controlled the NRA when *Chiang Kai-shek* (qv) withdrew from public life in 1927.

He joined Li in 1929 as one of the leaders of the *Kwangtung-Kwangsi* clique and when the clique recognized the Nanking government's authority he was appointed chief of staff of the Military Affairs Commission. He held various staff appointments during the war against Japan but no operational ones although Li was given command of a war zone.

After the war he became Minister of the National Defence but disagreements with Chiang Kai-shek over the need for a unified command between the *Yellow* River and the *Yangtze* led to his being assigned the new Chiuchiang Command in 1948. In 1949 he held the key central command in southern China until he was defeated.

Yen Hsi-shan (b. 1883)

Commander 2nd War Zone/Director, Taiyuan Pacification Area (1945–1949). Governor of Shansi (1917–1949), Minister of National Defence (January to April 1949).

'The Model Governor' was born in Shansi, and attended the provincial military college then the Japanese Army's military academy which left him an admirer of Japan's military prowess. With the revolution in 1911 he became military governor and in 1917 he seized absolute power in the province by driving out the civil governor.

He was one of the leading warlords in northern China but in 1927, facing the growing power of Kuomintang, he allied himself with the NRA. However, two years later when faced with a threat to his provincial autonomy he raised the banner of revolt. Militarily defeated he was too powerful for Chiang Kai-shek to destroy and in return for a considerable degree of freedom within Shansi he acknowledged Kuomintang authority. It was during the 1930s that he undertook a 10-year economic development plan.

In 1937 he became commander of the 2nd War Zone but subsequently he found himself squeezed between the Communists and the Nationalists. The latter, under Hu Tsung-nan, made their first incursions into Shansi and as a result Yen came to an understanding with the Japanese without recognising their puppet Chinese government.

After the war he regained his province but found himself under ever tightening constraints. By accident or design he was away from his capital, Taiyuan, when it fell in 1949 and briefly held the position of Defence Minister in Li Tsung-jen's administration.

Biographical Sketches of Important Civil War Figures

Communist

Chen Yi (b. 1901)

Commander of the Central China/East China (later the Third) Field Army.

The son of a Szechwan district magistrate, after primary and secondary education Chen travelled to Europe with a group of students in 1919 to study social conditions. He was expelled from France in 1921 but later attended the Sino–French University in China and during this time joined the Chinese Communist Party (CCP).

In 1925 he joined the political department of the Whampoa Military Academy (See Chou En-lai) and subsequently became Chu Teh's political officer. His association with Mao began in 1930 and he distinguished himself as a guerilla leader but due to wounds he did not participate in the Long March but remained behind in Kiangsi.

With a few survivors he helped to found the New Fourth Army in 1937 and after the destruction of its headquarters in 1941 he became its commander, with Liu Shao-chi (qv) acting as his political officer for a time. At the Seventh National Congress in 1945 he, like all senior military leaders, was elected to the Central Committee.

Chou En-lai (b. 1898)

Vice Chairman of the People's Revolutionary Military Council, member of the CCP Central Committee and of the committee's Secretariat.

Born in Kiangsu but largely raised in Manchuria he became interested in Marxist theory while a university student in Japan. In 1919 he met Mao Tse-tung (qv) but the following year he left for Europe with other Chinese students as part of a working-study group. In Europe he became a Marxist and founded the European branch of the CCP.

He returned to China in 1924 and, until removed in a purge of Communists, was the deputy director of the Whampoa political department. Political activities in Shanghai followed in 1926 and 1927, during which time he was elected to the Central Committee.

During the late 1920s he made several visits to Moscow which no doubt helped him maintain his political position when Stalinists came to dominate the CCP during the early 1930s.

Their penchant for conventional operations threatened the existence of the Communist bases and Chou helped plan the break-out which became the Long March. During the March he identified with Mao's faction.

In Shensi his talents as a negotiator enabled him to make contact with the Sian plotters and he is generally credited with saving Chiang's life. An affable and persuasive personality made him the ideal choice for negotiations with the KMT during the war against Japan and he accompanied Mao to Chungking in August 1945.

He remained in Chungking, and later Nanking, after Mao's departure and later became the principal Communist negotiator serving with Marshall on the supreme arbitration committee. He did not leave Nanking until November 1946 and then joined Mao first in Shensi and later in Hopeh. With the creation of the People's Republic of China (PRC) he became the First Foreign Minister.

Chu Teh (b. 1886)

Member of the CCP Central Committee, member of the Secretariat of the CCP Central Committee, member of the Politburu, Commander in Chief of the Eighteenth Army then the People's Liberation Army (PLA).

Born in Szechwan into a family from Kwangtung, Chu's first job was as a school teacher but in 1909 he joined the Yunnan Military Academy. He became an officer in the Imperial Army and later in Szechwan warlord forces where he had some success.

Despite meeting Sun Yat-sen in 1921, the following year Chu became a member of the Chinese worker-study group in Europe. He worked in France and Germany, became a member of the CCP and met Chou En-lai before being deported from Germany in 1926.

He returned to China to become a political officer in the NRA and in 1927 was one of the key figures in the Nanchang Uprising. Following the defeat there he wandered to Kiangsi where he met Mao Tse-tung and became one of the leaders of the Red Army. During the Long March he became commander in chief of the Red Army and during the war against Japan he became, in rapid succession, commander of the Eighth Route Army then the Eighteenth Army and concurrently deputy commander of the 1st War Zone.

During the war against Japan he was one of the key figures in the 'Hundred Regiments Offensive' which was probably conducted against the wishes of the Central Committee. Despite the consequences of this disastrous offensive Chu Teh retained his command and in 1945 became the second ranking member after Mao Tse-tung in each of the CCP's three key organisations. With the formation of the People's Liberation Army in 1946 he became its commander in chief, a position he retained until 1954.

Liu Shao-chi (b. 1900)

Vice Chairman of the People's Revolutionary Council, member of the Secretariat of the CCP Central Committee. Second Vice-Chairman of the Central Government of the PRC.

Born in Hunan, the son of a landowner, Liu was educated at Changsha where Mao Tse-tung (qv) was one of his school friends. He displayed a keen interest in Leftwing politics and went to Moscow in 1920, founding a branch of the CCP there the following year.

He returned to China in 1922 and became closely associated with the trades union movement becoming General Secretary of the All China Federation of Labour in 1927. Although he participated in the opening stages of the Long March he later worked underground in enemy occupied areas especially in cities. He was instrumental in attracting many students and graduates into the CCP.

From 1936 he was secretary of various regional bureaux in the CCP and from 1939 developed a position as CCP theorist only second to Mao. He worked with Mao in the sinification of CCP philosophy and by the summer of 1945 was the third ranking member of the Central Committee. When Mao was in Chungking, Liu acted as his deputy and it was he who masterminded the move into Manchuria.

His de facto position as deputy chairman of the CCP was underlined during the civil war although he held no military posts. When Yenan was abandoned in March 1947 Liu was despatched with part of the Central Committee and Secretariat to Hopeh and Mao, with the remainder of the leadership, did not join him until the following spring. Consequently it was Liu, a man usually associated with urban rather than rural activities, who chaired the vital National Land Conference during the autumn of 1947 which reshaped CCP land reform policy.

Liu Po-cheng (b. 1892)

Commander in Chief CHINCHILUYU Field Army then the Central Plains (later the Second) Field Army.

The 'One-Eyed Dragon' had a military education then joined Szechwan warlord forces in whose service he lost an eye. He joined the CCP in 1926 and distinguished himself in the NRA but from 1927 to 1930 he was improving his military education in the USSR. He resumed his military career upon his return to China and his forces were the spearhead of the Long March.

When the Red Army was merged with the Nationalist Army in 1937, Liu commanded the 129th Division of Eighth Route Army with Teng Hsiao-ping (who ultimately became Mao Tse-tung's successor) as his political officer, the two remaining together until after the end of the civil war. Under this formidable duo Communist forces expanded eastwards during the war against Japan and by the beginning of the civil war Liu's forces controlled a large part of northern China.

Lin Piao (b. 1907)

Commander in Chief of Northeast Democratic United/Northeast later Fourth Field Army.

As a teenager Lin entered Whampoa as a cadet but increasingly he sympathised with the Communists and in 1927 became a member of the CCP. He participated in the Nanchang Uprising of 1927, which is now regarded as the founding of the People's Liberation Army, then joined Mao in Kiangsi the following year.

His military competence ensured his progress. He played an important part in defeating many of the Bandit Suppression Campaigns in the early 1930s as well as becoming commander of the Red Army Academy. He accompanied Mao during the Long March and in 1937 he again became commander of the Red Army Academy (later renamed the Anti-Japanese Military and Political University) and concurrent commander of the Eighth Route Army's 115th Division.

Injured in 1938 he was taken to the USSR for medical treatment and for further military education. Upon his return to China in 1942 he emerged as a strong supporter of Mao Tse-tung but he was given staff appointments, probably because of doubts about his health. However, he also assisted Chou En-lai in abortive negotiations during the early 1940s to resolve the growing crisis between the Communists and the Nationalists. In 1945 he was appointed commander in chief of Communist forces in Manchuria.

Mao Tse-tung (b. 1893)

Concurrently Chairman of the Central Committee, Chairman of the Politburo, Chairman of the Military Affairs Committee, leader of the Secretariat of the Central Committee until the establishment of the PRC.

Mao's education was interrupted for three years from 1906 but he went on to work in the library of Peking University. In 1920 he read the Communist Manifesto and the following year he was one of the founders of the CCP. However, he was not elected to the Central Committee in 1923 and uncharacteristic illness soon forced him to relinquish the position.

Instinctively he drew away from Marxist orthodoxy with its emphasis upon the urban proletariat in favour of revolution by the rural proletariat and in 1927 he became head of the National Peasant Association. With the failure of the Communist revolt in that year he withdrew to the Kiangsi mountains where he was able to put his theories to the test.

During the late 1920s his star was in the ascendant; he joined the Central Committee and in 1931 became chairman of the central executive of the All-China Congress of Soviets. However, during the early 1930s the Russian-dominated Comintern re-established control over the CCP, restored Marxist orthodoxy. Mao's star waned and in January 1934 he lost the chairmanship. During this time the various soviets were brought to the brink of ruin and flight was the only salvation and this led to the Long March which began in October 1934.

Mao's enemies might have left him to his fate but he eventually participated in the Communist exodus and in the following months he and his allies gradually regained control of the CCP. After the Communist arrival in Shensi in 1935 and the Sian Incident the following year he began to refine his political philosophy.

His rural-based revolution became the CCP's official policy and the supremacy of his views, together with his personal standing, were confirmed in the Rectification Programmes of the early 1940s. During the civil war his energies were largely concentrated on the political field defining CCP policy especially on land holdings where he veered from Left (from 1946) to Right (from the end of 1947). He may not have created the CCP's political programmes but he certainly acted as the final arbiter of their interpretation.

Nieh Jung-chen (b. 1899)

Commander-in-Chief at CHINCHACHI (later North China) Field Army.

The son of an Imperial official, Nieh was given a technical education and he was a member of the work-study group which went to France in the 1920s. He joined the CCP in 1922 and two years later went to Moscow to study at the Red Army Academy.

He returned to China in 1925 and joined the Whampoa political department. His career until 1937 was exclusively in the military–political field and it was not until November 1937 that he was given command of a military district. His success here ensured that he continued to hold operational positions until the end of the civil war and the establishment of the PRC.

1

The Rude Awakening: China 1936–45

ACCORDING to an old saying, there is a small upheaval in China every 30 years and a great tumult every 100. When the nation's leader, Generalissimo Chiang Kai-shek retired to bed near the ancient city of Sian, capital of the Province of Shensi, on 11 December 1936 he was quite unaware that China was about to embark upon the greatest tumult in its three millennia of recorded history ... the Communist revolution.

Chiang was the leader of the Nationalist Party (the Kuomintang) who had driven their former allies, the Communists, from their bases south of the Yangtze river two years earlier. For nearly a year thereafter, the Communists, under Mao Tse-tung, had sought sanctuary, travelling some 9,600 kilometres in what was to become known to the world as 'The Long March'. The exhausted survivors arrived in Shensi, where Chiang urged his local commanders, the Manchurian 'Young Marshal', Chang Hsueh-liang, and the Northwestern leader 'Old Yang' (Yang Hu-cheng) to finish them off. Neither was enthusiastic because the siren song of national unity against the encroaching Japanese was drifting from the new Communist capital, Yenan.

Chiang had flown to Sian to demand an offensive but was rudely awakened in the small hours of 12 December to find his bodyguards battling with the 'Young Marshal's' forces. He soon found himself hurrying, barefoot and without his false-teeth, through the hills. In a sense, his fortunes continued downhill until he reached Taiwan some twelve years later.

Chiang was soon re-captured and confronted by the 'Young

1

Marshal', who explained that he and his fellow conspirators were determined to force him into an alliance with the Communists against the Japanese invaders. Meanwhile, the Communists, who had had no knowledge of the conspiracy, despatched Chou En-lai to Sian to negotiate an alliance with the Generalissimo. Despite all the efforts of the 'Young Marshal', Chou managed only to obtain a vague, verbal undertaking. Chiang returned to his capital, Nanking, on Christmas Day, accompanied by the 'Young Marshal' who impulsively demanded that he should be punished for his mutinous temerity. He was duly court martialled and received a token jail sentence. However, Chiang Kai-shek ensured that he never regained his freedom and, two years later, imprisoned 'Old Yang'.

The Japanese Invasion

Surprisingly, despite its flimsiness, Chiang did not renege on the Sian agreement although the existence of a formal undertaking was not revealed until 22 September of the following year, by which time war had broken out in earnest with the Japanese around the former capital, Peiping.[1] By this time, the Generalissimo sought to avoid a war on two fronts while the Communists wished only for a breathing space to consolidate their base. They now pledged to end their revolutionary activities, to place themselves under the direction of the Kuomintang and to follow the principles of its founder Sun Yat-sen. The promises were as ephemeral as those of the Nationalists, who undertook to end military operations against the Communists and to recognise the Communist administration around Yenan but national unity was now to take priority.

For the next two years, China's ramshackle forces fought a losing battle against the Japanese Army, which occupied much of the north of the country before extending Tokyo's rule along the valley of the Yangtze. Faced by their irresistible force, Chiang could only withdraw into the interior, hoping that the sheer size of the country would ultimately prove an insurmountable barrier to Japanese ambitions.

The Japanese invasion was like a flood whose waters quickly abate and return to their natural channels – in this situation, those channels were the railways and the areas contiguous to them. Specifically, these were along the Peiping–Hankou (given

2

the Chinese acronym PINGHAN) and Tientsin–Pukou (TSINPU) lines, which linked northern and central China, as well as the two lateral railways, the Peiping–Paotou (PINGSUI) running from Hopeh to Suiyan and the Lanchou Lienyunkang (LUNGHAI) from Kiangsu to Shensi. The Japanese ignored the hinterland, from where most of the Central Government's officials had fled with the retreating Nationalist troops. This created a power vacuum, with each district (*hsien*) becoming a separate fiefdom of local leaders.

This situation offered the Communists a unique opportunity. Indeed, one commentator has observed: 'Without the international conflict that engulfed China ... the revolution could not have taken place.[2] In May 1937, Communist forces began advancing eastwards. To contemplate such a gamble when the Chinese Communist Party (CCP) had only 40,000 members and before the Shensi base was consolidated, reflected a growing confidence deriving from the adoption a sinified Marxist philosophy during the Long March.

The leading light in this philosophical development was Mao Tse-tung. Mao, who was 44 years old in December 1937, was a romantic intellectual, a school teacher by temperament whose fiery doctrine was matched by his love of peppery foods. His father, a self-made, rich peasant, whom he loathed, had forced him to live in the harsh real world of China. In so doing, he had given his son an iron constitution and an insight into the peasant mind which was reflected in the earthy language he used to communicate his ideas.

Mao's concept of revolution, based upon the countryside rather than the town, was anathema to the orthodox Soviet-trained, or Stalinist, leaders who had dominated the Party in the early 1930s. When the revolt against the Nationalists had failed in 1927 the Communists, led by Mao, had established mountain sanctuaries as bases for rural revolution. The Stalinists turned them into city-substitutes and within them they had gathered impediments more suited to urban than rural life. They included industrial machinery, electrical generators, radio stations, printing presses, a mint and a treasury with bullion. All were abandoned in the early days of the Long March. As the Party was driven westwards during 1934, the authority of the Stalinists was eroded and Mao's followers returned to the fore. Nevertheless, the lure of the cities, and a desire for an urban symbol of Communist power, remained strong within the Party.

China's Rural Problems

With 75 per cent of the nation's 500 million people living in the countryside, producing 65 per cent of the national output, and with rural society fast approaching crisis point, there were excellent reasons for seeking a rural-based revolution. The countryside had suffered from the same socio–economic ossification which had afflicted the Chinese Empire since the Middle Ages and had made it so vulnerable to the predatory ambitions of the industrial imperialists of the 19th century.

Average farm sizes were contracting remorselessly as hereditary tradition splintered the limited area of arable land, producing less efficient farms in the face of an annual population growth of 1.07 per cent. By 1937, one third of all households needed wages to supplement farm incomes and households tended to lease plots which were not economically viable.[3] Nearly half the country's 60–70 million farms had less than 10 *mou* (0.64 hectares or 1.6 acres)[4] of land and even this was often scattered around the village (*tsun*) in small plots, limiting the number of these which any one family could work efficiently.

To feed the growing numbers of mouths, Chinese agriculture concentrated upon grain, seeking two crops a year – a task that could be achieved only by an extensive use of manpower. During the 20th century, borrowing became an integral part of rural existence. Half the country's farmers were borrowing money or grain at annual interest rates of 20–40 per cent though sometimes this figure was 100 or even 200 per cent. Such a situation proved an ever growing source of social tension for, in the absence of any rural banking system, farmers inevitably capitalised upon the land, their only asset, as security.

For most of what is known as the Republican period (1911–49), the rural economy was stagnant or in decline. Nevertheless, domestic taxation and requisitions remained a constant drain upon the resources of the poor, making it ever more difficult for them to retain even the little land which they had. Thus rural poverty was always increasing. By the time of the Japanese invasion, barely one third of the men in China were in full employment and 58 per cent were working part-time.

The poverty of the small farmers and labourers contrasted with the prosperity of the larger landowners who acquired far more land than they could farm themselves and used it to provide extra income through leasing. Many of these were peasants, or the sons of peasants, who had expanded their land holdings through a combination of hard work, astute management, thrift and good luck. Such opportunities for social advancement provided a safety-valve for the ambitous; men such as Mao's father. Yet the insecurities driving such ambition were frequently expressed in an arrogance that could only exacerbate social tensions further.

The tensions were aggravated further still by the existence of absentee landlords, merchants who invested money in land for insurance or as a source of finance. Although such men rarely owned more than 10 per cent of the land of a village, their agents proved every bit as arrogant as their masters.

During the early Republican period, when central authority became eroded, the power of the notables (or 'the big trees' as the Communists called them) increased, giving them supreme power in the districts. The resentful poor had not only to defer to them but had also to treat them as near deities to whom gifts must be offered to secure patronage. If defied, the 'big trees' could call upon a host of supporters from their own families, retainers and clients to impose their will. Their position was strengthened by the administrative officials, whether centrally appointed professionals or locally selected amateurs, whose corruption earned them the title of 'blood-sucking devils'.[5] There was no redress against these officials, for Chinese local government was primarily interested in the collection of taxes, in the form of money, grain and service, the latter being the most dreaded by the peasantry.

The Communists were quick to exploit this highly volatile situation. The Sixth Plenum of the Central Committee of the CCP, which ended on 6 November 1938, reasserted the seizure of political power by 'armed struggle' as the Party's ultimate goal. Any semblance of adherence to the Sian agreement was clearly now a thing of the past and, in order to implement their new policies, they began to expand their political and military organisations. Their ability to exploit the spirit of nationalism provided them with a rallying call which penetrated the remotest districts. Yet, in some ways, it circumscribed their actions for to overcome political resistance throughout northern China, a subtle blend of political and military force was needed. By developing a military strategy based upon a new approach to guerilla warfare, they discovered a formula for success.

Guerilla Warfare

Although the Communists had adopted a guerilla strategy as long ago as 1927, following the defeat of their rebellious forces by the Nationalists, their leaders had tended to vacillate between guerilla tactics and conventional operations. Failure of the latter now forced them back to guerilla tactics and the need to win both the political and the military (or 'armed') struggle was the spur to new inspiration.

In war the goal is to defeat the enemy, and this is achieved by combining shock and manoeuvre followed by the occupation of territory. In conventional warfare these goals are achieved by destroying the enemy's forces through decisive action which usually involves the seizure of key terrain or communities. Because these are conflicts of material, conventional forces depend on their axes of supply upon which civilians may be employed. However, traditionally in conventional warfare civilians have had a non-combatant role although this has been blurred during the 20th century by the trend towards attacking civilian-based means of production.

In guerilla warfare, or insurgency, all of the civilian population are both combatants and battleground. The guerilla's purpose is to control the majority of the population usually by persuasion but by the selective use of violence where necessary. Military success is the most effective persuader but the guerilla's objective is not to destroy the enemy by decisive action but rather to erode his control and morale by diffused action. This is conducted wherever the enemy is perceived as weak or exposed. Control of the population brings the guerilla benefits in the form of intelligence and shelter as well as establishing a dispersed supply network based upon a myriad homes and small communities.

Success for a guerilla movement occurs when the enemy requires a disproportionate amount of military effort to maintain himself in an area. If this effort is not matched by any benefits the enemy will then be forced to abandon the territory.

For the insurgent the earliest successes will occur in areas of relatively little importance to their enemies by reason of remoteness. But to transform parochial success into regional and, ultimately, national triumph brings new problems.

Expansion brings the guerilla into areas which the enemy will regard as of great value and he will, therefore, be less willing to abandon them. Moreover, as larger areas come under the guerilla's control they lose the shield of concealment. Enemy forces can now focus upon the guerilla, attack him and possibly regain control of the population by demonstrating the guerilla's impotence in providing security. As the guerilla expands, therefore, territorial security becomes a growing requirement and ultimately it can be achieved only through conventional operations either through the assistance of friendly conventional forces or by the guerillas establishing their own.

The cross-over from guerilla to conventional warfare occurs as the insurgent expands regionally and aspires to national power but the change is never clear-cut. In China there emerged during the 1920s and 1930s two distinct guerilla philosophies which remain to the present day.

Initially the Chinese Communists adopted what might be termed the 'European' form made famous by the Spanish during the Peninsula War of 1807 to 1814. As such it retains a considerable degree of Latin machismo by assuming the automatic support of the civilian population and concentrating upon the destruction of the enemy's security forces. Political action is largely confined to terror tactics, such as bombings and assassination, both to cow opponents and as gestures of defiance. Only when there is a reasonable degree of territorial security is political and military mobilisation attempted and this is symbolised by the creation of conventional forces.

However, this style of guerilla warfare reflects the urban dominance of European life and the largely subservient role of rural interests. In Asia, as the Chinese Communists soon discovered, this position is reversed, indeed the lemming-like desire to fight a conventional war brought the Communist cause to the verge of ruin in 1934.

Here regional and parochial interests have always been strong and usually paramount. The peasants, such as those in China, tend to be introspective in their struggle against a harsh existence and to be subservient to the landlords (the

'Big Trees'), who naturally oppose any attempt to overthrow the established order.

Faced by the realities of this situation, and by such extensive and entrenched opposition, the Communists realised success would depend upon positive action amongst the populace to generate support. For this reason they developed a distinctly 'Asian' form of guerilla warfare in which what they now termed 'the political struggle' became of equal importance to the 'armed struggle', the two melding into a single strategy.

'Political struggle' seeks not only to establish the foundation for a military force but also a political and administrative organisation, having the triple aim of generating support for the movement, removing political opposition and providing resources for the 'armed struggle'. Such organisations provide multiple centres of resistance whose existence helps to sustain dominance and to divert and dilute the enemy's counter-guerilla effort.

In this way the Communists wove their webs first around the villages before gradually extending their network into the smaller towns throughout a province. They could operate either secretly or overtly and the flexible and resilient nature of the structure they had created was capable of absorbing heavy blows from either the Nationalists' counter-insurgency forces or the Japanese. Meanwhile, their own military forces could not only support the network when it was under attack but also could concentrate upon becoming a professional army in a situation where they could rely upon local support and prepare for the later phases of the grand design in which they would be involved in conventional warfare.

Laying the foundations of such a politico–administrative organisation was extremely difficult. It was conducted at district level by work teams who were directed by the Party's regional bureaux. Lightly armed, at best, the work team was a political battlegroup of flexible composition, having anything from 50 to half-a-dozen activists (also, and more generally, known as cadres) each of whom was assigned to a specific task. In Communist terms, their role was to 'mobilise the masses' so that they would re-mould their communities in the revolutionary image.

With the masses 'set in motion' (to use another Communist expression), each community would become part of the great social avalanche which was to sweep away the existing oppressive order, creating a new one in its place. While it was impossible to impose alien ideas upon the conservative villagers, they could be guided along the path of revolution. In the words of one commentator:

Like skilful theatre directors, work team cadres were supposed to guide the production of revolution authoritatively but inconspicuously...[6]

The cadres would cultivate potential activists and encourage the peasants to develop a collective voice by making them aware of social injustice and of their own potential strength. Thus encouraged, the villagers could become self-assertive and would participate in the new village administration.

A particularly good example of the operation of this new 'people power' was the handling of 'the big trees' by the Party. During the war against Japan there were few direct attacks upon them. Instead, by controlling local administration, the Party concentrated upon the erosion of the 'big trees' financial base and authority. This was achieved by insisting upon the strict observance of existing laws under which rents and interest rates had to be reduced. Introduced by the Nationalist Government before the war, these laws had been ignored by 'the big trees' while the government had made little or no effort to enforce them.

Communist Expansion

As more and more districts came under their control, the Communists built up their system of political administration through a series of provincial-level bureaux. Meanwhile, as the mobilisation of the masses gathered momentum, a steady expansion of the Communist 'Red' (or Eighteenth) Army took place.

The Army consisted of two 'corps', the Eighth Route Army in the north and the New Fourth Army in the south.[7] At the beginning of the war, in 1937, the Communists had some 45,000 men under arms. By January 1940, this number had increased to 500,000 and much of Hopeh, Shantung, Shansi, Honan, Anwhei and Kiangsu was under their control, the Nationalist guerilla forces in these provinces having been either destroyed or absorbed.

Though alarmed and angered by the Communists' success, the Nationalists were virtually impotent for, in 1938, they had withdrawn their capital to Chungking, in Szechwan, so that the administration effectively became a government in exile. It was to remain so until 1946. Nationalist fortunes were at their nadir in 1939; the Japanese were establishing their puppet régime in Nanking and their invasion had unleashed the centrifugal forces of Chinese regionalism expressed in the resurgence not only of Communist but also of warlord power.

The warlords had always possessed a considerable degree of regional autonomy in return for acknowledging the national supremacy of both Chiang Kai-shek and the Kuomintang but during the winter of 1939–40, they exploited Chiang's weakness by ignoring his call for a nationwide offensive. Chiang suffered this humiliation silently but determined to reassert himself by increasing pressure upon the Communists. This created new pressures which blazed into open conflict and reached a crescendo in January 1941, when the headquarters and rear-guard of the New Fourth Army were attacked and destroyed by Nationalist troops.

The Communists could do little more than protest over the Nationalist attack, having only recently suffered a severe reverse at the hands of the Japanese. Between August and December of the previous year, the Red Army demonstrated disastrous overconfidence by launching what came to be known as 'The Hundred Regiments' Offensive'. The invaders had reacted with a massive retaliatory operation that halved the population under Communist control, eroded popular support, severed communications with their capital Yenan and threw the regions back upon their own resources. A direct consequence of this set-back was that it forced the Communist hierarchy into a reassessment of their revolutionary policies which now became better refined. They also undertook a reappraisal of their subordinates, to ensure the personnel of the movement became better educated politically and better disciplined, although these objectives were not reached at the lower levels.

The experience also led to the completion of the sinification of their approach to Marxist philosophy, assisted by the central-isation of cadre training which politicised the Army and strengthened Party control. At the same time, the system of administration was simplified and the number of officials was greatly reduced, as each region was encouraged to become self-sufficient, thereby reducing the overall economic burden.

As a point of focus for Party loyalty, Mao now achieved a figurehead status which could be compared with that of Stalin in the Soviet Union. However, although he wielded great personal influence, it was not until the 1950s that he really controlled the Central Committee and the Party machine. Meanwhile, he could not dictate policy and frequently was forced to accept views contrary to his own, leading on occasion to displays of petulance.

China's American Allies

In 1941, the Japanese extended the war throughout the Pacific Rim and from 1942, as the Japanese faced the growing American threat, the pressure upon the Communists eased. As the Japanese troops withdrew, they were replaced by Chinese units of the puppet régime established in 1940 by Wang Ching-wei, a former Kuomintang leader who had defected to the invaders. Many of Wang's regiments had come over from the Nationalist Army and had little enthusiasm for fighting their fellow countrymen. Their passiveness enabled the Communists to expand cautiously from 1943 so that within two years they could claim control of 678 of the 914 districts in occupied China.

In practice, the degree of control exercised was related to the distance from the Communist sanctuaries so that in the remoter areas a loose alliance was established with the 'big trees'. Even where control was tightest, the authority of the Party was eroded by the poor quality of the junior cadres and activists at village level, which made revolutionary progress uneven. Nevertheless, confidence within the Party was boosted by growing superpower recognition – a Soviet mission arrived in Yenan in May 1942 and this was followed by an American one just over two years later.

By contrast, the extension of the war weakened the Nationalist position and so their authority. The Japanese invasion of Burma in 1942 physically isolated Chiang, who maintained his war effort on the weak economic and industrial base of China's poorest provinces. He also became committed to conventional operations in alliance with the Western Allies, who were fighting to re-open the Burma overland route – the only available route into China from the West.

In these operations the American and Chinese effort was commanded by General Joseph W. Stilwell (known to history as 'Vinegar Joe') who was also Chiang's American deputy. Stilwell was a man with all the qualifications for command in such a situation but with none of the personal qualities, so that he was a constant source of friction not only with Chiang but also with his British allies.

The Americans were quite unable to comprehend Chiang's difficulties nor did they recognise the state of exhaustion which pervaded the Chungking administration after so many years of struggle. In consequence, they became irritated by the Nationalists' demands for aid and were critical of their conservatism. In contrast, their mission in Yenan, when it arrived in 1944, appeared to find a Shangrila of social and economic justice, efficient government and patriotic fervour. Sino–American tensions boiled over when Chiang demanded the recall of Stilwell after a series of blazing altercations arising from Stilwell's tactless dealings with the Generalissimo. Exasperated by this demand, President Roosevelt acceded to it and replaced Stilwell with General Albert C. Wedermeyer. By this exchange, Chiang gained a more cooperative and understanding deputy but lost his principal supporter in Washington.

The political situation in China and relationships with the United States became increasingly confused as the war progressed. Although American long-term policy was based upon China exercising a stabilising influence in Asia, the State Department recognised that hopes of this were compromised by the Communists' control of the north. Despite their deep seated opposition to one another the two Chinese factions managed to maintain a facade of national unity, but by 1944 even this was crumbling and the two sides had clearly reached an impasse. Seeking to achieve a peaceful solution, the United States offered to provide a mediator. The offer was accepted by both parties with enthusiasm, not so much in a spirit of optimism but because each saw the prospect of wringing concessions from the other.

As his personal envoy for this mission, Roosevelt despatched Patrick J. Hurley, a colourful businessman from Oklahoma who knew nothing of Chinese politics and under-estimated Communist radicalism when he visited Yenan in November 1944. For their part, the Central Committee believed that his mediation represented superpower recognition and, in an atmosphere of amiable incomprehension, agreed to enter into a coalition government with the Nationalists. Unfortunately for Hurley, this agreement was unacceptable to the Kuomintang because it would have deprived them of control of the 'liberated areas' under Communist dominance and threatened what they saw as their monopoly of political power.

As light dawned upon them, the Communists too became conscious of this question of where the power was to lie. Without their share of real political power, they refused to surrender control of their forces through integration in a new national army. Like twin peaks in a Chinese landscape painting, these two issues now dominated the political scene and, while other issues might temporarily cloud them, they would always re-appear.

In vain did Hurley seek a solution but his failure to have implemented his own agreement exasperated the Communists, who soon dubbed him 'The Great Wind', the implication of this term being left in no doubt. As for the Kuomintang, even Hurley's appointment as United States Ambassador in January 1945 failed to wring any concessions from the Generalissimo.

Communist Resurgence

This latest American move made the Communists more sceptical than ever of their intentions and they now decided to seize power themselves, the political and military processes to effect this being initiated during the Seventh Party Congress which was held from April to June 1945. As an interim measure, moderate rural policies were to be retained but revolution remained the ultimate aim. The secret decision was taken to mobilise and the Red Army was expanded by some 57 per cent by dint of upgrading guerilla units. By March, it had 880,000 troops of whom 600,000 were in the Eighth Route Army, 260,000 in the New Fourth Army and the remainder in southeastern China. A simultaneous decision was also taken to expand Communist control into Manchuria.

In the wake of the Japanese invasion in 1931, the Communists had supported the local Manchurian guerilla movement. However, the Japanese garrison, the Kwantung Army, and their Manchurian puppets, the Manchukuo Army, had proved too strong. By 1940, the surviving guerillas were either in jail or had fled to the Soviet Union. Despite these early failures, the Communists believed Manchurian bases offered greater potential than their existing ones, which possessed neither the human nor the economic resources to enable them to survive a long war. Manchuria, on the other hand, had them in abundance together with an extensive industrial base.

Control of the region now became a vital new feature of Communist strategy, especially as the prospect of Soviet 'fraternal assistance' would compensate for Yenan's cooling relations with the United States, following the debacle with Hurley. Soon after the Seventy Party Congress, a 600-man expeditionary force, led by Tseng Ko-lin, was despatched northwards. But the Japanese were determined to prevent any Communist incursion into Manchukuo and by early August 1945, Tseng was surrounded and in danger of annihilation. He was saved by the nuclear attacks on Hiroshima and Nagasaki on 6 and 9 August, which ultimately led to the Japanese surrender on 2 September. Spurred by the Hiroshima attack, the Soviets completed their mobilisation and, with indecent haste, struck on 9 August, swiftly over-running Manchuria. Unknown to the Chinese, the Americans and British had bought Soviet entry into the war against Japan at Yalta, in February 1945, with commercial concessions in Manchuria.

No sooner had their troops entered Manchuria than the Soviets bullied the Nationalists into accepting these commercial arrangements and incorporating them into a Sino–Soviet Treaty of Friendship, which was signed five days later on 14 August. In return for unequivocal support for Chiang's government, the Soviets had acquired commercial guarantees relating to Manchuria which '... eased Soviet fears that the region might become an industrial and strategic base harnessed to the American threat to the Soviet Far East'.[8] As for the Chinese Communists, despite the mauling which Tseng's small force had received, they were also to benefit in the post-war race for power.

The Race for Power

With the Japanese offer to surrender on 10 August, the post-war race for power in China had begun. Chiang saw in this new situation an opportunity to secure the authority of the Kuomintang as the bedrock of the new China.

Although aloof, Chiang was a charismatic figure whose facade of calm confidence concealed profound emotions, occasionally expressed in spontaneous acts of violence and, later in the civil war, to insomnia. The resolution with which he protected China's independence was not matched by any profound depth of intellect, certainly in matters of political, social and economic significance, for to these he was indifferent. Yet political leadership was vital if the nation's post-war problems were to be overcome.

During the Second World War, exile had led many European governments into a political renaissance. Tragically, China enjoyed no such renaissance of the Kuomintang which remained a factionalised movement with posturing conservatives and liberals, whose ideas barely passed the city walls of the capital. Thus, by default, the real power lay in the hands of the Army, dominated by the Generalissimo, who, like many soldiers, was contemptuous of both politics and politicians. As he wrote in his diary: 'Politics make men lead a dog's life. . . . Where is morality? Where is friendship?'[9]

The son of a Chekiang landowner, Chiang was an autocrat whose decrees were restricted by financial, political and provincial special interests. A Christian, with staunch Confucian values, he was a mystical pragmatist naive enough to believe that he could change a nation simply by setting a personal moral example. Essentially, he was China's greatest warlord, the supreme practitioner of the art of military-political manoeuvre designed to secure power for its own sake. Thus it was that at the end of the war against Japan, he at once set about curbing warlord power in a process which was to last until the New Year of 1946.

With American help, Chiang now transferred loyal units from the southwest to occupy cities in the former Japanese-held zone so depriving most of his warlord rivals of their power bases. At the same time, he issued orders to both warlord and Communist forces, restricting their movements. Under contingency plans prepared in July 1945 for the sudden end of the war, the United States allocated 200 long-range Douglas C-54 Skymaster transports to an operation which flew 26,237 men from three corps into Nanking and Shanghai during September. From these points, they flew a further 5,000 men to Peiping. Then, from October, the American 7th Fleet moved another 280,000 men by sea in a programme lasting until May 1946.[10]

While all this was being accomplished, southern warlords, such as 'Little Tiger' Hsueh Yueh and Li Tsung-jen, were separated from their troops and given prestigious, but empty, new commands in the north, where Chiang's supporters were in real control. At a stroke he rendered most of the major warlords impotent although he was. forced to move against only one warlord, Governor Lung Yun of Yunnan. Against minor warlords Chiang and the Chungking administration used the need to rationalise the Army as an excuse to disband 110 of their divisions by the end of 1945 and to sandwich others into loyal corps. In addition, southerners were often used to counter-balance northerners, such as 'Model Governor' Yen Hsi-shan, Hu Tsung-nan and Fu Tso-yi, who were, in any case, dependent upon Chiang for supplies.

The Communists Move into Manchuria

Although the Americans rationalised their intervention in China as a stabilising measure in the chaos of Japanese surrender while they also sought to act as mediator in the negotiations to prevent civil war, the Communists saw it as an unwarranted interference in Chinese affairs in support of their enemies. However, it was also a surprise which forced their leadership to review their strategy in the aftermath of the Japanese ceasefire. Furthermore, it brought the sudden realisation that the prospects of taking Manchuria were far brighter than they had previously supposed following the near defeat of Tseng Ko-lin's expeditionary force (see page 14).

The Japanese surrender had saved Tseng Ko-lin and his troops and they had marched to Kalgan, capital of Chahar, before entering Manchuria on 30 August. Soviet trains moved them to Mukden where they arrived on 6 September to establish a token administration. As early as 11 August, Chu Teh had despatched 15,000 reinforcements northwards. To these the Soviets gave Chengte, the capital of Jehol, before assisting their further advance into Manchuria in mid-September. Both Chahar and Jehol were predominantly Mongolian and the Communists astutely courted popular support by creating the Inner Mongolia Autonomous Movement Association in

November 1945. This soon led to the Mongolian leaders pledging support to them in return for autonomy.

Even as Chu's reinforcements reached Manchuria, the Soviets flew Tseng Ko-lin to the Communists' headquarters at Yenan. Here his report to the Central Committee was so favourable that, without further reference to Mao in Chungking (see page 19) the acting chairman Liu Shao-chi authorised a major commitment of military and political resources to Manchuria. When Tseng flew back to Mukden he was accompanied by Peng Chen, secretary of the Party Directorate, and a team which became the nucleus of the Party's Northeast Bureau.[11] A further massive reinforcement of 80,000 troops from both the Eighth Route and the New Fourth Armies were ordered northwards ultimately bringing the total commitment in Manchuria to nearly 11 per cent of Red Army strength.

These moves shifted the balance of power between the Great Wall and the Yangtze into the hands of 400,000 Japanese and 275,000 Chinese puppet troops who awaited their fate with trepidation.[12] At the time of the cease-fire, Chungking had warned the Japanese that they must hold their positions and surrender only to Nationalist troops – and this, with the exception of about 30,000 men, they did. For the puppet troops, many of whom came from former Nationalist formations, Chungking dangled the carrot of reinstatement.

With the loss of Kalgan and Chengte to the Communists, Chungking demanded from its former enemies a more active role. On 23 August they were ordered to recover any positions lost to the Communists (described by them as 'irregular forces'). Still smarting from their wartime defeat, the Japanese responded with enthusiasm and, by the end of September, recovered a score of towns, some of their troops remaining active until early in the following year. The puppet troops, however, were markedly less enthusiastic and some defected. When relieved by Nationalist units, the puppets were either disbanded or down-graded to a paramilitary status.

By this use of former enemies and traitors against his own countrymen, Chiang deprived the Communists of territory but tarnished the reputation of his régime. Even greater damage to its good name was done when the Nationalists finally arrived in the territories formerly occupied by the Japanese, for they continued to employ Chinese puppet officials and police, thereby souring the joy of liberation. The bewilderment of the liberated was compounded by the attitudes of the Nationalist officials, who descended like locusts upon the occupied areas displaying sanctimonious arrogance, venality and corruption. They alienated the people and wrecked the commercial and industrial assets of the Nationalist heartland in Shanghai. This wanton destruction made it impossible to treat the pandemic of inflation, born of excessive public expenditure and inadequate revenue. Inflation had been brought from unoccupied China like a plague virus and a year-long moratorium on the land tax, the government's prime source of revenue, helped spread it nationwide.

By contrast, the Communists maintained moderate fiscal and social policies to consolidate and expand support in the territories still under their control. However, even here there were problems, arising chiefly from the earlier raising of the peasants' expectations, so that the hound of revolution was straining at the leash with many cadres allowing attacks on the 'big trees' under the guise of settling accounts with former collaborators. The leadership, on the other hand, with their army in a state of flux, realised the time was not ripe for such action on a national scale and that they must buy time in order to consolidate their territory.

Chiang and Mao Meet

With the cease-fire, the Communists at once began to spread throughout northern China, ignoring instructions from Chungking to remain in their present positions but their own sudden decision to reinforce Manchuria disrupted the rest of their expansion plans. Despite initial Soviet help, with the signing of the Sino–Soviet Treaty they realised they could now expect little fraternal assistance from Moscow upon which, perhaps not unreasonably, they had pinned their hopes. In late August Liu Shao-chi led a delegation to Moscow and sought in vain to change Stalin's mind. Stalin's response was to advise the Chinese to follow the example of the West European Communists by participating in a coalition government and merging their forces into a national army. Disappointment fed an internal Party dispute in Yenan over the policy of 'armed struggle' and, only by using the lever of his personal prestige, could Mao maintain the Party on the twin-tracked course of 'political' and 'armed' struggle.

Thus it was a combination of internal and international pressures which compelled Mao Tse-tung to accept Chiang's invitation to visit Chungking on 28 August for negotiations over a post-war government for the Chinese people. While personally sceptical about the outcome, Mao realised that public war-weariness made a gesture of reconciliation essential. At least the negotiations would buy a little time, enabling him and the Central Committee to re-evaluate the prospects for the revolutionary process.

The meeting concluded on 10 October, producing agreements in principle for a more democratic government, recognition of the Kuomintang's political opponents and the unification of the armed forces. A Political Consultative Conference (PCC) would be convened to consider government organisation and to draft a constitution. Mao refused to concede control of the northern 'liberated areas', including Manchuria, but voluntarily abandoned those in southern China, thereby enabling the Communists to replace the troops which they had redeployed earlier from northern China to Manchuria.

However, the negotiations then ground to a deadlock and, convinced that only the military option now remained, Mao flew home to Yenan on 11 October. Chou En-lai remained in the Nationalist capital until 25 November when, unable to make any further headway, he too returned to Yenan.

Meanwhile, a new problem had blown up in Communist-held territory when the Americans landed a force of United States Marines during October, increasing the Communists' distrust of their intentions. General Wedermeyer, seeking to balance the Soviet occupation of Manchuria, had asked for reinforcements and was allocated the IIIrd Amphibious Corps, of 53,000 men, to occupy Shantung.[13] When the Communists learned of this plan, they were doubly alarmed for they were shipping men and material into Manchuria through the ports of the province. The Communist commander-in-chief, Chu Teh, protested vigorously to Wedemeyer and implied that any landing would be opposed. As Wedemeyer's orders forbade any United States involvement in a civil conflict, he now divided the Marines between Tsingtao and Hopeh[14], thereby protecting the Peiping–Mukden[15] (PEINING) railway and controlling the rail link into Manchuria.

First Clashes

The desire of both sides for a military solution grew irresistibly throughout the remainder of 1945, leading to a number of set-piece battles, despite the talks in Chungking between the two leaders. This is an aspect of the Chinese civil war which is without parallel – the seemingly inextricable tangle of a country in which two major political factions engaged in an internecine struggle while seeking to gain some advantage from the presence of troops of two superpowers within their national boundaries. Simultaneously the superpowers, with rare accord but with different motives, made fruitless efforts to achieve national unity. The whole is so confusing that it more closely resembles the story of Alice in Wonderland than real life. Whatever the superficial picture may have revealed at any one time, in plain truth this was a life and death struggle between the forces of conservatism (the Nationalists) and revolution (the Communists).

During the autumn of 1945, the Nationalists regained most of the major cities. As their strength increased, so did their self-confidence rise. They now sought to re-open the PINGHAN and TSINPU railways in order to gain the necessary mobility which would enable them to reduce the Communists' bases in detail. But large sections of both lines were in Communist hands and while the PINGHAN line in northern China seemed the easier option, the Nationalists' hopes there were dashed by a series of defeats.

In late August, they had attempted to take Changchih, in the heart of the Shantang mountains, in south east Shansi, in order to strike into Honan or Hopeh. Although the force entered the city, it was quickly trapped there by Liu Po-cheng and, after a relief force had been destroyed in an ambush on 1 October, the Changchih garrison had to abandon the city a few days later.

However, undeterred, the Nationalists now began a 200 kilometre advance up the PINGHAN railway on 14 October to reach Shihchiachuang. The operation was directed by Sun Lien-chung, the 11th War Zone commander in Peiping, but he lacked the strength to support it and allowed the Communists of Yang Te-chih's CHINLUYU Military Region to prepare a conventional defence in depth.

The Nationalist task force, of seven divisions, took Anyang and crossed the River Chang (Chang Ho) on 22 October but within two days, Yang Te-chih's troops had fought them to a standstill south of Hantan. Liu Po-cheng then conducted a double encirclement, leading a task force from the Shantang mountains in the west to meet an advance by Sung Jen-chiung from the east on 29 October. Meanwhile, Yang's troops had contained a relief operation from Anyang in a bridgehead on the northern bank of the Chang. On 31 October, the northern pocket was overrun when Kao Shu-hsun, a Nationalist corps commander with a grudge against the régime, defected opening the pocket's western side. Facing annihilation, the remaining Nationalist defenders, with a courage born of despair, smashed their way through the southern siege ring to reach the Chang River bridgehead, which was evacuated on 2 November.

In both battles, the outnumbered Communists, by skilful manoeuvre, inflicted heavy defeats upon their Nationalist enemies, who lost a total of 50,000 men and much equipment including 30 guns. Although the Communist losses were also severe, Liu Po-cheng and his troops had thwarted a fleeting opportunity for the Nationalists to split Communist territory at a time when the Eighth Route Army was at its weakest.

Further north, the Communists had checked another Nationalist advance along the PINGSUI railway, by Fu Tso-Yi's 12th War Zone after it had reached Chining on the Great Wall and was threatening to interrupt the flow of men and supplies into Manchuria. The Communist forces involved were Nieh Jung-chen's CHINCHACHI Military Border Region and Ho Lung's CHINSUI Field Army. These responded to the threat by making a double envelopment from the east and the south, cutting the railway at a point east of Kueisui on 18 October and forcing the abandonment of Chining. Then, while Nieh besieged Kueisui, Ho isolated Paotao. However, both cities held out against their attacks until Fu was able to launch a counter-stroke on 3 December, driving off the Communists. Nevertheless, the Nationalists' losses were so heavy that they were unable to re-take Chining for a year.

Dramatic though these events had been, it was Manchuria which was to prove the litmus test of the nation's political future and upon which superpower attention was focused. The root of the problem was the power vacuum created by the Soviet invasion which had left in place no Nationalist leader of even regional status, apart from the 'Young Marshal' who was still under restraint. Rather than restore him, and create a new warlord threat, Chiang set up a new regional leadership in the form of a triumvirate with nominal supreme authority given to an experienced administrator, Hsiung Shih-hui, as Director of the Northeast Headquarters. Chiang's eldest son, Ching-kuo, represented the Foreign Ministry while Tu Yu-ming became commander of the Northeast Garrison General Headquarters as a reward for overthrowing Governor Lung Yun of Yunnan.

By contrast, the Communists permitted native Party members, including members of the Central Committee, to participate in the administration of the area. They were supported by 45,000 cadres (representing 2 per cent of the Party membership), and a presence was established in all the important towns and cities of southern Manchuria. But regional parochialism soon produced tensions and strained relations, with the newcomers being called 'southern louts' by the Manchurians who, in their turn, were contemptuously dismissed by the southerners as 'yokels'. These divisions were encouraged by the Soviets who remained concerned by the political heresy of their Chinese comrades and sought to encourage more orthodox views.

The newly appointed Communist commander of the forces in Manchuria, Lin Piao, soon discovered upon his arrival in late September 1945 that the political divisions were also reflected in military ones. Lin, selected because of his training experience and familiarity with the Soviet Army, had some 100,000 troops but could only rely upon the Eighteenth (Red) Army men in southern Manchuria. In the north, Chou Pao-chung commanded the Soviet-sponsored Northeast People's Self-Defence Army which had been created from survivors of the Manchurian guerillas and volunteers from the former Japanese puppet force, the Manchukuo Army.

The Nationalists were unaware of these divisions and consequently did not exploit them, but suffered serious problems of their own for the Soviets would not allow them to create an effective administration in Manchuria. The Soviets, still officially pressing for national unity, provided little help because they had a vested interest in maintaining a situation in which Stalin could exercise the balance of power while exploiting Manchurian resources to support his own war-battered economy. He was seeking a friendly and neutral China to safeguard his Asian flank, but the sudden appearance of United States Marines close to the Manchurian border must have driven him to re-evaluate Sino–Soviet policy. As superpower tensions increased, the spectre grew of the Nationalists permitting the establishment of American air bases in Manchuria.

The Russians Oppose Chiang

Under the terms of the Sino–Soviet Treaty, the Soviets had been due to withdraw from Manchuria within three weeks of the war's end. Facing this deadline the Nationalists were desperate to establish their authority in the region before the Russian withdrawal. In late September 1945 (while the talks between Chiang and Mao were still in progress in Chungking), six Nationalist divisions were despatched northwards in American ships and, on 1 October, Chungking sought formal approval through the Soviet Embassy to land at Dairen.[16] The Soviets refused and told Chungking to discuss the matter with Marshal Malinovsky, the Soviet commander in Manchuria who had his headquarters at Changchun from where he had a radio–telephone link to Moscow, giving Stalin personal control of the negotiations.

The situation in Manchuria was becoming daily more confused for it will be recalled it was at this time that General Wedermeyer had sought to land the United States IIIrd Amphibious Corps in Shantung as a counter-balance to the Soviet presence. Despite the fact that Washington forbade this move, and the Marines were redeployed, the very idea added to the growing maelstrom of political pressures on the area.

Stalin's restriction of Nationalist access to Manchuria now gave the Communists time to establish themselves more firmly, aided by limited access to Soviet stocks of captured Japanese weapons. In this situation Stalin gained leverage in his search for access to the region's mineral and industrial resources. Devastated Soviet industries were already being rebuilt with 'war booty' seized in Manchuria at an ultimate cost to the Chinese economy of some US$2 billion. However, the Soviets did not strip Manchurian industry bare. Although they left a potentially powerful industrial base, as the Nationalists recognised, it was soon ruined by the incoming Nationalist officials.[17]

Soviet 'booty' was flooding out of the region as Hsiung Shih-hui arrived in Changchun with an advance party of the

Nationalist Northeast Headquarters and as the first troop convoy dropped anchor off Dairen on 12 October. Although the Soviets now grudgingly conceded the use of Manchuria's smaller ports, these were already occupied by the Communists. Furthermore, the Soviets refused to intervene in the matter or even to allow the Nationalists to fly troops into the area.

In consequence, they had no alternative but to disembark Hsiung's troops at Chinhuangtao in northern Hopeh on 1 November and to march along the PEINING railway.[18] Four divisions struck up the railway from 5 November entering the LIAOSI Corridor, the narrow plain between the mountains and the sea. By a series of outflanking movements through the mountains over the next three weeks, they drove the Communists, some 20,000 strong, out of the Corridor. On 26 November, they took the port of Chinchou. Here the Generalissimo halted the advance. At a cost of only 750 casualties, they had inflicted a loss on the Communists of one fifth of their strength and had captured a substantial quantity of equipment.

Nevertheless, this success did nothing to make the Soviets more co-operative, so Chiang decided to break the impasse. On 17 November, he ordered Hsuing Shih-hui to return to Peiping from Changchun as a gesture of public protest at Stalin's obstructionism. Stalin was unruffled and only on 23 November did his minions reveal that the price of Soviet co-operation was a substantial stake in Manchuria's industrial and mining enterprises. That demand was ill-timed and ill-starred, for the fall of Chinchou had given the Nationalists access to the Manchurian heartland. Meanwhile, on the same day, Hurley resigned as United States ambassador, an act which once more focused American attention on China.

The Soviet demands struck a particularly sensitive nerve in the United States where commerce was preparing to exploit the post-war market in Asia. During the 19th century, the Western Powers had forced the Chinese empire to adopt an 'Open Door' policy, preventing the erection of trade barriers to foreign commerce. As the United States still supported the 'Open Door' and was now China's largest trading partner, the Soviet demands represented a serious threat to American commercial interests. Washington therefore lodged a diplomatic protest with Moscow while also serving notice that the United States would not stand idly by as Stalin compromised Chinese territorial integrity.

Stalin now recognised that the two superpowers were on a global collision course. Like President Truman (who had succeeded Roosevelt), he regarded Europe as the prime theatre of conflict and had no wish to see a secondary one, such as China, become the flash-point. Faced with just this possibility, Stalin rapidly back-tracked and, amid profuse apologies about 'misunderstandings', his people in China agreed to assist the Nationalists and to curtail Communist activities. On 5 December, Malinovsky, on Stalin's orders, agreed to the airlift of three Nationalist divisions, one to Changchun and the rest to Mukden. The Soviet withdrawal was delayed until 1 February 1945, presumably thereby giving the Nationalists some moral support as they consolidated in their new locations.

On the other side of the coin, the Soviet fraternisation with their enemies must undoubtedly have aroused bitterness at the private meetings of the CCP. Nevertheless, profound divisions within the Northeast Bureau remained, with many, including Peng Chen, wishing to retain their hold over the cities, despite the Nationalist–Soviet rapprochement. Just before Nationalist troops were flown in, a meeting of the Bureau appeared to reject this policy when it ordered Party members to take to the countryside, a decision which was endorsed by Yenan on 25 December in a directive demanding the establishment of rural base areas. Yet the lure of the cities, as a symbol of Communist power, remained strong and was to bring the cause to the verge of disaster during the coming spring.

American Intervention

The mounting Manchurian crisis emphasised the need for intervention by the United States if an all-out civil war in China was to be avoided. While both superpowers were in accord in their desire to avoid conflict in Asia and to create a stable China, it seemed in Washington as if events in Manchuria were raising the spectre of a Communist Manchukuo, with all its historic implications. On the other hand, while Chiang's control of the region would allay American fears, as a long-term solution it would be regarded with concern in Moscow.

Wedemeyer, who still retained some influence, suggested the

alternative of placing Manchuria under international control – but this was unacceptable to the Chinese of both persuasions. In Washington, the State Department, while recognising that the Chinese body politic was ill, and that without treatment the illness could prove terminal, was quite unable to agree within its own walls upon the treatment needed. The greatest obstacle to reform was Chiang himself, but his prestige, together with his personal control of both the Kuomintang and the Army, made his position impregnable.

As the world's most powerful post-war nation, the United States dominated China's foreign trade. The United Kingdom trailed far behind, although Hong Kong had by now recovered its position as a major entrepôt. Inevitably, the decline in British commercial importance[19] was matched by a decline in influence, something that was underlined symbolically on New Year's Day 1946, when China's road traffic switched to the American pattern. The depths of China's economic crisis were not yet revealed and, with the United States military presence being rapidly eroded by demobilisation, the only leverage left to Washington was military aid.

The short-term solution was to honour the war-time commitment to provide sufficient Lend–Lease aid to equip 39 divisions and an air force of 25 squadrons (8⅓ groups). This gesture offered some balm for the running sore of wartime Sino–American relations, caused by the miniscule amount of such aid which had reached China during the war.[20] In the event, the Chinese managed to equip no fewer than 58 divisions with Lend–Lease material. In addition they were able to re-equip the remaining military and paramilitary forces from the substantial booty gained on the mainland and in Formosa (now renamed Taiwan) after the Japanese surrender. As a consequence, the Americans gained nothing whatsoever in terms of influence.[21] The Japanese military treasure trove also gave Chiang insurance against any attempt by the United States to force his hand by means of an arms embargo. Meanwhile, Europe also provided an alternate source of war-surplus and new military equipment.

Marshall

Deprived of any means of exerting influence, Hurley had left Chungking for Washington in late September, ostensibly on grounds of ill-health but in truth because he was sick with disappointment.[22] After brooding for two months, he resigned on 26 November, blaming the professional diplomats for his failure.

On the following day, an inter-departmental committee agreed to continue to support Chiang's efforts to regain Manchuria, to retain United States Marines in northern China and, while transporting Nationalist troops, to make every effort to arrange a truce and political settlement. President Truman sought to create a genuine coalition government which would include the Communists, thereby emulating the successful policies of both France and Italy, where strong administrations had been created while keeping the Communists under some form of restraint. Although his influence was limited, Truman believed it to be strong enough to enable him to wring some concessions out of Chiang.

In these circumstances, the task of persuading both sides to negotiate called for a very remarkable man. Truman casually, but astutely, selected the recently retired Army Chief of Staff, General George C. Marshall, whose negotiating skills had played so important a part in shaping the war-winning strategy of the Allies. Marshall's initial objective was to be the extension of Nationalist authority into Manchuria without provoking a hostile Soviet reaction. To achieve this, he would first have to win Communist support. Although permitted to use his own judgement and initiative over pledges of military and economic aid, Truman warned Marshall that the United States would not abandon Chiang, even if obstructed. On this cautionary note, Marshall departed on his Herculean task.

How much Chiang knew of Marshall's instructions is a matter for conjecture. However, it must have irked the Generalissimo, the very personification of Chinese nationalism, to have a foreign envoy interfering into his country's internal affairs. Yet he had no other choice but to acquiesce for, as he well knew, the situation was of his own making, even if the Japanese had acted as the catalyst which parked off the first explosion.

At bayonet point, he had succeeded in achieving some nominal form of reunification of China during the 1920s after a decade of regional warfare between the warlords. Lacking the political philosophy or apparatus to consolidate victory, he remained under pressure from warlord-led regional interests which continued to challenge his authority until 1936. The Communists exploited the political vacuum but, at the point at which this book opens, in 1936, they were still reeling from a series of military defeats. The rebellion of the 'Young Marshal' and 'Old Yang' at Sian in December of that year, inspired by a combination of regional and national interests sparked by the Japanese encroachment, had led to a fragile reconciliation between Chiang and the Communists. However, when Nationalist authority was driven out of northern China by the Japanese in 1937–8, a power vacuum was created which the Communists were quick to fill – as we have seen.

Throughout the Japanese invasion, Chiang was unable to mobilise either the political will to oppose the Communists or the military resources to defeat them. The American material assistance he had received as the internationally recognised head-of-state had ultimately enabled him to neutralise the warlords. But the Communists were a far more formidable problem, for they had come to dominate Manchuria, a situation which Chiang had wrongly assumed to be part of a deep Soviet plot. By late 1945, a combination of circumstances and external pressures from the superpowers had made him realise that an interim political solution had, if possible, to be found.

However formidable a problem they may have seemed to pose for Chiang, the Communists were only too conscious of their military weakness, in real terms, and of their international isolation. Both Chiang and Mao well knew how exhausted the nation had become after eight years of war and bitter internal strife which left a profound dread of further civil conflict. In Marshall both leaders saw an opportunity to wring significant concessions from the other and even to achieve their own long term goals by negotiation. His arrival was therefore profoundly welcomed throughout China.

2

A Lifetime of Regret:
The Politics of Defeat
1946–49

GENERAL Marshall's arrival in China on 20 December 1945 seemed like manna from heaven to both the Nationalists and the Communists, both sides having realised that they lacked the strength to force the issue on the battlefield. Consequently, whatever private reservations each had about this new turn of events, publicly, they welcomed his mission.

The conciliatory mood of both parties enabled the modest, friendly, but exceedingly shrewd Marshall rapidly to secure the concessions necessary to establish a foundation for peace. The most important was the agreement of the Kuomintang to surrender their monopoly of power and to permit the establishment of a Political Consultative Conference (PCC) in order to frame a new constitution. To reduce tension while the PCC deliberated, both sides agreed, on 10 January 1946, to an unconditional cease-fire based upon the status quo. The participation of the Americans in the monitoring teams which supervised this agreement ensured their effectiveness while Marshall himself acted as one of the national arbitrators, together with the Nationalist Chen Cheng and Mao's representative Chou En-lai. In return for the Communists' agreement to his reinforcement of the existing Nationalist garrison in Manchuria, Chiang gave an undertaking not to advance in Chahar and Jehol.

Marshall's Successes and Frustrations

The PCC met from 11–31 January 1946 and resolved the major political and constitutional problems, proposing a cabinet-style government with a popularly elected National Assembly whose first task would be the adoption of a new constitution. However, there was a fly in the ointment. The proposal that the provinces should retain a degree of autonomy, with local elections for officials, alarmed the Kuomintang Right, led by the Renovationist (Ko-hsin) Movement, of which the most powerful element was the CC Clique led by Chen Li-fu.[1] While recognising that reform in the Kuomintang was the key to the future this movement also demanded the restoration of the traditional authority of the central government. So it was that when the Kuomintang Central Executive Committee considered the PCC's proposals in early March, the movement contrived successfully to add amendments to curb provincial authority and to perpetuate the presidential form of government. However, the Communists, who regarded the PCC's proposals as binding, demanded their acceptance by the Kuomintang, refusing further participation in the constitutional process which, by the end of April, had become paralysed.

This development prevented the implementation of Marshall's plans to integrate the forces of both sides into a national army of 60 divisions of which 10 would be Communist. Although an agreement to this effect had been signed on 25 February, the Communists became noticeably more reluctant to implement it in the succeeding weeks as the pace of political reform began to flag. To Chiang, the commitment of the Communist forces to the new army was the litmus test of their sincerity and his suspicion of their motives began to increase.

In truth, neither side had been optimistic about the prospects of a negotiated settlement and by March their worst fears were confirmed. However, the facade of achievement was sufficiently encouraging for Marshall to leave for Washington to organise a package of economic aid which he hoped would help bind the uneasy coalition. Meanwhile, the military agreement led Wedermeyer to organise a military mission to train the new national army.[2]

Disputes in Manchuria

Unfortunately, Marshall's departure removed the hand of restraint and the embers of mutual suspicion were fanned into a blazing conflict by factional rivalry among the Communists in Manchuria. There the Northeast Bureau leadership remained divided between the Stalinists, who wished to hold the cities – with their industries and urban proletariat – and the Maoists who sought a rural-based revolution. Peng Chen, secretary of the Party Directorate, sided with the Stalinists, possibly in an attempt to retain support in a region where Moscow had as much influence as Yenan. He was opposed by Lin Pao whose forces faced the Nationalist Army and would be particularly vulnerable if they were concentrated to hold any of the cities. The dispute remained unresolved into the spring.

Perhaps because the Communist Party was so weak, its Northeast Bureau stridently opposed the strengthening of Chiang's grip on Manchuria where, with Soviet support, Hsiung Shih-hui's Nationalist Northeast Provisional Headquarters had created 10 token municipal administrations during January. From New Year's Day 1946, the Bureau unleashed a propaganda campaign against the presence of Hsuing and the Nationalist forces, demanding, in essence, that the area should come under total Communist control.

Such demands were deeply embarrassing to the Central Committee in Yenan, who publicly supported the Nationalist presence as a symbol of national sovereignty. In Chungking, Chou En-lai sought to reassure both the Nationalists and the United States but, inevitably, there was a credibility gap. He may have been dissembling but, given the Communists' weak military position, it is probable that he was trying to paper over cracks in Party unity. In all this, the Nationalists merely saw further evidence of Communist duplicity and the conservatives' resolve to reimpose central authority and oppose regionalism was strengthened.

Conservative fervour was further roused by the publication of the terms of the Yalta Treaty, in February 1946, while Chiang's conciliatory policy in Manchuria bewildered them. During the momentous Kuomintang Central Executive Committee meeting in March which amended the PCC proposal, they launched an indirect attack upon Chiang by moving a vote of censure on Hsiung Shih-hui. Although Chiang's personal intervention thwarted this move, he could not persuade the Committee to support economic concessions to the Soviets in Manchuria, where the Sino–Soviet honeymoon quickly ended. There the Soviet troops had failed to withdraw from Manchuria on 1 February 1946 as agreed, claiming that there was not enough coal for the railways. Meanwhile, Stalin made half-hearted attempts to negotiate commercial concessions.[3]

By March it was obvious that no more could be wrung out of the Nationalists and Stalin reviewed his options. Marshall's presence underlined Chiang's pro-American policy, renewing Soviet fears of United States' air bases in Manchuria. This, Stalin was determined to avoid. As open opposition would have brought conflict with the Americans, he decided to destabilise the region by using the Chinese Communists as a surrogate army.

While some of the captured war material from the Kwantung Army had already been scrapped, the Communists were now given what was left. By these means Stalin hoped not only to prevent the Nationalists from consolidating their authority but also, possibly, to gain sufficient leverage to extract from them those commercial concessions which had so far eluded him. His long term objective may well have been the creation of a more traditional Communist Party in China.

There is some dispute over the quantity of arms involved for while the Kwantung Army was known to be desperately short of equipment in August 1945, at the time of the Japanese surrender, the Soviets claimed to have captured much war material. What we do know is that in the spring of 1946 they began large scale deliveries to Communist-held cities in the north and that in the south of the region they simply abandoned numerous arms dumps.[4]

The Communists Take Changchun

The expectation of a Soviet withdrawal in February led to clashes in the Liao valley during January as the Nationalists moved slowly towards Mukden. During the first half of that month, they occupied Changchun and Yingkou. In addition, some 8,000 men supplemented the Soviet garrison in Mukden. In mid-February, Lin Pao, the Communist commander, personally directed a short spoiling operation while his guerillas remained active along the whole PEINING railway, preventing the Nationalists from running any trains from Mukden to Peiping until 18 April. The line was under continual attack within the LIAOSI corridor but elsewhere in the region an uneasy calm descended in anticipation of the uncertain date of the Soviet withdrawal.

The Soviets concealed their intentions from both sides and only on 11 March did they inform the Nationalists that their army would complete its evacuation by the end of April. As part of that operation, the Soviet Army quit Mukden on 19 March with the Nationalists quickly occupying the city. However, Lin Piao's Northeast Democratic United Army (as the Communist forces were known from January) was in an arc north and east of the city. Formidable as this may have appeared, the truth is that Lin Pao's troops were united in name alone. He appears never to have visited Chou Pao-chung's Northeast People's Self Defence Army, whose 55,000 men regarded themselves as a separate entity.

For Chou and his Soviet-influenced forces, the lure of the cities was irresistible and drew them to Changchun when the Soviet Army withdrew on 14 April. Four days later, supported by 200 Japanese gunners and tank crews, whom his men had recruited from prison camps, Chou attacked the city. The defence, a heterogeneous force of some 14,000 men, known as the New 27th Corps and commanded by a former puppet army officer, Chiang Peng-fei, was quickly overwhelmed. Chiang Peng-fei was captured and subsequently tried and executed in Harbin five months later.

The confusion which dominated the Chinese scene at this time was intense. The Soviets were backing one side against the other, within the minds of all other parties there were uncertainties which existed about the true significance of the American presence, while there remained a deep division within the Communist ranks over policy. All this occurred against the background of Marshall's desperate efforts to induce some form of cohesion into the move towards a national government and despite the fragility of the so-called cease-fire, now hopelessly ruptured by Chou's attack on Changchun.

That flagrant violation of the cease-fire hardened Nationalist hearts and they now resolved to regain Changchun before resuming the constitutional process. However, they had a tough nut to crack, for Lin Piao's main force lay between them and Ssuping, the key to the regional rail network, controlling as it did the range of low hills between the Sungari and Liao valleys through which the Harbin–Mukden railway line passed. That line was the main axis of the nine-division Nationalist advance but this was offering an exposed right flank. To cover this flank four divisions were assigned but the spring thaw now turned the plain on the flank into a huge swamp, making progress impossible.

The Ssuping Campaign

The offensive got off to a very slow start from 19 March because Lin had demolished the bridges and culverts along the railway and his guerillas kept up harrassing attacks on the Nationalist lines of communication. In addition, his 70,000 men had feverishly prepared extensive field fortifications in front of Ssuping and the exhausted Nationalists had to halt when they reached them in mid-April. For a fortnight they launched successive, uncoordinated, piecemeal frontal assaults with in-adequate artillery support – repeating tactical weaknesses which their American military advisers had observed in operations against the Japanese often by the same formations.

Only in late April, as the ground dried and dense clouds of dust blew across the Communist trenches, did the tide of battle turn. Protection of the Nationalists' open right flank had at last been achieved by a thrust from Mukden which now outflanked Lin Pao's left, as attacks on his right prevented him from meeting this new threat. On 18 May, supported by tanks, the Nationalists began a double envelopment of Ssuping, forcing Lin Piao to withdraw that night to positions further north. The city fell on 19 May and Changchun four days later. As the withdrawal continued towards the sanctuary of the River Sungari, Communist morale collapsed. Some 2,000 were captured, many finding that their hiding place had been betrayed by Manchurian peasants.

*　　*　　*

Upon returning to China after an absence of five weeks, shortly before the fall of Ssuping to the Nationalists, Marshall found his framework for peace collapsing like the proverbial pack of cards. After their seizure of Changchun, the Communists had not only refused to surrender the city but also had sought to capitalise their success by strengthening their position in Manchuria. After the Nationalist success at Chungchin in May, Chou En-lai had become more conciliatory in his dealings but Chiang was now determined to extract concessions at bayonet point.

Worried and depressed, Marshall now sought to drag both sides back from the chasm of civil war. Adopting the role of mediator once more, he vainly warned Chiang against over-extending the army and thereby ruining the prospects of peace, but the heady triumphs of victory in the field had deafened the Generalissimo. Once the Communist armies were destroyed, he said, then anything could be discussed. He claimed that he had heard nothing from his field commanders since the fall of Ssuping and decided to fly to Manchuria to take personal control. Desperate and exhausted, Marshall now compromised his role as mediator. In a gamble to stop the Nationalist advance, as he learned of the fall of Changchun, he offered Chiang the use of his own aircraft to speed him on his way – an offer which was promptly accepted.

However, when he reached the battlefield, Chiang urged his generals to continue the advance, asserting that he would only accept a cease-fire if the Communists re-opened the railways in northern China. At a meeting with Marshall in Nanking on 3 June, however, he allowed himself to be persuaded to accept a 10-day cease-fire pending negotiations, not only for the re-opening of the railways but for the integration of the Communist forces into the national army. Marshall's success had come only because he had threatened to abandon his role as mediator and Chiang had feared that such a step would jeopardise his American support. He felt confident that he had inflicted a decisive defeat upon Mao in Manchuria but he warned Marshall, nevertheless, that this would be his last diplomatic effort.

Even as Marshall and Chiang were negotiating, Tu Yu-ming's Nationalist troops had seized a bridgehead over the Sungari and were poised to take the Communist capital of Harbin. When the cease-fire order was issued on 6 June, Tu protested bitterly but to no avail and the order became effective at midnight.

Despite an inauspicious start, the campaign had been a tremendous success for Chiang, whose troops had inflicted some 20,000 casualties on the Communists at a cost of only 7,600 men to themselves. However, the Communist armies were still intact and the paper-thin bonds of trust so carefully created by Marshall had been torn to shreds. Although the events in Manchuria were not the only cause of the open breach they were certainly the catalyst.

*   *   *

Chiang's view of the situation that now prevailed was inspired by the experience of his personal hero Tseng Kuo-fan, who had defeated the revolutionary Taiping movement in the 19th century. After many disappointments, Tseng had achieved victory by purely military means, defeat turning the rebel movement in upon itself.[5] By the summer of 1946, Chiang clearly believed that history was being repeated, that the Communists had reached the limit of their endeavours and that he could now annihilate them.

Certain of ultimate triumph, he may well have hoped that the process would be facilitated by schism within the enemy camp. 'Given time' he told Marshall, 'the ripe apple will fall into our laps'.[6] Provided that his own forces kept up the pressure, for Chiang the negotiations were simply a matter of drafting the terms for the enemy's capitulation. Meanwhile, his own contribution to that pressure took the form of a unilateral announcement that the National Assembly would convene in Nanking on 12 November to ratify the revised constitution drafted by the Kuomintang. Understandably, this dismissal of the constitution prepared by the PCC was seen by the Communists as a violation of the political understanding reached in January and, until it was restored, they refused to attend the Assembly.

The Cease-Fire Collapses

Nevertheless, the Communists continued to negotiate in order to buy time in which to strengthen both their army and their control of the countryside. They now reverted to their twin-track approach of the previous autumn, with Chou En-lai seeking a negotiated solution, using Marshall as a mediator, while Mao, in Yenan, supervised preparations for war. The cease-fire was extended, ultimately to 1 July, with both sides claiming that they had issued orders for a cessation of offensive operations while the search for a political solution continued. Yet, once again, that search was overshadowed by the insurmountable twin peaks of Kuomintang power and military integration. The situation was further aggravated by unrealistic Communist demands which included a return to the status quo south of the Great Wall in January and north of it on 7 June as well as confirmation of their rule in both Jehol and Shantung.

Meanwhile, cease-fire or no cease-fire, fighting became increasingly intense as the armies sought to strengthen the hands of their negotiators. The cease-fire eventually suffered 'the death of a thousand cuts' inflicted by a succession of snipings, patrols, ambushes, artillery barrages and local counter-attacks, with only token attempts at restraint.

In mid-July, campaigns directed by Chiang from his summer holiday resort of Kuling, were opened to clear Anhwei and northern Kiangsu. For their part, the Communists now struck the Tsinan–Tsingtao railway while, to the south, their garrison abandoned the Tapieh Mountains and marched westwards across Honan to Shansi. The Mad Hatter's Tea Party was now in full swing! In a kaleidoscopic situation, negotiators daily went through the motions of presenting demands which had been overtaken by events on the battlefield. Nationalist political action was used by the Communists to justify their own 'armed struggle' which, in its turn, was used to justify new Nationalist advances. In truth, both sides now sought a military solution but neither wished to bear the odium of publicly provoking civil war.

On 20 July 1946, the Communist Central Committee ordered the senior Party echelons to prepare for 'a war of self-defence' to defeat Nationalist military action. Perceptively, the Committee noted that despite United States aid, the Nationalist economy was in difficulties. The Committee therefore demanded the preparation of long-term plans, the adoption of mobile warfare and the temporary abandonment of indefensible cities. Land reform was now regarded as the prime means of mobilising the masses, whose support was to be strengthened by improvements to their quality of life.[7]

As the shift to open war fast became unstoppable, Marshall strove valiantly to keep some semblance of peace, aided by the newly appointed US Ambassador, Dr John Leighton Stuart, a distinguished academic. Communist propaganda now became more stridently anti-American. During July there were two incidents involving United States Marines in Hopeh, the second involving an ambush in which several Americans were killed (see page 71).

Marshall's position became further eroded over the question of American aid to China. Under pressure from Congress to reduce public spending and to assist China, the Truman Administration responded with a policy of financial favouritism. On 28 June, shortly before it concluded Lend-Lease arrangements with its other allies, the Administration had extended US$51.7 million worth of Lend-Lease credit to Nanking and on 30 August it sold millions of dollars worth of war-surplus property to them which lay scattered throughout the Pacific rim.

While these actions were regarded in Washington, with the dispassion of an accountant, as symbols of a policy of financial prudence and as foreign aid to a government recognised throughout the world, the Communists in Yenan took a far more jaundiced view. Since Marshall, as the US envoy, adopted a neutral stance in his efforts to avoid civil war, these measures of the Truman Administration, which could only help the Nationalists, were regarded as acts of the deepest duplicity.

Following the extension of Lend-Lease credit in June, Marshall managed to recover a little credibility by securing an arms embargo on China – a measure which could only affect the Nationalists[8] and one which, it will be remembered, Chiang had feared (see page 26). When he learned of the sale of war surplus property, Marshall was driven to give Chou En-lai the lame excuse that the agreement only covered medicines and equipment for the economic rehabilitation of the country – but, not surprisingly, the Communists were unimpressed and most certainly not convinced.[9] Meanwhile, behind the scenes, President Truman had tried twice during August to coerce Chiang into a political compromise by hinting that the absence of a settlement would hinder further American aid, but Chiang ignored these threats since he knew that the two countries were close to the conclusion of a commercial treaty and realised that the President was merely saving face.

Open Warfare Breaks Out

Nothing would now deflect Chiang from his crusade. Indeed, he commented that were he to cease hostilities there would be no way in which he could force the Communists to attend the National Assembly. During July he had already demanded the withdrawal of Communist forces from various strategic locations including the vital railways and it was this demand which ultimately led to the collapse of the rickety edifice of the peace process.

Ever since the Japanese surrender in the previous August, the Communists had maintained a 'corridor' from Hopeh into Manchuria. It crossed the PINGSUI railway and threatened the Nationalist-held PEINING railway. Since the Nationalists held Tatung, which they might well use as a base from which to strike eastwards along the PINGSUI railway, both sides felt under some form of threat in the existing circumstances. So, in August, they attempted simultaneously to resolve their military problems in and around the 'corridor'. In the east, Tu Yu-ming led to a Nationalist offensive from Manchuria into Jehol to secure the PEINING railway while the Communists besieged Tatung from mid-August, thereby giving the Nationalists an excuse to advance along the PINGSUI line to retake Chining on 16 September and relieve Tatung four days later.

With these successes behind them, the Nationalists were now determined to exploit their advantage and, on 30 September, publicly proclaimed an advance upon Kalgan, the last provincial capital in Communist hands. This direct threat to Communist political authority led Chou En-lai to warn that such a move would be seen as proof that the Nationalists were no longer interested in a negotiated peace. Despite Marshall's pleas for restraint, Chiang refused to hold back and Kalgan fell on 10 October. On the same day, the Nationalists announced the reintroduction of conscription and on the next they confirmed that the National Assembly would convene on 12 November.

Open warfare now spread across the whole of northern China but, for cosmetic reasons, the Assembly's opening was delayed by three days, ostensibly to allow the Communists time to reconsider their position. Not surprisingly, the Communists refused to recognise the authority of the Assembly and on the day after its inaugural meeting, Chou En-lai requested air transport to Yenan. He left on 19 November, leaving a small mission which remained in Nanking until February 1947, when the Nationalists 'requested' its departure.

During December, the Assembly adopted most of the PCC constitutional proposals with their Kuomintang amendments. Although the Assembly confirmed the ending of the Kuomintang's political monopoly (an important demand by the PCC) it was given a year's grace during which to prepare for the introduction of democracy. By accepting the diluted proposals put forward by the Kuomintang, the Assembly also endorsed the view that provincial interests should be subordinated to those of the central government and the supremacy of the movement in the nation's political life.

In the light of these far-reaching decisions, the political consensus, essential if the Nationalists and Communists were to be able to negotiate their way away from civil war, was shattered. Moreover, by reducing provincial political power, the Assembly dashed hopes of political compromise for the move was clearly aimed at the Communists' power base.

Marshall Departs

Although he had been convinced since September that mediation was futile, Marshall remained in China and, on 1 December, made a last effort to persuade Chiang to make the political and social reforms vital to the survival of the régime. He warned that the war could not be won purely by military means and that the economy would collapse if the government continued with its present policies. Chiang rejected both arguments, claiming that the rural-based economy of China was more resilient than the American believed. Marshall remained in China for a few more weeks, hoping by his presence to moderate the actions of the National Assembly but left for home on 8 January 1947. Chiang's delight at Marshall's departure turned to chagrin when he learned on the same day that President Truman had nominated George Marshall as US Secretary of State. Simultaneously with this announcement, the State Department released Marshall's final statement on the situation in China in which he blamed the hostilities upon deliberate sabotage by elements of both sides.

*   *   *

Marshall had failed either to avert war or to stimulate the process of political and social reform in Nationalist China which would have laid the foundations of a stable nation capable of acting as a stabilising factor in Asia, as both Washington and Moscow had hoped. Although rival political parties did now exist in China and the Kuomintang monopoly of power had, theoretically been broken, in truth the Kuomintang continued to dominate the political scene until the end of 1947, those of its opponents which it did not ban or absorb being reduced to ciphers. Although the conservatives strengthened their hold within the Kuomintang, this did not prevent the Central Executive Committee from proposing an elaborate programme of reform in mid-September 1947.[10] Chiang rejected the programme, claiming that it was unnecessary, provided that the movement gave effect to its promises of the past two years – yet he then did nothing to implement them.

One consequence of the official ending of Kuomintang political monopoly was that elections were held in late 1947 for both the National Assembly and the Executive Yuan (or Cabinet). In the race for power, the Renovationist Movement dissolved into factions of which the CC Clique remained the strongest. Its members and supporters won most of the seats, despite the fact that both Chiang and the government had sought to have a significant proportion of non-Kuomintang representation in the legislature. Realising that the delicate balance of power was threatened by this situation, Chiang forced the government to persuade some of the CC Clique's candidates to withdraw.

The loss of face and personal prestige which this move caused for the candidates concerned fuelled a parliamentary revolt when the Assembly met on 28 March 1948 to elect a President and Vice-President. While Chiang's candidacy for President was unopposed, his choice for Vice President of Sun Yat-sen's colourless son, Dr Sun Fo, was firmly rejected by a strong liberal-led revolt and Li Tsung-jen was elected. Li was a leader of the Kwantung–Kwangsi clique which had proved a thorn in Chiang's side before the war with Japan and his election caused Chiang to threaten his withdrawal from the race. The CC clique and many generals now announced that they refused to co-operate with any government not led by him (a threat which was to become reality a year later). With great reluctance Chiang then accepted Li's election. However, the vice-president was pointedly ignored at the inaugural ceremony and promptly retired in a huff to his military headquarters in Peiping.

For all the liberals' hopes, Li was to prove a political lightweight. The habit of military discipline and the absence of any national political organisation made him not only unwilling to, but also incapable of, challenging the Generalissimo, whose position was beyond serious challenge with a new cabinet (Executive Yuan) made up of a familiar collection of Kuomintang hacks. Only the Premier, Dr Wong Wen-hao, a world-famous geologist, was of unquestioned integrity but he was without political experience.

The Financial Crisis

The principal problem facing the new government was the state of the economy, which had been deteriorating rapidly for two years. Thanks to the former government's failure to relate income to expenditure, inflation was rampant. Only 35 per cent of expenditure was covered by taxation and reserves, the deficit being made good by printing money. In consequence, the currency's value had decreased in ratio to its volume, the financial barometer of the US:Chinese dollar exchange reflecting the seriousness of the situation. For example, the official exchange rate, set in August 1945, at the end of the war with Japan, had given the US dollar a value of CN$3,350. By January 1947 its black market value had fallen to CN$7,700 and by August of that year it had plummeted to CN$45,000. This, then, was a measure of the depth of the crisis faced by the new government.

Its predecessors had remained complacent and reluctant to impose any form of financial discipline. There had been little effort either to broaden the financial base of the economy or to redistribute the burden of taxation. Attempts to restrict imports had been half-hearted and of short duration. As it had become clear that the government had no solution to offer, both civilian support and army morale had steadily eroded. The war with the Communists, which was still raging, had been a prime factor in the growth of inflation for it disrupted the national economy. The Communists not only occupied the prime timber and cotton-growing areas but had strangled, and continued to strangle, the national system of distribution, by repeatedly attacking the railways. Thus, when good harvests occurred, the government was unable to transport the large quantities of grain available to the cities, where rocketing prices and seasonal food shortages provoked riots.

In the countryside, the economic crisis was even more destructive than in the cities. Prices for agricultural produce were lower in real terms than they had been for years and could not keep pace with inflation, so undermining and eroding rural incomes. Meanwhile, taxes and the costs of production rose unchecked, giving the peasant little incentive to produce any more food than he needed for his family. Thus even though the Nationalist armies gained territory, paradoxically, grain collections had declined when compared to their original quotas; by 43 per cent in 1946 and 48 per cent in the following year. To meet these deficits, the government relied increasingly upon imports, draining the reserves of foreign currency and further eroding the national financial base.

Above all, it was the direct cost of the years of warfare, over which the government could exercise no control, which had really crippled the economy, absorbing more than 70 per cent of the national budget. This was despite the fact that the armed services themselves were surprisingly frugal in fuel, munitions and spares expenditure for, in the war against Japan, the habit of thrift had been essential to survival. Incomplete data suggests that, even in the field, the average monthly ammunition consumption for a Nationalist division was less than 25 tonnes. Similarly, the air force firmly restricted sortie rates, despite the pleas of their American advisers who pointed out that this was hamstringing training and affecting operational efficiency.[11] However, in direct contrast to this spirit of frugality born of necessity, feelings of logistic insecurity had led the Nationalists to spend more than US$400 million upon military equipment – and this figure included no less than US$141 million for a new navy which was irrelevant to the prosecution of the war.[12]

A rapid conclusion to the present war was the obvious solution to Chiang's predicament but it was one that was becoming less and less attainable with every month that the economy haemorrhaged. In February 1947, soon after Marshall's departure, the government had attempted to solve inflation by an arbitrary wage and price freeze. However, as it was unable to impose these restrictions outside the major cities, they merely aggravated the problem. By the end of that year, the spiral was accelerating into hyper-inflation and the Nationalists had been driven to seek economic aid from the United States in return for offers of political reform.

Marshall, who by now was heavily involved in his massive programme of relief for Europe, for which he desperately needed Congressional support, agreed to the Chinese request with some reluctance and categorically refused to provide a permanent prop for the tottering Nationalist economy. On 22 December 1947, the United States Administration requested approval from Congress for a four-year programme of aid for China at a cost of $1.5 billion, with an interim package of $570 million to provide a breathing space for internal reforms. But Congress, mindful that 1948 was a presidential election year, slashed the package to $338 million (see pages 52).

It was like prescribing aspirin to cure cancer. By the summer of 1948 a crisis of confidence was developing in China where 68 per cent of the expenditure was now being met by printing worthless banknotes. In order to restore confidence in the currency, Chiang authorised a cosmetic alternative similar to that which saved the economy of the Weimar Republic in Germany in the 1920s – he created a new currency. The Gold Yuan (GY) was based upon a bullion and jewellery reserve, GY1 being worth CN$3 million or 25 US cents. Introduced on 19 August 1948, it was supported by a package of economic reforms which included a wage-price freeze and an increase in commodity taxes. To increase public confidence, the architects of the new measures, Premier Dr Wong and his Finance Minister Wang Yun-wu, pledged to restrict the quantity of notes printed.

For five weeks the measures worked – but the basic problem remained. On 31 October, Dr Wong and Wang Yun-wu resigned, the government being forced to admit that it had reneged upon its promise to limit the issue of new notes. The inevitable collapse of public confidence occurred just as the Communists, who had rebuilt their army, accomplished the destruction of Nationalist military power north of the Yangtze, paving the way for their advance into southern China.

Nationalist Rural Policy

The story of the ineptitude of the Nationalists' handling of rural affairs almost rivals that of their mismanagement of the economy, the effect of which, by 1948, had been the creation of a rural economy based upon barter. We have already seen how the diminishing return of grain had embarrassed the government, driving them to importing. Nevertheless, Nanking maintained its traditional indifference towards the countryside which it milked mercilessly, ignoring the warnings of the provincial administrations, who were only too keenly aware of the dangers. Now, in 1948, the government demanded ever greater requisitions of grain despite the further warnings of the provincial governors that the peasants had reached the limits of their endurance, having already lost a third of their grain to requisitions of one sort or another.

Land tax, which had been reintroduced in June 1946, was a major source of discontent. Not only were the records inaccurate but, as Chiang himself was well aware, contributions were in inverse proportion to wealth, so that the poorest paid most, often with the connivance of officials. It is little wonder that a sense of despair permeated the countryside with some peasants fleeing to the cities, some turning to banditry while others committed suicide. Small wonder too that Chiang's rural subjects often welcomed Communist rule to escape the crushing burden of the fiscal obligation imposed upon them by the government.

In newly recaptured territory, Nationalist economic mismanagement and exploitation was often exacerbated by the rapaciousness and brutality of returning landlords. They reimposed high rents and reintroduced high interest rates, ignoring not only the Nationalist law of 1930 but also an even more favourable one of 1945. They demanded back rents for the period of Communist rule and, ignoring official decrees, took revenge upon activists prominent in Communist land reform movements. Thousands of countryfolk perished or were imprisoned, some having surrendered under promise of an amnesty. After an initial period of shock, the peasants realised that they had little option but to store their resentment and await an opportunity for revenge.

The army was aware of these problems and, in October 1946, the Supreme National Defence Council had discussed a scheme for rent and interest rate reductions in pacification areas – but, in the end, took no action. However, at about the same time, T. V. Soong, Chiang's brother-in-law and President of the Executive Yuan, set up a pilot project in some 80 districts by which large land holders sold to the government those plots which they could not work. The government, in its turn, leased the plots to peasants with little or no land.

That apart, Nanking made little further effort to appease rural land hunger until September 1948. Then, in the face of Communist advances, Nanking and some provincial governments proposed buying more land from landlords and redistributing it to the peasants. However, these later measures were still the subject of discussion when the Nationalists lost control north of the Yangtze.[13]

Communist Policies in the Countryside

In direct contrast to their Nationalist enemies, the Communists increasingly committed everything to the countryside. However, their control remained uncertain in many areas until the middle of 1948.

In the aftermath of the Japanese surrender, moderate policies had officially been in force but the 'settling of accounts' with collaborators had excited revolutionary passions. During the winter of 1945–46 the clamour for wholesale land reform had increased and as war with the Nationalists became inevitable, the need to mobilise peasant support forced the Party's hand.

On 4 May 1946, the Central Committee had issued a directive on 'Liquidations, Rent Reductions and Land Problems' which called for the redistribution of land and property to benefit the poorest peasants. This measure reversed the Party's attitude to the class struggle during the war with the Japanese, when the need to establish Communist administrations in the villages had forced it to adopt conciliatory policies towards the rural leadership. Now the imminent prospect of civil war had made it imperative that the authority of the 'big trees' should be destroyed by means of uniting the peasantry against them. Later, in order to consolidate its control, the Party would find that more conservative policies would be needed. Thus it was that radicalism flourished in inverse proportion to military success – increasing as the Nationalists advanced and diminishing as they retreated.

The seizure of the 'big trees' property was controlled by the poor peasant organisation under the guidance of cadres. It involved what were known as 'struggle sessions' in which luckless men and women were systematically stripped of all they possessed. So important was this process seen to be that it was even carried out at gun point behind enemy lines by work-teams operating on a hit-and-run basis. Fearing retaliation from either side, peasants in contested areas and villages left much of the land to lie fallow, a development which caused the Communists greater concern than any amount of peasant suffering. By February 1947, the Party claimed that some 60 million poor peasants had each received up to six *mou* (0.40 hectare) of land. It was now the poor who dominated village life with many activists becoming cadres. The cadres were responsible for distributing property and were directed to exploit the villagers' gratitude in order to secure supplies and recruits for the People's Liberation Army (PLA).[14]

Communist Excesses

However, land reform proved something of a poisoned chalice. In many villages it was only half completed and in others hardly begun; 'half cooked rice' and 'uncooked rice' in Communist jargon. This occurred largely because of a shortage of experienced cadres who had had to rush the process, leaving it to new cadres who were not only politically, but sometimes educationally, illiterate. Many of these proved both incompetent and corrupt, arousing discontent which was aggravated by the seemingly interminable process of distribution. In practice, widespread distribution of the property of 'big trees' brought only minor benefit to the poor and this, in its turn, created further discontent which the inexperienced cadres tried to deflect by finding new victims among the rich and middle peasants. These poor wretches were now subjected by the poor to 'struggle sessions' with beatings commonly administered, mutilation not unknown and executions all too frequent.

Mao and the other senior Party leaders became aware of these problems during 1947 although their principal concern lay in falling production rather than in human suffering. There was also a major political threat, for one result of land reform was that now up to half the peasants were in the middle category of affluence, which supplied up to 40 per cent of the PLA.

There was considerable unease in the army at this time, a disquiet which was only partly allayed by a campaign of political education designed to sustain the troops' loyalty to the Party. Despite this campaign, doubts clearly remained, especially about post-war Party policy. These lingered on for some years so that many Chinese prisoners taken in Korea after 1950 refused repatriation.

All these rumblings in the countryside and the army caused growing concern within the Party, provoking considerable debate about the limits of land reform and the attitude which should be adopted towards the 'middle peasant'. These issues surfaced at the National Land Conference, held at Hsipaipo, near Shihchiachuang, in Hopeh in September 1947 with Liu Shao-chi as the chairman. This conference led to the publication of the Outline Agrarian Law on 10 October, allowing the redistributed land to be treated as private property. During the conference, and in the discussions which followed when the regional branches considered the new law, there was considerable criticism of the work of the cadres. However, in the first instance it was the conservative or 'Right Tendency' cadres who came in for this criticism rather than the radical 'Left Tendency'. In consequence the middle peasants continued to suffer from the excesses of the latter.

Realising the need for action, Mao hinted to the Central Committee, on Christmas Day 1947, that middle peasant support needed cultivation. Within two months, a new policy had been hammered out and on 22 February a new directive was issued. This called for protection for middle peasants and effectively halted land reform in areas where more than half the population were in that category. Where more than half were poor peasants, however, the process was to continue on a voluntary basis. A particularly interesting aspect of the directive was that it contained official encouragement to surviving landlords and rich peasants to invest in both industry and commerce.

One consequence of the Communists' investment in land reform was a large dividend in the form of a wave of recruits for the army. This included 1.5 million poor peasants, many of whom had been persuaded to leave their newly acquired land by the cadres playing on their justified fear of the landlords' revenge. This great influx produced not only more fighting troops but large numbers of *min-fu*, unarmed peasants who transported supplies, evacuated the wounded and repaired the roads.

The mobilisation of the countryside greatly assisted the Communists' triumph in the field – providing manpower in abundance together with logistic support. Simultaneously the reforms consolidated Party power in the rear areas – as had been hoped. Indeed without this political activity, the Communist cause could never have triumphed.

As their area of control increased, the Communists amended their February directive at the end of May with a view to assisting further the process of consolidation. In future, land reform would only be carried out in areas which were militarily secure and where there were enough cadres to implement it.

With measures such as these, the advancing Communists were welcomed almost everywhere, everywhere that is except in the political strongholds which they had established between the Yellow River and the Yangtze from 1938 to 1946. The reason for this was clear enough, for many of those areas had been overrun by the Nationalists in 1946–47, exposing the peasants to the savage retribution of the returning landlords. All too often, the cadres had refused to face up to this ordeal and had abandoned the unfortunate peasants to their fate while they themselves sought sanctuary in the Communist bases. A few cadres did something to salvage tattered Communist prestige by joining surviving activists in hiding, from where they organised resistance on the part of the poor peasant organisation. Using 'sparrow tactics' (low level guerilla warfare), they gradually regained control of villages and even districts, frequently by the liberal use of terror against the 'big trees' and their 'running dogs'.

Later, when the Communists returned to such districts, they encountered far greater difficulty in rebuilding their organisation than they did in areas which had never previously been under their control. The peasants cursed the cadres for abandoning them to the vengeance of the landlords. Indeed, they refused even to attend open meetings, they were unwilling to provide any help to the PLA or even to supply it with information.[15] Only gradually did confidence return when, shielded by the PLA, the peasants were able to take their revenge against the remaining 'big trees' and begin the process of land reform.

*   *   *

Marshall Examines the Options

As the tide of war turned perceptibly against the Nationalists during 1947, the United States had remained an agonised observer. It was not surprising that, in the light of his own experience in China, Marshall put in hand a review of Sino–American policy soon after his appointment as US Secretary of State. The review was completed in the spring of 1947 but its findings were no different from those given earlier to Marshall by Ambassador Stuart in Nanking – that there were three options: to withdraw, to provide aid in exchange for political and economic reforms, or to do nothing.

Even before Marshall's appointment, the loss of the 1946 Congressional elections by the Democrats had meant that there was in any case little scope for radical action with Congress now under Republican control but with a Democrat still in the White House, facing the prospect of a Presidential election in 1948. The American State Department, and Marshall in particular, had no illusions about the incompetence and inefficiency of the Nationalist administration in China and its obstinate refusal to countenance reform. Yet the abandonment of China to the Communists was unacceptable to either shade of political opinion in the United States for strategic, economic and political reasons as the slide towards the Cold War continued. There was really only one option to pursue, the second. However, the decision to end the United States arms embargo, taken on 26 May 1947 effectively signalled the abandonment of any serious attempt to put pressure on Chiang, who in any case had two other good cards up his sleeve.

The first was the growing public affiliation between the Chinese Communists and the Soviet Union. During Marshall's time in China, the Communists had publicly criticised the Americans for appearing to support the Nationalists. Their own support for the Soviets had been more muted, not least because, at times, Soviet policy had seemed to play one side off against the other. However, during 1947 that support had become more strident, culminating in Mao's statement in December entitled 'The Present Situation and Our Tasks', in which he firmly aligned Revolutionary China with the Soviet-led 'anti-imperialist camp'.[16]

Chiang's second card was the assurance of a sympathetic hearing from the Republican Party in Washington, with its isolationist policy towards Europe and interventionist leanings towards Asia. That the Republican Party now dominated the Senate was a boon when he pleaded with the Administration for aid. Such pleas were dictated more by prestige than necessity, especially where military equipment was concerned, for there were no shortages of that until 1949. Because Washington would deal only through his régime, Chiang's international and national status was enhanced while his control of military supplies helped to regulate the political ambitions of his military subordinates.

A good deal of uneasiness was still being felt in Washington about Chiang's prospects and, in July 1947, this disquiet led to General Wedermeyer being sent back to China at the head of a mission to assess the situation in mainland Asia. Wedermeyer was appalled by the deterioration which had set in in China within a year. However, when he reported back to Marshall on 19 September, he could only endorse the State Department's existing policy, although he did recommend stricter supervision of aid by the United States. Fearing that this would lead to an open-ended commitment to China and because of Wedermeyer's advocacy of an international trusteeship for Manchuria, Marshall unwisely suppressed the report, fuelling Republican suspicions of a Communist fifth column within the State Department.

For all the concern expressed in Washington about China, few believed it to be a short-term problem, unlike the rapidly deteriorating situation in Europe. The Truman Doctrine, pronounced in March 1947, had already signalled the Administration's determination to intervene there and, to that end, even as the Wedermeyer Report was being digested, a massive programme of aid for Europe was being prepared by the State Department. With the Republican watchdogs in Congress determined to reduce the Federal Budget, the Administration recognised the need for Republican support.

The price exacted was an aid programme for China – a package of $1.5 billion, spread over four years, being proposed in December 1947.

Even if the package had been proposed earlier it was too late. The Kuomintang's shortcomings were now displayed on the battlefield where the Communists increasingly seized the initiative. By 1948 the tide had turned remorselessly in their favour yet still the scale of the impending catastrophe to American fortune was not perceived.

The United States' Presidential Election

In the light of the Nationalists' growing economic crisis, the proposed package of aid was later amended to provide $570 million worth of economic aid over a period of 12 months. However, a parsimonious Congress slashed the economic aid package to $338 million when the China Aid Act was passed on 2 April 1948, although there was a special allocation of $125 million for military equipment to be supplied at President Truman's discretion. The Act, as one historian has observed, was a programme of half-measures with no prospect of success and proved unpopular with the Chinese, who regarded it as something that would prolong the war.

The Nationalists believed that the Act heralded massive United States assistance which would follow the 1948 Presidential election campaign, now rapidly gathering momentum. The colourless Truman and his policies were widely unpopular within the United States so that the election of the Republican candidate, Governor Thomas E. Dewey, was generally regarded as a foregone conclusion. As we have seen, Chiang had been carefully cultivating Republican support ever since their 1946 victory in the Congressional elections and now, in the run-up to the election, he concentrated his wooing upon Dewey, who responded by raising Nationalist hopes with a pledge to provide both financial assistance and military advisers. It was against his background that the Nationalists had taken their decision to introduce the Gold Yuan (see page 44).

The Collapse of Nationalist Fortunes

The Presidential election provided a period of reflection for the State Department. In the face of growing Communist military success Washington, from late October, pondered on its response to the anticipated Communist occupation of northern China. The optimists took the view that the tide of nationalism would produce a schism between China and the Soviet Union, as had recently happened in Yugoslavia. In those circumstances, it was hoped that economic factors would protect American interests and lead to a resumption of good Sino–American relations.

But it was not to be for the election produced a political shock which no one had foreseen. On 2 November, as Mukden fell to the Communists, bringing a triumphant end to their second Manchurian offensive, Truman's astonishing victory in the election was announced. Despite the passage of the China Aid Act in April, the newly elected President soon took his revenge upon Chiang for his involvement with Dewey, responding to all his pleas for aid and assistance by sharply reminding him that the United States had already provided no less than $3.8 billion's worth.

The sharp change in American foreign policy was now underlined by Marshall's replacement by Dean Acheson on 21 January 1949. Whether by accident or design, Chiang Kai-shek officially withdrew from public life on the same day, ostensibly to ensure the success of negotiations with the Communists (as we shall now see).[17]

* * *

As the loss of northern China become daily more certain, the pressure upon Chiang to negotiate a settlement increased. The failure of the 1948 economic reforms only served to accelerate the decline of his prestige. As the crisis deepened during the autumn, he was bombarded with telegrams from the provincial governors, led by the former Minister of National Defence, Pai Chung-hsi, urging him to start negotiating.

Until New Year's Day 1949, he refused but the imminent loss of his Peiping and Hsuchou garrisons now led him to indicate to the Communists that his government was willing to enter into negotiations. The offer was contemptuously rejected, as were the government's pleas on 8 January for foreign intervention. On 11 January, Mao set out the Communist terms which, like Chiang's of three years earlier, amounted to a demand for unconditional surrender. Despite the severity of his demands, there were many among the Nationalist leadership who favoured a period of negotiation to buy time while the Yangtze defences were being strengthened. On 16 January, the situation was discussed by the cabinet and such leading figures as Pai Chung-hsi, Yen Hsi-shan and Hu Tsung-nan. Failing to dissuade the meeting from their determination to negotiate, Chiang now fired his Parthian shot by placing the responsibility for the defence of his own province upon the shoulders of each governor. Meanwhile, he (Chiang) would continue to defend the Nanking–Shanghai area.

This pronouncement was the first step in a strategy designed to restore the prestige of the Generalissimo and to help him to defeat the Communists. Having secured his political power, his ultimate and wildly optimistic military aim was to launch a counter-stroke across the Yangtze as he had in August 1927. It was now that he began to use his control of supplies and the air force (see page 153) to neutralise provincial power, forcing the provincial governors to become suppliants for aid. As an added measure of security, he also prepared an impregnable redoubt on Taiwan.

There a dramatic change in Nationalist fortunes had occurred since 1947, when the inhabitants had rioted in protest against the rapacious policies of the governor, General Chen I, hundreds of them perishing in his brutal reaction.[18] In May of that year, Chen had been replaced by a civilian, Wei Tao-ming, whose conciliatory policies had recovered support for the government. This having been achieved, Chiang summarily replaced Wei by Chen Cheng while his own son, Chiang Ching-kuo, became head of the island's Kuomintang.

It was now that Chiang, having secured his military position and neutralised his warlord rivals, took steps to restore his national prestige. With defeat clearly imminent the Generalissimo resorted to his favoured stratagem by which he would allow others to bear the odium while at the same time he demonstrated his personal importance. On 21 January 1949 Chiang announced his withdrawal from public life before a crowd of weeping dignitaries. Yet it should be noted that he was careful not to renounce his title of President, which he had assumed on 19 April 1948.

Retiring to his birthplace at Fenghua, in Chekiang, Chiang still maintained contact with the key figures in both the forces and the government, even building his own airfield to provide ease of access to him when they were summoned. Meanwhile, the Vice-President, Li Tsung-jen, was given the title of Acting President, a title which carried no constitutional status and so rendered Nationalist China's new leader impotent, as he prepared to defend the south of the country against the growing power of the Communists.

3

From the Barrel of a Gun: The Armies and the War 1946–49

MAO OBSERVED that power grows from the barrel of a gun, and indeed the success of the Communist revolution was decided upon the battlefield. The two opposing armies in China were boughs from the same trunk, but which had grown very differently. This 'trunk' was the National Revolutionary Army (NRA) which had conquered China in the 1920s.

In 1927 several Communist-led corps of the NRA had participated in an uprising against Chiang Kai-shek's authority. The revolt was quickly suppressed but the remnants of rebel regiments became the foundation for the Red Army. Even in 1936 the commands of Lin Piao, Liu Po-cheng and Ho Lung could trace their lineage to the NRA whose 'loyal' forces became the Nationalist Army.

Their differences were clearly shown in the basic matter of recruitment which both sides drew from the vast pool of rural manpower. The peasants dreaded military service, as much out of fear of leaving their district as of the dangers and hardships of campaigning. Yet during the civil war the overall quality of the PLA (People's Liberation Army) soldier was far superior to that of his enemy, many of whom were later to join the Communist army.

Until conscription was reintroduced in October 1947 the Nationalist Army relied upon a trickle of volunteers which proved so inadequate that formations were forced to maintain strength by using press gangs. These would literally rope in any unfortunates without the money to evade service and were so feared that the merest hint of their presence would send peasants fleeing. Conscription was theoretically fairer, for it was based upon ballots organised at district level, but the inevitable corruption ensured only the poorest were selected.

The Nationalist Soldier

The unwilling recruits were assembled at holding depots in the major cities where their training was largely confined to drilling before joining their regiments although veterans did provide some rudimentary field training. There the recruits would be robbed of their remaining personal possessions and suffer general ill treatment. Yet, as in the Royal Navy of the 18th century, once the recruits overcame their initial despair they came to regard the formation as their new family.

Like the French soldier before the Petain reforms of 1917, the Nationalist soldier was largely left to his own devices when not in action. This lax discipline meant he could pilfer at will which not only provided him with a sense of power but also helped to bond men who became comrades in crime. Although there was always a trickle of deserters when formations acted as garrisons, once in the field the new recruits appeared to have carried out their duty without complaint. It is noteworthy that, even in adversity, formations would fight to the last and that the impetus for mass surrender or defection came from their leaders.[1]

The Communist Soldier

Communist troops also did their duty but with greater enthusiasm because they were supposed to be volunteers. In practice even the egalitarian Mao recognised the need for professional forces and this led to the emergence of a three-tier structure through which filtered a military elite. At the lowest level was the Village Self Defence Corps, an ill-armed militia drawn from all men between 15 and 55, who operated within district boundaries. The best of these armed civilians were turned into professional soldiers when they were recruited into the regional forces, who are often described, like the self defence corps, as guerillas. Both were controlled by the Party regional bureaux, reflecting their political–military role which was to support the work teams' challenge to enemy political and social authority. Both had auxiliary roles in conventional operations, being responsible for reconnaissance, harassment and sieges, and they would engage the Nationalist Army under field army command only when stiffened by the field forces.

The regional forces usually operated within provincial boundaries and their best men were selected for the mobile field forces. Often described as 'regulars' they were the cutting edge of the PLA and, theoretically, could be deployed anywhere in China. Their role was to engage the enemy army, either to assist the expansion of the Party's administration or to protect it from attack. As the PLA adapted to conventional warfare the recruiting process was also modified with regional forces being upgraded en bloc into the field forces while recruits were drafted directly into field force regiments.

All Communist recruits were supposed to be volunteers, and some undoubtedly were, but most were dragooned into volunteering. Peasants were supposed to join the PLA in gratitude for the benefits of land reform which actually provided an incentive for them to remain in their villages to secure the spoils of revolution. This posed a dilemma for cadres who were assigned recruiting quotas, usually 30 to 80 men per village, but who had no powers of conscription. Instead they used Party influence to put communal pressure upon families, especially those who had most benefited from the revolution, into providing a 'volunteer'. In return the Party had to guarantee the 'volunteer's' interests, even ensuring their wives would not divorce them while they were away.

The use of regional force regiments within provincial boundaries broadened the recruit's outlook while reducing his homesickness, a potential source for desertion. Political officers also encouraged veterans to help the recruit feel at home by sharing some of the few luxuries, such as soap. The presence of political officers throughout the command spectrum not only ensured the army would loyally carry out the Party's bidding but also helped *esprit de corps*. Political 'education' encouraged troops to regard themselves as the leading edge of a political and social crusade which would bring the people a better life. It was a belief which the PLA retained after the war and carried it to international disgrace at Tien-an Men (Tianamen) Square in 1989. During the war it created an atmosphere of mutual confidence and an environment in which the recruit could concentrate upon developing professional skills.

Such professionalism in the fields of camouflage, co-ordination, infiltration and weapon proficiency was both encouraged and demanded by the field army commanders. At battalion and regimental levels considerable attention was paid to planning and preparation, with NCOs and other ranks encouraged to participate. Whenever possible there would be a debriefing session, sometimes attended by the wounded, in which collective and individual actions would be examined and the lessons analysed. It was by these means that the PLA rapidly gained a significant tactical advantage over its enemies.

Nationalist Officers

As a post-war Nationalist study admitted their troops were reluctant to engage in hand-to-hand combat, they were terrified of operating at night, were road-bound and possessed poor fire discipline. Reconnaissance was cursory, patrolling inadequate while in attack there was a propensity towards frontal assault with initiative conspicuous by its rarity. In the field, troops marched along roads in close-order columns with inadequate flank protection which made them appallingly vulnerable to ambush.

The tactical inferiority of the Nationalist Army reflected the poor quality of its officers at all levels. Below regimental level the only thing expected of an officer was that in battle he conduct himself bravely and with dignity to act as an example to the men; tactical ability was a bonus. Only 27 per cent of the regimental to divisional commanders had enjoyed formal military education while the remainder were promoted from the ranks.

Military academy graduates dominated the higher levels but their education had focused upon classical theory with little attempt to study modern warfare and few subsequently received any form of formal military education. Consequently planning was cursory and ignored terrain, intelligence or logistics while staff work was little more than the issue of outline orders whose detailed execution was left to lower echelons. Staff officers were generally regarded as little more than clerks while the graduates of specialist schools endured a similar status because their ill-educated seniors regarded expertise as a threat to their authority.

Communist Officers

By contrast the PLA tried hard to improve officers' education, for its leaders recognised the benefits which would accrue in improved battlefield performance. Most field armies had some form of training organisation which became more sophisticated as the demand for specialists grew to meet the challenge of conventional warfare. The traditional Chinese respect for education provided these graduates with a far higher status than in the enemy army. A senior Nationalist officer was later to observe that within the Communist armies, advancement depended upon battlefield success rather than personal background, connections or educational background.[2]

The implied criticism of the Nationalist Army leadership was well-founded, for its performance in the field was mired by a swamp of personal relationships. Loyalty to superiors was the prerequisite for command and in return the patron would provide supplies, equipment and replacements together with advancement. So tight was the strait-jacket of loyalty that all ranks would ignore orders from an officer outside the formation's chain of command, unless he demonstrated he had the commander's authority.

Rivalries within the Nationalist Army

This system of patronage hid rivalries which, like the flaws in an uncut diamond, appeared with shattering consequences at moments of crisis. Within the army there was a mutual antipathy between the provincial and Kuomintang (or Central Army) military leaderships, both of which were also riven by factionalism. For the provincial leaders the struggle for power and influence before the Japanese invasion had created a miasma of mistrust between individuals. Among the Kuomintang generals, or Whampoa Clique,[3] the prime divisions were between the supporters of Chen Cheng and Ho Ying-chin. Chen, whose star was in the ascendant during the civil war, was Chief of the General Staff from June 1946, while Ho was in the United States from October 1946 to March 1948 before succeeding Pai Chung-hsi as Minister of National Defence. Together with divisions between the generations of Whampoa graduates, these rivalries made mutual support in the field at all levels almost impossible. On numerous occasions surrounded units were abandoned to their fate by comrades who could easily have relieved them.

Personal rivalries were aggravated by organisational ones. The Nationalist Army followed the German pattern in creating a general staff, responsible for operational matters, and the Ministry of National Defence, responsible for administrative ones. Each encroached upon the other but the Chief of the General Staff had the advantage of direct access to the Generalissimo, who remained the ultimate authority. Yet neither Chiang nor the general staff could impose that authority upon the regional commanders. Instead, as in the Imperial Japanese Army which so influenced the Nationalist generals, decisions were reached by a consensus. Divisions also existed in the vital field of intelligence where the army and the Kuomintang maintained their own apparatus. The Whampoa Clique dominated the Bureau of Investigation and Statistics of the National Military Affairs Commission which was led by Tai Li. After his death, the bureau was supposed to be merged with the Bureau of Investigation and Statistics of the Kuomintang Central Executive Committee,[4] itself dominated by the Kuomintang's Organisation Bureau. But both organisations retained their independence and were extremely jealous of each other.[5]

PLA Cohesion

By contrast the PLA, while physically divided, retained an enviable cohesion. Its titular head was the Military Affairs Committee at Yenan which could not control operations in detail. Instead its executive arm, the Revolutionary Military Council headed by Chu Teh as commander in chief of the PLA and Yeh Chien-ying as chief of the general staff, developed general concepts of operations. They then sought to co-ordinate the field commanders' actions, usually by means of an insecure and unreliable radio link. Essentially the two organisations remained a military secretariat until a provisional capital was established at Shihchiachuang in the summer of 1948 when they were able to adopt a more conventional role.

Much depended upon the field commanders and while personal rivalries undoubtedly existed it did not prevent them responding to pleas for support even when hard-pressed themselves. This was, indeed, a significant feature of the operations conducted by Liu Po-cheng and Chen Yi in central China. The demands of guerilla warfare forced the Communists to adopt a more pragmatic policy towards commanders, for only the skilful and the lucky survived. Li Hsien-nien, for example, succeeded in evading entrapment in the Tapieh Mountains of Central China during the summer of 1946 but his command was wrecked and Li was transferred to political duties. A degree of military and political patronage certainly existed within PLA ranks and most field army commanders had supported Mao during the Long March. Yet he would quickly have removed them if they failed on the battlefield where their success allowed them to replace most of Mao's much touted theories of people's warfare with a more conventional approach.[6]

Higher Direction of the War

However, in studying Communist strategy against the Japanese in 1938, Mao produced the blueprint for the Communist strategic concept of the civil war. In 'Problems of Strategy in Guerilla War Against Japan' Mao emphasised operations based upon mobile warfare with aggressive tactics even when the Communists were on the defensive. Confrontation with the enemy was to be avoided, except in the most favourable circumstances, until he was dispersed. This process was to be encouraged by large scale guerilla warfare which would erode enemy strength, place him on the defensive and eventually seize the initiative from him.[7]

The process involved three strategic phases which he detailed in 'On Protracted War'. In the first, as the enemy advanced, the Communists would adopt a strategic defensive but a tactical offensive using both mobile and guerilla operations to erode enemy strength. This would lead to a stalemated second stage when the enemy tried to consolidate the newly conquered territory but found his authority challenged through large scale guerilla warfare. Eventually the enemy would be placed on the strategic defensive and the mobile field forces, supported by guerillas, would drive him into the cities which would then be isolated and stormed.[8] In practice guerilla operations, 'sparrow warfare' in Communist terminology, played a smaller role than Mao had envisaged because the field army commanders placed greater reliance upon mobile conventional operations.

Despite possessing Mao's blueprint, neither the Communists nor the Nationalists attempted detailed strategic planning until 1949 because their forces were too dispersed to be effectively controlled. The Nationalists were largely confined to the valleys, the plains and corridors along the main railway lines. The Communists were in the mountains and marshes which were difficult for the enemy to penetrate and even more difficult to secure. These dispositions created a strategic jigsaw which neither side could complete until late 1948. The Nationalists sought to control the railways, then to destroy the enemy bases in detail, while the Communists sought to control the people and to bind their enemies to the cities. Neither side was capable of applying the traditional 'horizontal' (west–east) or 'vertical' (north–south) Chinese strategies and instead they struggled at 'operational'[9] level for regional supremacy in three theatres; Manchuria, the area north of the Wei and Yellow Rivers, and finally the area between the Yellow and the Yangtze Rivers.

The Nationalist Army's 'operational' concepts were a mixture of experience gained during the warlord years and the successful pre-war 'bandit extermination campaigns'. The emphasis was upon possessing the major towns and cities to provide secure bases and the railways to provide freedom of 'operational' movement. However, the warlord influence was such that many commanders were reluctant to risk the destruction of their forces in battle and when large Communist forces were encountered there was a tendency to meet them by deploying formations piecemeal. Once they achieved urban security the Nationalists would theoretically begin to sweep the countryside clear of enemy guerillas, surround their bases and slowly crush them. However, in practice Nationalist commanders were primarily concerned with protecting their own bases and their refusal to support each other made it almost impossible to surround any enemy base.

By contrast the Communist 'operational' philosophy relied upon a Ying and Yang of military and political action to erode enemy control of the countryside. In this philosophy the acquisition of territory was an abstract concept, control of the people being the central truth.

However, within the Communist Party there had always been a dichotomy of thought about military operations. Mao believed guerilla operations, 'sparrow warfare' in Communist parlance, would in itself destroy Nationalist political and military power. He envisaged the enemy gradually losing control of the countryside and eventually being restricted to the cities where they could be starved, or stormed into, submission.

His generals, whose views were to dominate during the civil war, were less optimistic. They believed the issue would be decided by large formations destroying the enemy in the field by means of conventional operations involving firepower and maneouvre. Yet at the same time they recognised their own military weakness, especially in firepower, which moulded their conventional or 'mobile warfare' tactics in the guerilla image.

'Mobile warfare' was based upon light infantry who could move quickly across the most difficult terrain and covertly over the featureless plains. Their mobility enabled the PLA, like a martial arts fighter, to surprise the enemy and deal devastating blows then withdraw before he could recover.

Yet there remained the daunting prospect that the enemy might force the PLA into prolonged and bruising engagements. The Japanese demonstrated this during the Hundred Regiments' Offensive as did the Nationalists on several occasions during 1946. However, the Communists learned from their mistakes and from 1946 there evolved the concept of striking the enemy throughout his 'operational' depth. By threatening the enemy rear in support of 'political struggle' the regional and self-defence forces diluted enemy strength because Nationalist troops were diverted to protect communications, installations and cities. This reduced the size of the strike forces which the Nationalists could commit against the PLA's mobile field forces. These fast moving regiments were then free to erode strike force strength further by selecting killing grounds and drawing individual formations into them. Experience led the PLA's commanders by 1948 to evolve their tactics of encirclement into an 'operational' concept of single or even double envelopment of multiple enemy armies.

As the strike forces were decimated the Nationalists were forced on to the defensive around the cities which in turn opened more areas to 'political struggle'. Yet without the mobilisation of the countryside by Party activists the mobile field forces were helpless, for it was this mobilisation which provided most of the sinews of conventional war. This support was assured even in 'enemy territory' allowing the mobile field forces to the Nationalists' vital areas. It also made the PLA relatively indifferent to the occupation of terrain or cities which were contested only when they offered either 'operational' freedom of movement or opportunities to erode the enemy strike force.

The Nationalist Army

For all Mao's talk of people's war the combined armies of the two sides struggling for the destiny of China's 400 million people never totalled more than 7 million men.[10] In 1946 the Nationalists continued to reduce their wartime army both to save money and to remove a potential political threat. Although the conflict intensified during 1946, Nationalist Army strength fell from 3 million to 2.6 million, but the following year it was expanded to a wartime peak of 2.7 million, of whom approximately a third were in support formations and organisations.[11]

It was supported by three uniformed paramilitary organisations; the Peace Preservation Corps, the railway police and the traffic police, created to protect communications and small towns from bandits. These lightly armed forces were under constant pressure from the Communists who milked them mercilessly of arms and equipment. The Peace Preservation Corps was the most numerous, drawing most of its personnel from the army but training and morale were poor. While the police continued to be organised into regiments, the Peace Preservation Corps was herded into larger units, up to brigade size, but without any improvement in effectiveness. The villages also had their own militia as protection against bandits but the men were poorly armed and in the civil war their loyalties inevitably lay with the stronger side.

The People's Liberation Army

In contrast to the Nationalist Army the PLA continued to expand after VJ Day and by June 1946 it had 1,278,000 men and women. During the next 12 months it expanded to 1,950,000 despite numerous defeats and heavy casualties. With the tide of victory flowing strongly, PLA strength swelled to 2.8 million by June 1948 aided by the defection of disgruntled Nationalist troops. This trickle became a flood in the following months and nearly doubled PLA strength which reached 4 million with the fall of Peiping in February 1949.[12]

Organisation

This expansion broke the cocoon of wartime organisation and with new field armies being created, a fundamental reorganisation became essential. On 1 May 1946 the Eighteenth Army became the PLA and field armies were assigned to support the party bureaux whose titles they shared.[13] There were six of these field armies; the Northeastern (Manchurian), the Shansi–Kansu–Ninghsia (known by its Chinese acronym of SHENKANNING), the Shensi–Suiyuan (CHINSUI), Shansi–Chahar–Hopeh (CHINCHACHI), the Shansi–Hopeh–Shantung–Honan (CHINCHILUYU) and the East China. In February 1949 the field armies were retitled the 1st (North West), 2nd (CHINCHILUYU), 3rd (East China), 4th (North East) and North China (CHINCHACHI) Field Armies.[14]

Nationalist Formations and Logistics

Nationalist 'operational' organisation was less radical with the wartime zone headquarters renamed commands which bore the name of the city where they were located i.e. Peiping, Hsuchou, Chengchou, Sian and Wuhan.[15] Each consisted of several armies, and most also controlled a number of pacification areas which were responsible for newly occupied territory. In the summer of 1946 these commands had a number of corps with two or three triangular divisions but few divisions had more than half their 10,977 man establishment and a process of consolidation followed. In a three-phase programme divisions were renamed Reorganised Brigades with two (three from May 1947) infantry regiments while the corps headquarters received artillery and engineer units and was redesignated a reorganised division. These changes were carried out in stages and confined to commands south of the Great Wall but were never universally applied so that corps and reorganised divisions frequently fought side-by-side. In September 1948 most of the reorganised divisions reverted to their original title of corps while brigades became divisions.[16]

Although 'formation' establishment was between 6,000 and

10,000 men, in practice it was usually around 5,500. Establishment tables were utopian, given China's shortage of equipment and technically trained manpower which made it impossible to fill many places[17]. Because the rifle regiments required only cannon fodder they were probably closer to their authorised strength. While many commanders presented padded rolls for reasons of personal profit there was a very practical reason for this practice. Pay was often in arrears and by building up his own financial reserve the commander could avoid discontent. It also helped to grease the supply system[18] which was so chaotic and corrupt that formations could not be certain of receiving their daily entitlement of 60 tonnes. This strengthened Nationalist Army habits of conservation and incomplete data suggests that a 'formation' operating in the field, and in intermittent contact with Communist forces, would consume 1.5 tonnes of shell, 2 tonnes of mortar bombs and 20 tonnes of rifle-calibre ammunition per month.[19]

In the absence of a modern road network, railways were the prime means of 'operational' movement, with motor transport used to distribute supplies from the rail head. It was more rarely used for troop transport while maintenance was, at best, rudimentary reducing the numbers of vehicles available. Tactical transport depended upon muscle power: bovine, equine and human, with the last the most important. The rural economy sustained only a limited number of draft animals while the Communists controlled the grasslands which were the prime source of horses and mules. Consequently the Nationalist Army found it impossible to meet more than a fraction of its requirements for draught animals. In 1947 it needed 100,000 horses and mules but could obtain only 8,000 while by October 1948 the Nationalist Army had barely half of its 400,000 establishment. Increasingly formations forced peasants to act as porters and carters, further undermining the rural economy and increasing the army's unpopularity.

PLA Formations and Logistics

The PLA also had its difficulties and its formations, too, were under establishment due to shortages of equipment. Until the winter of 1946–47 field army organisation reflected the whims and prejudices of the military and Party leaders. Regiments of two to four battalions existed although average regimental strength was about 1,500. Regimental groupings varied not only from region to region but also from district to district. Two or three could make a brigade, a division or a column while in some regions a division could have two or three brigades.

By the spring of 1947 this chaotic structure was being rationalised into a triangular pattern similar to that adopted by the Nationalist Army. The mobile field forces were organised into columns, each of three brigades or divisions. While the terminology may reflect command preference there is evidence to suggest brigades had only around 4,000 men while divisions had about 7,000 against an establishment of about 10,000. In most cases the brigades were gradually expanded to divisional strength. Regional forces were organised into battalions of 300 to 400 men or regiments of around 1,000 men. Later they were expanded into divisions and brigades although these were never as strong as the field force formations, probably with 4,000 and 2,000 men respectively.

Much of the PLA's equipment was captured, often from Nationalist paramilitary forces, and this especially applied to arms and ammunition.[20] Smuggling undoubtedly supplemented this source but manufacture was largely thwarted by a shortage of plant and machinery as well as the absence of a chemical industry to produce large quantities of modern explosives. However, it was possible to collect the raw materials of gun powder for grenades and mortar bombs.

It was the Party's regional bureaux who provided the sulphur and saltpetre as well as other essential materials through a supply organisation which appears to have been more efficient and more reliable than their opponents. The bureaux collected and distributed food, clothing and footwear, organised workers, (*min-fu*) to transport supplies, to act as engineers and even to provide casualty evacuation with each village providing an eight-man stretcher team. Bureaux would be informed of the PLA requirements for an operation and would delegate responsibility for meeting them to district cadres, each of whom would be assigned a quota. The organisation was extremely responsive to the PLA's needs but care had to be exercised to regulate demand for fear of exhausting the district.

The *min-fu* provided labour, their own transport and their own implements, literally risking everything on the battlefield, yet in the early months of the war were not even provided food or shelter. They had the deepest dread of air attack and in some theatres by 1947 were displaying a marked reluctance to volunteer. To ensure the flow of supplies the Party was forced to pay compensation for injuries or lost property while the Army agreed to provide the *min-fu* with rations. Although primitive the *min-fu* system could still meet most of the PLA's daily needs of 36 to 45 tonnes per division.[21] Porters could carry 30–40 kg loads up to 55 kilometres a day or 40 kilometres at night, half a tonne could be carried in a squeaking wheelbarrow while carts could carry a tonne.

Without this supply system the Communists would not have won the trial of strength which began in July 1946 and lasted until January 1949. The struggle was largely confined to China's more populous provinces north of the Yangtze and the axes of operations were usually defined by the major railway lines while major rivers confined theatre-level movement.

Situation in 1946

In the summer of 1946 the Communists held most of the territory between the Great Wall and the Yellow River leaving the Nationalists holding two enclaves. In Shansi their 2nd War Zone was confined to the area around Taiyuan while in Hopeh the 11th War Zone held an area from Peiping to Shihchiachuang. Their only link was a narrow corridor along the Taiyuan–Shihchiachuang branch railway line. Another exposed rail link, along the LIAOSI Corridor, joined the Northeast Garrison Command in Manchuria with the 11th War Zone.

Not only did the Communists control most of Hopeh and Shansi but also they held a deep belt of territory running eastwards from Shensi into northern Shantung. In addition they continued to hold the corridor which cut the PINGSUI Railway northwest of Peiping then ran through Jehol. This corridor remained a conduit for supplies into Manchuria and also isolated the 12th War Zone in Suiyuan and Chahar.

The fragmentation of Nationalist military power in northern China meant the impetus for relieving the enclaves had to come from the south with the option of three axes; along the TUNGPU, PINGHAN and TSINPU Railways. With the 1945 Chang River campaign having demonstrated the vulnerability of the PINGHAN route, Nationalist strategists decided to exploit the others. There were considerable resources available south of the Yellow River and in the Anyang salient for the Chengchou and Hsuchou Pacification Commands, together with the Wuhan Provisional Headquarters, possessed 123 (46 per cent) of the army's 267 formations. But, south of the LUNGHAI Railway, the PINGHAN and TSINPU lines were being harassed by the enemy and during the summer of 1946 priority was given to relieving this pressure by clearing Anhwei and northern Kiangsu.

The TUNGPU route, from Taiyuan to the Yangtze, appeared promising and during the summer of 1946 the line was briefly re-opened but it proved impossible to secure the heights on either side. Moreover the half-hearted commitment to the operation of Shansi's Governor Yen Hsi-shan, allowed the Communists to expand their control through the province.

Once the area south of the LUNGHAI Railway was cleared, the Nationalists concentrated upon opening the TSINPU Railway in Shantung. As their spearhead they used the Hsuchou Pacification Command whose 81 formations were the largest concentration (30 per cent) of the total force committed against the Communists. In August it drove into the west Shantung plain but became enmeshed in a struggle with Liu Po-cheng which hindered progress up the TSINPU Railway. Liu gained time for his colleague, Chen Yi, to withdraw his surviving field forces from Kiangsu into central Shantung. Throughout this period the 11th War Zone (later Peiping General Headquarters) was unable to assist this vital operation because it was supporting the general assault upon the Manchurian corridor together with the 12th War Zone and the Northeast Garrison Command. These commands succeeded in reopening the PINGSUI Railway and clearing Jehol by the end of 1946.

In the second half of 1946 alone, the Communists lost 174,000 square kilometres of territory and 165 towns. They were later to refer to the 12 months from July 1946 as the 'defensive phase' and at the end their 'liberated areas' consisted of 191,000 square kilometres and 18 million people.[22] During this period the PLA suffered heavy casualties, 358,000 men including 19,500 'missing', indeed in the second half of 1946 the PLA probably lost about 15 per cent of its overall strength.[23] The scale of these losses was partly due to attempts to fight conventional positional battles due to over-confidence in PLA abilities. Yet few doubted in ultimate victory although even optimists did not expect it before 1955, while pessimists thought it would take 10 years after that. Morale was shaken but did not crack and the PLA maintained pressure on the enemy throughout their 'operational' depth, eroding strength. Optimistically the Communists claimed to have inflicted 966,200 casualties and to have captured 1,630,000 men, although total Nationalist losses were probably about 300,000.

The loss of territory caused deep concern among the Communist regional leadership for these were the very districts where the Communists claimed to have had their greatest political success. In such districts the cadres had often followed 'The Left Tendency' and attacked the middle peasants. No preparations were made for guerilla operations and frequently all the cadres decamped for safer districts. Those who remained behind displayed remarkable resilience using work teams and the surviving activists to strike back at Nationalist administrations. Village leaders were assassinated or cowed and within a few months the Communists were recreating their own administrations, indeed they were often able to continue land reform.

Militarily this political success led to the resurgence of self-defence and regional forces who challenged Nationalist control of the countryside. They were active between the River Sungari in Manchuria and the Yangtze in central China and every day there were new reports to Nationalist headquarters of sentries being sniped at, railways torn up, convoys or foraging parties ambushed and installations raided. Two examples will illustrate the pattern of events which faced not only the Nationalist Army throughout northern China and Manchuria but also the United States Marine Corps in Hopeh and Shantung.

Attacks on US Marines

Peiping and Tientsin were linked by one of the busiest roads which, at its half-way point, ran due north through wheat fields to bisect the village of Anping. On 29 July 1946 a Communist regional force[24] blocked the road near the village bus station with ox carts and rocks, then set up an ambush in the southern outskirts along a line of trees east of the road. As a convoy of 22 vehicles approached around midday, the ambush party, 300 strong, could not have known it was a US Marine convoy escorted by 41 men and carrying unarmed replacements together with supplies for the Marines' Peiping garrison.

The lead jeeps skidded around the rocks but stopped near the carts. As the men dismounted they were felled by a shower of grenades and the main body came under heavy fire from the tree line while the rearguard was engaged from positions covering both sides of the road. The Chinese drivers and the replacements dived into a roadside ditch while the rearguard, under an experienced NCO, laid down a barrage of machine gun and mortar fire which prevented the Communists approaching.

The Marines' two radios were short-range sets and Anping lay in a 'dead spot' preventing the convoy summoning assistance, so an hour elapsed before a jeep-load of Marines broke out to the south. The convoy remained under sporadic fire for another three hours, then the disappointed Communists withdrew having failed to loot the vehicles. When the survivors were certain they were safe they collected the casualties (three dead and 12 were wounded, one fatally). Having removed the barricades, they continued their journey to Peiping which they reached in the early evening. Meanwhile a 400-man relief force summoned by the jeep party rushed up the road with air and artillery support. But the Communists, who lost an estimated 15 dead, escaped.

Nine months later another 350-man regional unit assaulted an isolated US Marine ammunition supply point at Hsin Ho, six miles from Tangku. The site was shaped like an Isosceles Triangle with individual dumps running parallel to the sides, sentry posts at each corner and a mobile jeep-borne patrol with three men. The main guard post was outside the site in a group of Quonset huts.

In the early hours of 5 April 1947 a bugle sounded and the northernmost sentry post was raked with small arms fire although it was 10 minutes before the last of the two guards died. Meanwhile two enemy parties staged a diversion in the north of the site as the main party struck in the east seizing a dump of artillery and mortar ammunition. While the Communists frantically dragged out crates of shells and mortar bombs, the jeep patrol and the guard-house party tried to intervene. Intense fire killed the jeep party, wounded eight men from the guard house and drove back the remainder.

Pinned down, the guards could only await relief which was despatched within half an hour. The relief column, a 5th Marines' company, drove up a road from the south but the Communists had anticipated such a move and had laid mines which disabled the lead vehicle, a self-propelled gun. This blocked the road which was raked with fire by some 40 men in a nearby irrigation ditch. When the Marines took cover, eight were wounded as two waves of Communists rushed up bombed them with grenades.

Meanwhile the main body had packed the ammunition into ox carts or tied them to mules. Once they had all the ammunition they could carry they blew up the remainder then withdrew northwards, crossed the Chin Chung River by ferry and escaped into the countryside beyond. They had lost six dead and some 30 wounded, but inflicted losses of five dead and 16 wounded upon the US Marines. It must, therefore have been a relief for the Marines when orders arrived a fortnight later to hand over the site to the Nationalist Army.[25]

In neither case was any warning provided by local people who probably sympathised with the Communists. The agricultural economy in these and surrounding districts was becoming commercialised reducing poor peasants to labourers while driving middle peasants into tenancy which affected 15 per cent of households. This further polarised rural society and encouraged support for the Communists.[26]

The railways had a similar effect not only upon the districts through which they passed but also upon the neighbouring ones. This hamstrung the defence of the rail network which came under daily attack from regional and self-defence forces who hamstrung enemy 'operational' movement. Throughout China trains came under small arms fire, locomotives were derailed, and fortified installations such as bridges and stations were attacked. The permanent way was rarely secure for at some point or other guerillas would tear up the rails, which would be warped by throwing them onto burning sleepers (cross-ties in American parlance). When repair teams came along they too would be attacked forcing a major commitment of forces to ensure new lines could be laid.

Nationalist Problems

The scale of the damage was formidable with 16,515 kilometres of line either captured or destroyed by the Communists between VJ Day and the end of 1947, of which only 6,398 kilometres could be reopened. During 1947 alone 2,057 kilometres of rails (930 kilometres repaired), 1,089 bridges (630) and 236 railway stations (60) south of the Great Wall were destroyed. To keep open the railways the Ministry of Communications maintained a reserve of 525 kilometres of rails, 2,480,000 sleepers and CNC$300 billion (US$7 million). Few figures are available for Manchuria but Wedemeyer reported that during the summer of 1947 the Nationalists controlled only 1,647 kilometres of Manchuria's 11,336 kilometre-long rail network and only 41 per cent (2,362 kilometres) of the 5,749 kilometres in northern China. At the end of 1957 the Communists announced they had replaced 10,500 kilometres of damaged track, most of this damage being caused by their own forces.

The Nationalist Army could not meet this threat for it possessed no concept of counter-insurgency operations. At a tactical level it continued to act as though the Communists were mere bandits who would be overawed by the army's presence and the strength of its fortifications. There was no attempt to win support among the peasants whose experience of the army consisted largely of robbery and rape. Chiang Ching-kuo did attempt to generate support by organising, in 1947, a 30,000 man corps whose task was to assist the peasants in recaptured districts. But following the August economic reforms in 1948 the corps was withdrawn to Shanghai.

Increasingly the Nationalists relied upon fortifications even in the major cities where the traditional walls were supplemented with trench systems, barbed wire, pillboxes and land mines. The facade of strength gave their garrisons a false sense of security which they were refused to compromise by going far beyond the fortifications. Consequently morale slowly seeped away and the men became interested only in their creature comforts. Holding cities became the criteria of success for senior Nationalist generals, indeed an examination of an official war history suggests only 10 per cent of the Nationalist Army was in the field at any one time.

As roads and railways were cut the Nationalists were forced to rely upon the slender reed of air transport. The Chinese Air

Force (CAF) had approximately 150 C–47 Skytrain and C–46 Commando transports which could be supplemented by some 90 civil aircraft of the three airlines.[27] However, maintenance standards were poor and the vital support infrastructure of good airfields, navigation aids and an efficient meteorological service was inadequate. Crashes were tragically frequent and in 1946 claiming the lives of four members of the Communist Party Central Committee (8 April) and the head of Chiang's secret police Tai Li (6 June)[28].

Air power might have been a valuable asset for the Nationalist cause but it was frittered away. At the end of 1945 the CAF had a first line strength of some 350 aircraft with a further 650 transferred from the US Army Air Force in China in storage. But by April 1947 some 430 aircraft had been destroyed or damaged beyond repair, while of 425 aircraft available on 1 April 1947 only 318 were operational.[29] Three months later, despite US assistance which raised strength by 76 aircraft, only 277 were operational.[30] Nanking's meagre air power was fragmented with the fighter and tactical bomber squadrons dispersed among commands at Mukden, Peiping, Sian and Wuhan while the heavy bombers, transports and reconnaissance aircraft were at Nanking and Shanghai. Economic considerations restricted operations, to the despair of US advisors, and the average daily combat sortie rate per theatre does not appear to have exceeded 42. Such a low level of effort had only a marginal effect in the conduct of Nationalist operations and failed to impress the PLA. Their first encounters with aircraft taught Communist troops prudence and their formations learned to conceal themselves during daylight and to move at night or in bad weather. Yet it was not until the Korean War that the PLA came fully to respect the awesome strength of tactical air power.

The Situation in 1947

Despite the defeats of 1946 the Communist Military Affairs Committee appeared to regard the situation with equanimity. On 1 October 1946 its report to the Central Committee expressed confidence in ultimate victory following a protracted war. It claimed the Nationalists had been forced to commit more than half the 190 formations it was using against the Communists (the actual figure was 205) to garrison duties. It added that while the Nationalist advance continued their mobile strike force would be weakened as units were diverted to protect communications. It was also claimed that 25 formations had been destroyed in the previous three months (an exaggeration) and a similar figure would be destroyed during the next three months enabling the Communists to check the enemy offensive, recover lost territory and, even more important, gain the strategic initiative.[31]

Optimistic in the short term, the directive proved more accurate in the long term. In Manchuria Lin Piao regained the initiative during the winter of 1946–47, then prematurely attempted a decisive blow at Ssuping, the heart of the Nationalist rail network. He suffered a tactical defeat but an 'operational' victory by seizing the initiative and forcing the enemy to abandon their conquests of autumn 1946. During the autumn of 1947 he exploited the situation to erode enemy strength and strengthen the Communist hold on the region. One of his deadliest tactics, a common one in the PLA, was the 'mousetrap' ambush which the Communists called 'pulling the stupid cow'. The PLA recognised that by sending relief forces to beseiged garrisons the Nationalists were exposing regiments and even formations. They therefore targeted these relief forces and drew them into pre-prepared ambushes having attacked a garrison which became the 'cheese' in the trap. Few Nationalist formations which fell into such a trap had the tactical skill to escape and after such disasters there was a noticeable reluctance to assist other isolated garrisons which then became vulnerable to assault. As a result of these tactics, by the end of the year the Northeast General Headquarters, now expanded to 34 formations, was on the verge of collapse.

Many commentators have criticised Chiang for committing too many resources to the Manchurian theatre, yet even in January 1948 less than 15 per cent of the total anti-Communist force of 233 formations was in this region. The greatest concentration of anti-Communist forces, 125 formations or 53 per cent, lay below the Yellow River and during 1947 it was here the war was decided both militarily and politically.

Militarily the Nationalists were able to advance deep into Chen Yi's Shantung base but he and Liu Po-cheng turned the area between the Yellow River and the LUNGHAI Railway into

TABLE 1

Nationalist formation losses: 30 June 1946–30 September 1948*					
Quarter	Lin Piao	Nieh Jung-chen	Peng Te-huai	Liu Po-cheng	Chen Yi	Total
1946 III	–	–	–	–	5	5
I	–	1	–	–	15	16
II	2	–	2	1	6	11
III	2	7	2	4	10	25
IV	3	3	1	1	–	8
1948 I	11	1	4	–	–	16
II	–	–	–	7	1	8
III	2	1	10	–	2	15
	21	13	19	16	31	107
Percentage (To two decimal places)	(19.62)	(12.15)	(17.75)	(14.95)	(36.44)	

These statistics are for formations which suffered 50 to 100 per cent casualties or which defected. Data based upon published PLA claims and upon Civil War.

a vast killing ground starting with Chen's spectacular I-tsao victory in January 1947. The PLA's tactics, described as '. . . based on mobility, deception, distraction, surprise, concentration of superior forces at the vital point, a "short attack" and speedy disengagement . . .',[32] destroyed or savaged 37 formations or 29 per cent of the Chengchou and Hsuchou Command strength. Nationalist casualties here were some 180,000, or some 45 per cent of the 400,000 men lost during 1947. As Table 1 shows, half of the Nationalist formations lost during the civil war between 30 June 1946 and 30 September 1948 fell victim to Chen and Liu.

The Communists exploited enemy discomfiture when Liu struck southwards on 30 June 1947. His march to the Tapieh Mountains, where he arrived in September, was the most significant strategic move of the war for it threatened both the enemy granaries and communications network. It also eased pressure in Shantung as the Hsuchou Command was stripped to meet the new threat. Throughout the winter of 1947–48 some 39 formations battered in vain at the Tapieh Mountain base but the hard pressed Communists survived and during March 1948 secured western Anhwei.

The most serious defeat suffered by the Communists was the loss of Yenan which fell on 19 March 1947 after the Nationalists committed 21 formations in a vain attempt to decapitate the Communist movement. The Communist leadership escaped and for the rest of the year played a lethal game of hide and seek in the mountains of north Shensi close to the Yellow River. The pursuit, by Hu Tsung-nan's Sian Pacification Command, was handicapped by the need to defend southern Shansi where the last stronghold (Yuncheng) fell at the end of the year. The Communists steadily tightened their hold on Shansi during 1947 and isolated the provincial capital of Taiyuan. They were assisted by Nieh Jung-chen who constantly harassed enemy communications here and in Hopeh, emulating the tactics of Chen Yi and Liu Po-cheng until the autumn. Then he brilliantly exploited Nationalist caution to take Shihchiachuang, their last bastion in central Hopeh. Soon the city became the Communist capital and the headquarters of the PLA.

For the Communists 1947 was the decisive year when, at the price of some 400,000 casualties (equivalent to 20 per cent of their strength), they seized the initiative in every theatre. Referring to the successes, which left the Nationalists controlling less than 15 per cent of northern China, an exultant Mao informed the Central Committee in December 1947 that they had reached a turning point in history.[33] The change of fortunes left Chiang tired, depressed, and plagued by insomnia which he could conquer only with the soporific effects of whisky. His tension was displayed in an increasing tendency to interfere with operations over the heads of his theatre commanders, undermining their authority without any noticeable benefit.

The Situation in 1948

By the beginning of 1948 the Communists, by employing 45 per cent of their field force divisions, had compelled the Nationalists to commit 54 per cent of their divisions between the Yellow River and the Yangtze. Yet this concentration of force brought no benefits for the government during the first half of 1948. On 9 March Liu Po-cheng's troops took Loyang to cut the LUNGHAI Railway, greatly assisted by Chiang's decision to strip the city of 23,000 defenders to reinforce Hu Tsung-nan. The troops were needed because Hu suffered a serious defeat at Watzuchieh in early March yet Chiang's action succeeded only in isolating Shensi. By taking Loyang the Communists were able to create a corridor between the Shansi bases and central Honan where they steadily tightened their hold until they took the provincial capital Kaifeng in June. In Shantung the Tsinan–Tsingtao Railway was cut by late April leaving only the terminii in Nationalist hands while southern Shantung was cleared by the end of June.

TABLE 2

	Nationalist formations	Communist field force divisions
Manchuria	39	48
North China	36	21
Shensi–Shansi	31	21
CENTRAL CHINA		
Hsuchou Command	86	39 (East China FA)
Chengchou Command	10	36 (Central Plains FA)
Chiuchiang Command	19	
Wuhan	10	

Based upon data from Major General Chang Chao-jen

The most ominous feature of the Communist successes was their ability to take cities, itself a reflection of the continuous improvement of quality of the PLA. By the summer of 1948 it was clear the Nationalists were facing defeat and by the autumn their cause was threatened with military catastrophe as isolated garrisons were destroyed piecemeal. The fall of Tsinan, on 23 September 1948, was especially ominous for it followed the defection of a complete re-organised division. Increasing numbers of Nationalist troops were surrendering and were so well treated that 800,000 volunteered to join the PLA.

Sensing victory the Communists, who now controlled 168 million people, now declared they could overthrow their enemies within four years. Against this background the United States despatched new arms shipments to China under the US$125 million military aid package. These arms were sufficient to equip the equivalent of eight corps but they arrived in the autumn at a time when northern China had become a vortex sucking the Nationalist cause to its doom.[34] In the last quarter of 1948 the Communists launched three massive offensives which completed the destruction of enemy power north of the Yangtze.

The Liao–Shen Campaign (12 September to 2 November) saw the Nationalists driven out of Manchuria, the Huai–Hai Campaign (6 November 1948 to 10 January 1949) brought about the end of Nationalist power between the Yellow and the Yangtze Rivers while the Peiping–Tientsin Campaign (21 November 1948 to 27 January 1949) saw the surrender of the last major concentration north of the Yellow river. The price paid was high, about 590,000 men or some 20 per cent of its strength, but the PLA had brought its enemies to the verge of ruin.

The course of the campaigns by which the Communists captured the country north of the Yangtze between 1946 and 1949 are examined on a geographic basis in the following three chapters which cover Manchuria, northern China and central China respectively. The penultimate chapter relates the crossing of the Yangtze in 1949 and the capture of southern China while the last chapter considers the aftermath of the civil war.

4

Defeat into Victory: Manchuria

It was upon the Manchurian plains that world attention focused during the civil war for here were armies manoeuvering in the classic way all too familiar to a war-weary world. Yet the brilliance of the Communist commander Lin Piao has blinded later commentators to the fact that this was not the decisive battleground.

The terrain consists of rolling grasslands criss-crossed by numerous rivers and streams which hinder movement. In the summer of 1946 the Lower Sungari River (Sunghua Chiang) marked the border between the Communists and the Nationalists, with the former holding northern Manchuria, and the latter holding the broad valley of the River Liao. The prime battlefield was the Liao valley and the low range of hills which lay to the north and were crowned by Ssuping. To the west the grasslands dissolve into marsh and desert while to the east lie the densely forested mountains which run along the Soviet and Korean borders then down into the Liaotung Peninsula.

The region's weather pattern resembles that of the Russian steppes although rain is largely confined to the mid summer. The winters are literally Siberian with the Arctic winds cutting the temperature to −20 degrees Centigrade which the wind-chill factor aggravates. The spring thaw turns the streams into raging torrents while the earth roads become bottomless bogs.

In the absence of metalled roads the railways thread together the major cities like pearls on a necklace. From Harbin two lines run south to Mukden; one through Changchun and Ssuping, the other through Kirin and Fushun's coalfields. From Mukden

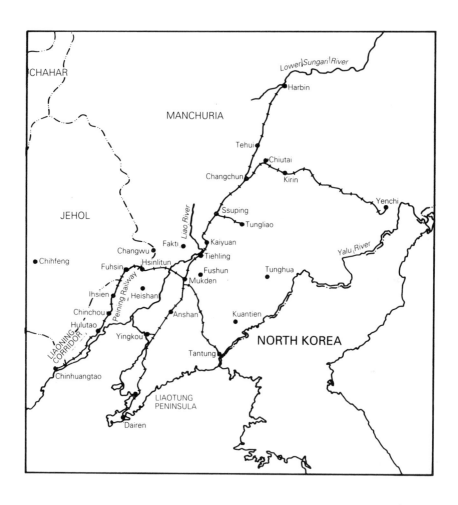

The Manchurian Theatre

another line runs southwards through Liaoyang and the Anshan steelworks to Dairen (Luta) and Port Arthur (Lushun). The PEINING Railway runs westwards to Fuhsin, turns south to Chinchou then runs through the LIAOSI Corridor to the Great Wall. A branch line runs through the Jehol hills from Ihsien (between Fuhsin and Chinchou) past Chengte to Peiping. There were two lateral lines to the Korean border; one running through Ssuping and Tunghua, the other from Mukden to Tantung.

The summer ceasefire prevented the Nationalists exploiting the victory at Ssuping but Hsiung Shih-hui's Northeast Provisional Headquarters was anxious to complete the re-occupation of the region. With the collapse of the ceasefire new thrusts into enemy territory were prepared by Tu Yu-ming, the commander of the Northeast General Headquarters, who had 228,000 men.

Tu Yu-ming and Lin Piao

Tu, aged 43, was dismissed by one commentator as 'one of Chiang's cronies'. Yet this son of a Shensi scholar was one of the most capable leaders in the Chinese Army. He had been one of Chiang's first cadets at Whampoa, but ability, as much as loyalty, gave him command of China's first motorised division. This was expanded into the 5th Corps which distinguished itself during the 1942 Burma campaign and earned Tu command of the US-equipped Y-Force.

After the war Tu deposed the Governor of Yunnan Province for Chiang, who rewarded the brash young general with the Manchuria command. The majority of his 23 formations were from the Central Army, many of them US-trained and equipped, but a quarter were former Yunnan provincial troops. They were of dubious reliability but, with Hsiung reluctant to use Manchurian recruits, the miserable Yunnanese were used for garrison duty.

When the rains ended in September Tu Yu-ming first cleared Jehol to secure communications with northern China and dam the flow of enemy men and equipment into Manchuria. The operation was coordinated with another thrust by the 11th War Zone into Chahar and against weak resistance most of Jehol was in Nationalist hands by the end of October. Heavy casualties were inflicted upon the enemy but the survivors continued to harass the railways and garrisons whose reluctance to pursue them into the hills allowed the Communists to recruit with impunity then rebuild their forces.

The offensive caused the formal break between the two sides at a time when the Communists were reeling in defeat on all fronts. Yet the isolation of Manchuria may actually have been received with relief in Harbin, the Communist regional capital, especially by Lin Piao commander of the Northeast Democratic United Army (NDUA). Lin, the 39-year-old son of a Hopeh textile manufacturer, was a stocky man with a sallow complexion and bushy eyebrows. As a Whampoa cadet he was introduced to Communism by Chou En-lai and in the 1930s displayed a remarkable talent for combining guerilla and conventional operations. He played a prominent part in the Long March, during which he became close to Mao Tse-tung, but the epic journey broke his health and left him with a chronic respiratory problem which was probably bronchitis.

A chest wound in 1938 aggravated his health and he was sent to the Soviet Union to recover and to improve his military education. He returned to Yenan in 1942 and realigned himself with Mao, demanding loyalty to 'our Nation, ... our Party, ... our great leader.' This stance led to his appointment as the deputy principal of the Central Party School and later his election as a regular member of the Central Committee in 1945. Lin concentrated upon training officers and creating specialist schools many of whose students were transferred to Manchuria where his combination of political loyalty, military education and command ability made him the unrivalled choice to lead the Communist forces. In the summer of 1946 the NDUA needed a leader of his stature to survive for it was a heterogeneous collection of north Chinese and Manchurian guerillas, Korean exiles, former Manchukuo troops, bandits and recruits. Lin was expanding and reorganising his troops but needed time to forge them into a sword which might smite the Nationalist dragon.

Lin Piao Prepares

In the aftermath of the Ssuping defeat the Northeast Bureau met at Meihokou and the military leaders rounded upon the First Secretary Peng Chen. They criticised not only his obsession with holding the cities, which cost the army so dear and took cadres from the rural revolution, but also his failure to reconcile the differences between the Party factions. Peng resigned and was replaced not by the Second Secretary, Kao Kang, but by Lin Piao. The reasons for the selection of a military leader are obscure but Lin's position allowed him to restrain Chao Pao-chung while the army was also the only source of trained cadres for expanding the rural base.

Some 12,000 soldiers, many of them experienced officers and NCOs were transferred to political duties during the summer. They represented 75 per cent of all the cadres the Party committed to its political offensive into a countryside made insecure by thousands of enemy guerillas. Their presence, and the continued strength of the 'big trees', strengthened fears of counter-revolution and encouraged the Northeast Bureau to adopt radical policies. On 7 July 1946 it ordered the confiscation not only of the remaining landlords' land but also that of the rich peasants. This exceeded the Central Committee's directive of 4 May but was justified by the bureau because the rich peasants had opposed the earlier moderate policy. The decision was a gamble but was essential both to confirm Communist rule in the provinces, 'building our own house' as one Party leader put it, and to mobilise the peasants in support of the war effort.

The following summer the class struggle intensified and thousands of landlords fled to Nationalist-controlled cities. Nanking ignored them, inflation soaked up their savings, there was no work and they starved. As the 'big trees' fell the PLA smashed the guerilla bands which were confined to the eastern mountains from 1947 and contained by intensive patrolling.

The knowledge that his rear was secure, to provide recruits and food proved a reasonable price for Lin Piao to pay for the loss of so many experienced men as cadres. In the meantime he and his subordinates worked night and day to prepare the army for its forthcoming campaigns. Difficulties in communication forced Lin to divide his command into five military regions, one behind enemy lines, and the 100,000 field force troops were organised into columns each with some 13,000 to 14,000 men. They were supported by up to 200,000 regional and self defence troops, but numbers alone do not make an army. Many of the men were raw recruits, discipline was uneven, while the standard of training was poor.

Lin Piao largely left the preparation of his forces for battle to his subordinates while he concentrated on their employment. On 30 September 1946 he published a text book, *Principles of Combat*, which echoed Mao-Tse-tung's thought in 'On Protracted War' and 'Strategic Problems of the Anti-Japanese War' but then expanded into extraordinary detail ranging from the tactic of street fighting to 'operational' principles. He warned the army it was not capable in the immediate future of achieving anything more than the destruction of isolated units, which required a 5:1 numerical superiority and this was to be attempted only when there was a 70 per cent chance of success.[1] He anticipated hit-and-run tactics would buy sufficient time to prepare the army for conventional warfare. While numerical superiority was essential, here too success also depended upon the employment of reserves, personal reconnaissance and attacks in echelon. Above all he stressed the need for commanders to use their initiative even when this meant disobeying their superiors.

The Tantung Campaign

The Communist generals had barely a month to digest his advice before they came under renewed pressure. Having cleared his western flank, Tu Yu-ming was now determined to clear the eastern mountains from where the Communists threatened the Mukden–Dairen Railway, and its branch line to Yingkou. Tu's goal was to extend Nationalist control into the Liaotung Peninsula and down to the Yalu River, the border with Communist North Korea. However, he had only 70,000 men to take 34,000 square kilometres of densely forested, sparsely populated mountains. No more men were available but following the Jehol campaign Tu probably believed the enemy would not offer effective resistance. This view was reinforced when Nationalist reconnaissance discovered that the enemy's East Manchurian Military Region (MR), under Hsiao Ching-kuang, had committed most of its 80,000 men to a conventional defensive battle in the rugged terrain.

On 20 October, seven Nationalist divisions struck the enemy defences and within a few days resistance collapsed, aided by mutinies among some regional regiments. Retreat turned into rout but the pursuit was cautious and Tantung, on the Korean border, was not reached until 25 October, giving the Communists time to demolish 30 kilometres of railway north of the city. The northern branch line through Kuantien was secured the following day and two Nationalist divisions pursued the Communist army northeastwards towards Tunghua. But on 30 October one division was ambushed and after a bitter two-day battle only 1,000 men escaped.

The momentum was recovered by bringing in a replacement division from Jehol and Tunghua was then taken to give the Nationalists control of the southeast Manchuria rail network. The victory cost the Nationalists some 11,000 casualties but they failed to destroy the Communist field forces which regrouped northeast of Tunghua.

The Winter Campaigns

Winter was imminent and soon blizzards would paralyse the battlefield but Lin Piao was too restless a personality to accept enforced idleness. He recognised that inactivity erodes morale and he had no intention of letting his men brood upon the recent spate of defeats. Instead he launched four large raids across the frozen Sungari with the triple objectives of relieving pressure upon the East Manchurian MR, reducing enemy strength and disrupting their communications.

Each raid was conducted with two or three columns and was based upon the tactic of the 'mousetrap' ambush. Their execution displayed considerable audacity with the first, beginning on the night of the 12–13 November 1946, involving a 250 kilometre march through blinding blizzards and mists although it achieved nothing. During the first quarter of 1947 there was a raid a month (confusingly dubbed the First, Second and Third Sungari Battles by the Communists) with the last ending in a desperate race with the thaw to the frozen Sungari. Only the First and Third Battles had any success, the former seeing the destruction of two regiments whose arrival time was discovered by tapping a telephone conversation. The raids succeeded in relieving pressure upon the East Manchuria MR and wrecking the rail network in central Manchuria. In the eastern mountains Hsiao Ching-kuang staged his own column-strength raid to contain the Nationalists around Tunghua which he isolated during the early spring of 1947.

Each side suffered some 10,000 casualties in these attacks which stretched Tu Yu-ming's resources to breaking point and made his garrison commanders wary of leaving their fortifications. Tu also had difficulty replacing his losses, unlike Lin Piao who expanded the field forces to 180,000 men, organised into eight columns and three artillery divisions with 100 guns. He also had some 150,000 regional and self-defence forces, including 10 regional force divisions. The men were physically fit, battle-hardened and with high morale, while the winter operations had given the young guerilla leaders experience in handling and coordinating the operations of large formations.

In any conflict a moment of balance is reached when even the smallest action may tip the scales and Lin believed that moment had arrived. If he was surprised at its speed he saw no reason to neglect the opportunity. Moreover, there were pressing political and economic reasons for a spectacular victory. Everywhere the White Sun was in the ascendant and from March it even flew over the Communist capital of Yenan. In Shantung the enemy were slowly driving Chen Yi from his mountain sanctuaries while Nieh Jung-chen and Liu Po-cheng could only harass the enemy, although this helped spread Communist political control.

Not only was victory vital for the national revolution but also for the Manchurian one. The region could not avoid problems encountered with land reform and there was a significant reduction in food production. To reduce urban consumption and to increase production some 150,000 city dwellers were unwillingly resettled in the country, sowing the seeds of counter-revolution whose harvest could be avoided only by reaping a victory.

Fourth Sungari Battle – The Siege of Ssuping

It was the enemy's passive response which lay at the heart of Lin Piao's 'operational' plan. He believed his forces were capable of a deep penetration operation which would destroy a large enemy force and to this end he drafted plans which have been described as 'aggressive, imaginative and dramatic'.[2] He intended to strike at Ssuping whose capture would secure the Sungari valley, give him access to the regional rail network and allow him to attack the Liao valley. It was a gamble which violated his own 'Principles of Combat' by allocating field forces,

PLATE 1. Pictured in 1945 are most of the senior leaders of the PLA. From left to right Peng Te-huai (Northwest Field Army), Chu Teh (Commander-in-Chief of the PLA), Yeh Chien-ying (Chief of the PLA General Staff), Nieh Jung-chen (CHINCHACHI Field Army) and Chen Yi (East China Field Army). Absent are Lin Piao and Liu Po-cheng (*Xinhua News Agency*).

PLATE 2. A Nationalist soldier stands guard. He is carrying a Thompson
M1A1 sub-machine gun (*Popperfoto*).

PLATE 3. Regional forces plan an attack upon an outpost with the aid of a model. The regional forces were professional soldiers whose task was to assist political expansion by eliminating strong points. They were also used to attack communications (*Popperfoto*).

PLATE 4. The remains of a stretch of the PINGHAN (Peiping to Wuhan) Railway. The rails have been torn up, burned on a bonfire of sleepers and then the road bed has been systematically dug up. On some lines railway embankments were razed to the ground and returned to agricultural land (*Popperfoto*).

PLATE 5. Nationalist troops climb into trucks in northern China. They are wearing captured Japanese helmets. Much Japanese equipment was used by both sides during the war (*Popperfoto*).

PLATE 6. Fu Tso-yi's cavalry brigade withdraws towards Peiping in December 1949. Cavalry were used extensively in Manchuria and northern China but acted largely as mounted infantry. The man in the right foreground is carrying a Sten gun, possibly of Chinese manufacture (*Popperfoto*).

PLATE 7. The 94th Corps prepares to re-open the PINGSUI (Peiping-Suiyuan) Railway in the autumn of 1948. This corps was one of Fu Tso-yi's fire brigades (*Popperfoto*).

PLATE 8. Nationalist gunners with a US M2A1 105 mm howitzer. Most divisions on both sides used 75 mm field guns, mountain howitzers or pack howitzers of Japanese and US origin (*Popperfoto*)

PLATE 9. Marines parade through Tsingtao to celebrate the Corps' 172nd anniversary in 1948. By this time the Marine presence consisted of two battalions with the designations of regiments; the 1st Marines (formerly 2/1st Marines) and the 3rd Marines (formerly 3/4th Marines), The Marine Corps suffered 54 casualties through Communist attacks and 22 in air crashes (*Popperfoto*).

PLATE 10. The People's Liberation Army (PLA) marches into Peiping on 31 January 1949 to receive a rapturous welcome as trucks drive towards Tien-an-Men Square. Forty years and four months later the PLA crushed student protesters in the same square (*Xinhua News Agency*).

PLATE 11. Nationalist infantry under fire during the Huai-Hai campaign at the end of 1948. The rifleman has a Chiang Kai-shek rifle, a Chinese made Mauser rifle, while the other soldier has a Thompson M1A1 sub-machine gun (*Popperfoto*).

PLATE 12. In the aftermath of the Huai-Hai Campaign Nationalist prisoners march past a captured US 105 mm howitzer (*Xinhua New Agency*).

PLATE 13. Wounded Nationalist soldiers are loaded into a C-46 Commando
transport of Civil Air Transport (CAT) during the Huai-Hai Campaign.
CAT was founded by Claire L. Chennault, leader of the famed Flying
Tigers during the Second World War. As the Communists took more of
the mainland CAT was used by the Central Intelligence Agency (CIA)
who eventually bought it and renamed it Air America (*Popperfoto*).

PLATE 14. A scouting party from the Third Field Army surveys crossing
points along the Yangtze in Kiangsu. The PLA used bugles extensively
for tactical signalling and a bugler is in the foreground behind an officer
(*Xinhua News Agency*).

PLATE 15. Nationalist troops wearing Japanese headgear prepare to fire a Japanese Type 4 150 mm howitzer during the Battle of Shanghai in May 1949 (*Popperfoto*).

PLATE 16. Exhausted and bemused, Nationalist soldiers in Nanking prepare to sell military equipment, possibly to earn enough for a bowl of rice (*Popperfoto*).

PLATE 17. Members of Chen Yi's Third Field Army march past the Park
Hotel in Shanghai in May 1949 (*Popperfoto*).

PLATE 18. Troops of the Communist mobile field forces in action. These
were the cutting edge of the PLA and by 1949 were well equipped
(*Popperfoto*).

PLATE 19. A battalion of the Nationalist 4th Army withdraws through Canton in October 1949 (*Popperfoto*).

PLATE 20. Nationalist soldiers of the 96th Corps cross a pontoon at Amoy on their way to Chinmen Island (Quemoy) in October. Although the United Kingdom imposed an arms embargo on China during the civil war many of these soldiers are carrying *British* Sten guns. (*Popperfoto*).

PLATE 21. A pause for lunch before the PLA continues driving the Nationalist armies westward in January 1950 (*Popperfoto*).

PLATE 22. Although of poor quality this photograph shows a PLA amphibious operation
conducted by the Third Field Army (B... of A...)

PLATE 23. Communist soldiers wade ashore to occupy the Choushan Islands in May 1950. Their occupation was made possible by the presence of a Soviet air force expeditionary force, including MiG-15 fighters, at Nanking and Shanghai (*Popperfoto*).

PLATE 24. Nationalist soldiers disembark from the Tien Hsing at Keelung, Taiwan after the evacuation of the Choushan Islands. While the men in the foreground appear to be carrying Kai-shek rifles those behind them are carrying the Johnson M1941 semi-automatic rifle. It appears that no Garand semi-automatic rifles were sent to the

rather than regional forces, for the assault upon the city. Yet the risk had to be taken for only the field forces had the training and the firepower for this task. To reduce the risk, regional and local forces were to strike throughout the enemy's 'operational' depth pinning down garrisons to prevent a counter-strike.

In early May the operation flared into life and for a fortnight Nationalist outposts and railways came under sustained guerilla attack. On the night of 13–14 May the field forces entered the fray when the North Manchurian MR crossed the Sungari as the Western and Eastern Regions began diversionary operations, the Eastern MR forcing the enemy to abandon Tunghua on 25 May. Lin's main force, four columns with 100,000 men, marched up to 40 kilometres a night towards Ssuping. In the absence of maps the Party organisation provided regiments with guides to bivouac areas, villages and farms where they dispersed before dawn to avoid the enemy aircraft which circled like vultures during the day. Other columns sealed off the Nationalist garrisons at Changchun and Kirin and with the arrival of Lin Piao's main force on the night of 21–22 May, Ssuping itself was isolated.

The scale and speed of the offensive shook the Nationalist commanders. It isolated three corps in the north leaving only five in the south and hardly any reserves. Tu Yu-ming's options were extremely limited; he could fight a static defensive battle with the few divisions available and lose Ssuping or he could collect a reserve for a counter-strike by abandoning territory. He chose the latter and abandoned his gains of the previous autumn to assemble six divisions while Fu Tso-yi agreed to provide another three from the LIAOSI Corridor. The Changchun and Kirin garrisons were also to participate, although the former had to abandon the Sungari bridgehead. Tu's decision, which was sanctioned by Chiang, broke the already strained relationship with Hsiung Shih-hui who delayed the abandonment of the east for a fortnight.

The success of the counter-stroke depended upon two divisions of Chen Ming-jen's 71st Corps holding Ssuping where Lin Piao received another two columns from the Eastern MR together with regional regiments. While this provided him with plenty of cannon-fodder it did not overcome his shortage of cannon and shell. Supplies failed to keep pace with the infantry due to air attacks which left Lin's artillery commander, Chu Jui, with few guns and a limited quantity of ammunition. Worse still, Lin had not planned the assault in detail and the time spent remedying this deficiency was exploited by the 29,000 defenders (including some 6,000 civilian volunteers). For 10 days they built fortifications within the city, perfected their artillery response and improved co-operation with the air force which struck the enemy day and night as well as parachuting in supplies.

Only on 2 June did the assault begin and drove back the defenders by sheer weight of numbers. Yet it took Lin's men a week to penetrate the city walls and there followed days of bitter street fighting. On 21 June the attackers reached the city centre and pushed the defenders into the northeastern quarter where they held out with air support.[3] Meanwhile Tu Yu-ming completed preparations for his counter-strike by assembling 11 divisions around Mukden. With these he struck northwards on 24 June while the Changchun garrison simultaneously struck south. The Western MR held back the Nationalists' southern thrust for a few days, but not enough for Lin Piao to adminster the *coup de grace* at Ssuping. On 28 June he reluctantly ordered a withdrawal which was completed smartly in torrential rain by the end of June.

The Communists Lick their Wounds

For the Communists the operation had been a terrible disappointment which cost them 40,000 men and created an atmosphere of mutual recrimination when the leadership met in Harbin during mid July. Lin Piao pre-empted criticism by a thorough public self-analysis in which he stressed his own errors in underestimating the enemy, failing to secure the outer line of the siege, delaying the assault upon Ssuping and inadequate planning. The failure of the supply system was blamed upon air attacks which had carved bloody swathes through the defenceless *min-fu*, the Nationalist airmen claiming to have inflicted 6,000 human and 4,500 equine casualties. This was an exaggeration but air attacks terrified the peasants and made them increasingly reluctant to act as *min-fu*.

Despite the defeat the 'operational' initiative was clearly in the Communists' favour. They had lost only six of the 42 districts they had taken and now controlled 166,000 square kilometres of territory and 10 million people. They had also seized large quantities of supplies and equipment while disrupting rail communications. A British observer reported that although the railway between Mukden and Changchun had been restored it had been more thoroughly destroyed than at any previous time. The Nationalists had lost 28,000 men, a quarter of them at Ssuping where two divisions had been decimated, and despite success morale plummeted. The loss of public confidence was reflected in an ever-increasing flow of capital from Nationalist Manchuria to Canton and Hong Kong.

The Communists rebuilt their shattered regiments and created another four field force columns and the troops, now redesignated the Northeast Field Army, pondered the lessons for the autumn campaign. As early as 7 July Lin Piao, in a morale-boosting message, emphasised the Maoist philosophy of driving the enemy into the cities and there destroying him. Yet he intended to achieve this by conventional operations and it was no coincidence that during the summer there was published a Chinese translation of a Soviet Army text book on front (army group) operations.

The emphasis upon Maoist doctrine came at a time when Soviet aid was steadily increasing. This was partly paid for in food and partly in consumer goods; 93 million roubles worth in 1947 (including 1.1 million tonnes of grain) and 151 million roubles worth the following year. Soviet missions helped both to operate and to repair the railways until the Chinese could perform this task themselves. Soviet military experts undoubtedly influenced the creation of Lin Piao's extensive network of specialist schools which prepared his army for the conventional battles of 1948.

The Soviets may also have supplied military equipment, for the Communists could not support their expansion merely from former Kwantung Army stocks and weapons taken from the enemy. There is circumstantial evidence of Lend–Lease material and Japanese equipment coming across the North Korean border after Li Li-san signed an agreement with Pyongyang for military assistance in return for food. However, the Korean Communist administration was not formally recognised by the Chinese until December 1947 although before then the PLA was transferring its Korean regional regiments southwards.[4] The process was accelerated the following year when the two Communist regimes created a joint military committee.

Exit Tu Yu-ming, enter Chen Cheng

By the late summer of 1947 the Communists were regaining strength and confidence for the turning point had undoubtedly been reached. On the Nationalist side the strain of snatching victory from the jaws of defeat broke Tu Yu-ming's health. His family requested he have medical treatment abroad and Chiang exploited a situation which he probably engineered. The Generalissimo recognised the problem with Manchuria lay with the region's divided command and in August Tu Yu-ming and Hsiung Shih-hui were recalled. Their commands were merged as the Generalissimo's Northeast Headquarters and placed under a dynamic new leader, Chen Cheng.

The rosy-cheeked 50-year-old general came from Chekiang and, after graduating at the Paoting Military Academy, was appointed artillery instructor at Whampoa where he became a close friend of Chiang who arranged his second marriage. In the war against Japan he held numerous responsible positions and was closely involved in creating the US backed Y-Force before succeeding his great rival Ho Ying-chin as War Minister in 1944. Chen was barely 5 feet tall and like many short men he was pugnacious. He was unquestioningly loyal to the Generalissimo and has been described as 'bold, impetuous, intolerant and impatient'.[5]

Exuding confidence Chen re-organised his command and incorporated large numbers of Manchurians into the Army. His predecessors had been reluctant to use men from the Manchukuo Army, whom they regarded as traitors, but some were used in the peace preservation force which had expanded to 11 brigades. Chen incorporated them into the army as the basis for four new corps each of which was stiffened with a reliable division. Nevertheless, he had still had to bring in 90,000 men from the south to improve his firepower and mobility and these included a corps from Kiangsu. No more reinforcements could be expected because of Liu Po-cheng's thrust towards the Tapieh Mountains, while increasing pressure in Hopeh meant Chen could not even be certain of assistance from that quarter.

To improve control he created five army headquarters; 1st at Changchun, 6th at Hopeh-Jehol Border at Chinchou, 7th at Ssuping, 8th at Kaiyuan, and 9th at Tiehling. He also took vigorous steps to tighten discipline and to end corruption but there were several distinguished victims of his purge. The most famous was Chen Ming-jen, the Hero of Ssuping, while another was Sun Li-jen who was transferred to a training command on Taiwan.

Chen Cheng awaited the end of the rains impatiently for he planned a decisive battle in which the enemy would be caught around the PEINING Railway by a strategically located three-corps force with mechanised support.[6] It was a challenge Lin Piao was willing to accept if it provided an opportunity to reduce Chen's 'operational' capability by disrupting his communications and destroying his forces piecemeal. Supported by Nieh Jung-chen, Lin's Jehol-Liaoning MR staged guerilla attacks upon the PEINING Railway and destroyed the important Alingho bridge near Chinchou. Then field forces were committed and two new columns cut the railway only 50 kilometres south of Chinchou wrecking two divisions in the process.

Fifth Sungari Battle

Chen Cheng alerted his forces, strengthened his reaction force with three more divisions and persuaded a reluctant Fu Tso-yi to place two crack corps in the LIAOSI Corridor. These preparations were still taking place when the Communists launched their main atack on 1 October with the secondary objective of capturing sufficient grain to cover any shortages in their own harvest. The Northern MR's troops again crossed the Sungari, bypassing Changchun and Ssuping to cut the Mukden-Ssuping Railway on 5 October. Meanwhile the Eastern MR swept down from the mountains to cut the Mukden-Dairen railway south of Anshan while the Western MR struck the PEINING Railway wreaking havoc with the 49th Corps, part of Chen's reaction force.

The Nationalist response was prompt; while Fu Tso-yi's corps struck from the west two of Chen Cheng's corps began a converging attack along the Ssuping–Mukden line but Lin Piao's forces escaped taking with them much grain. In the west the column which had savaged the 49th Corps made the mistake of engaging Fu-Tso-yi's corps and suffered a bloody nose. The battle proved inconclusive and while the Communists suffered some 30,000 casualties they retained the initiative.

Lin Piao continued to expand his forces, estimated by the Nationalists at 508,000 by the end of the year. Aware of their own failures, and growing enemy strength, Nationalist troops developed an obsessive reliance upon aerial firepower. Simultaneously aerial transport grew in importance as the rail system disintegrated.

As blizzards engulfed the region the Northeast Field Army began two hectic months of activity. The purpose was to improve operational efficiency, with Lin Piao demanding not only proficiency with individual weapons but improved interarms co-ordination. His experience at Ssuping made him determined to ensure his army could win not only battles of manoeuvre but also sieges, although he recognised the odds were still against him.

Calculating as ever, he decided to reduce these odds by developing, during the winer, a plan to attack each 'operational' flank and a key point simultaneously, the so-called One Point, Two Flanks policy. It was now feasible because the Communists controlled an extensive transport system including a well developed rail network. The latter suffered the handicap of severe rolling stock shortages and enemy air attacks, but 300 members of the Soviet Army's Railway Troops ensured it ran efficiently.

Lin Piao Strikes Again

By exploiting exterior lines Lin intended to threaten the Mukden's rail links at Chinchou and Yingkou in order to force the enemy to disperse his troops. This would open the way to Ssuping, thereby splitting Nationalist Manchuria into two. His plan was moulded by Chen Cheng's dispositions; the PEINING Railway was protected by the Hopeh–Jehol Border and 6th Armies (11 divisions), while the 1st, 8th and 9th Armies (16 divisions) were strung out along the Changchun–Mukden. In reserve at Mukden was 7th Army (8 divisions) leaving only six divisions south of Mukden.

After a nine-day guerilla offensive the field forces struck on 14 January protected from air attack by Arctic weather conditions and mist which restricted CAF operations throughout the campaign to an average of a dozen sorties a day. Eleven Northern MR divisions besieged Ssuping while two columns besieged Faku to prevent relief from the southwest. A Western MR column attacked the PEINING Railway north of Chinchou and on 5 January besieged Hsinlitun, from where a branch line led northwards to the Communist-controlled rail network. Lin Piao hoped to use the town as bait in a 'mousetrap' ambush but the mouse-like Nationalists failed to respond and on 23 January Hsinlitun was stormed. The garrison of neighbouring Fuhsin fled westwards to Ihsien.

These attacks finally enticed part of Chen Cheng's reaction force, the Manchurian New 5th Corps, from Mukden but on 24 January it was surrounded by two columns. The commander sought permission to withdraw eastwards but Chen Cheng hesitated for a day, hoping the nearby 9th Army (Liao Yao-hsiang) would relieve it. Liao himself feared attack from Faku and refused to move without a written order from Chen. The Nationalist leaders were still squabbling when the trapped corps was destroyed on 26 January.

On New Year's Day Chen had bombastically proclaimed his army had completed its battle preparations and that the crisis in Manchuria had passed but now his command was collapsing before Chiang's eyes. The Generalissimo had flown into Mukden for a conference before the enemy offensive and remained, possibly doubting Chen's ability. As Cheng panicked and committed reserves piecemeal these doubts grew. With the destruction of New 5th Corps an enquiry was held into Liao Yao-hsiang's conduct. Privately Chen admitted he was responsible and on 27 January Chiang relieved him, ostensibly because of an ulcer complaint. Chen remained in Mukden until 5 February when he was secretly flown out.

The Fall of Ssuping

He was replaced by the 50-year-old Wei Li-huang, dubbed the 'Ever Victorious General' for destroying a Communist base in the early 1930s. In the war against Japan his career was not distinguished, although he participated in the New Fourth Army Incident. Subsequently he helped plan the recovery of Burma but after VJ Day he was despatched upon an 'inspection tour' abroad. Soon after his return he assumed command of what was now renamed the Northeast Rebellion Suppression Headquarters but he was ignorant of both the theatre and Communist methods of fighting.

Before Wei could familiarise himself, Lin Piao personally led a nine-division raid which sliced into the soft underbelly of south Liaoning. He cut the railway south of Mukden on 28 January and, with the support of the Eastern MR, stormed all the cities along the line destroying three divisions in the process. Ominously, the fall of Yingkou on 25 February was due to the defection of a defending division. Although Lin Piao set up his headquarters at Liaochung, a mere 55 kilometres southwest of Mukden, he was never at risk for the Nationalists had only five formations to defend the city.

Simultaneously the Western MR consolidated its hold southwest of Ssuping taking Faku in mid February and destroying two divisions in the process. In early March its columns marched north to join the siege of Ssuping while Lin Piao transferred his headquarters to Faku for the *coup de grace*. The defenders were Peng O's 88th Division which had twice fought the Japanese for Shanghai. With attached units and support troops it had 19,000 men but in its last battle the defenders were outnumbered 5:1, the very ratio Lin preferred. After a week's bombardment by Chu Jui's 70 guns the main assault was launched on the evening of 11 March supported by tanks. By midday on 12 March the city was doomed although the surviving defenders succeeded in making a costly breakout led by Peng O. A column was then sent to take Kirin but before it arrived the Nationalists abandoned the city and transferred the garrison to Changchun.

Like a *kung-fu* fighter Lin Piao had bewildered his opponents before dealing stunning blows to which they could not respond. Both sides had suffered some 80,000 casualties but the Nationalists had lost 11 divisions, a quarter of their strength, and the Changchun garrison was hopelessly isolated. Wei Li-huang's command was now reduced to a few enclaves while the Northeast Bureau controlled 300,000 square kilometres of territory and some 13 million people. With this success behind him Lin moved to Ssuping and prepared for the final campaign.

The Communists Re-organise

One problem Lin Piao was forced to address concerned logistics in newly liberated territory. By supporting and compensating the peasants he had ensured supplies would be brought forward by the *min-fu* from established liberated areas. But such was the military situation that in early 1948 villagers were barely liberated before they faced Communist demands for supplies and recruits virtually at gunpoint. Rather than face a threat to his supply system Lin Piao deliberately waited six months before resuming the offensive and during this time he accelerated the land reform programme in captured districts.

The lull gave him time to expand his forces to 1,030,000 men (53 divisions) supported by 1.6 million *min-fu*. With victory inevitable he prepared for a conventional campaign exploiting artillery and armour. The winter campaign had showed it was impossible for his headquarters, or those of the military regions, to control all 13 columns (each with three field force and one regional division or some 25,000 men) simultaneously and he established four army headquarters. He retained control of the Third (Chen Chi-han) and Fourth (Teng Hua) Armies, together with Chu Jui's 'Artillery' Column of armour and artillery.

The First Army (Hsiao Ching-kuang) was left to mask Changchun assisted by regional divisions while the Second Army (Cheng Tzu-hua) was created in the west. The new army commanders were given intensive staff training, probably using Soviet Army manuals, while at all levels Lin again demanded extensive inter-arm training to make the maximum use of his newly acquired firepower. Demonstrations and minor attacks around the Mukden enclave completed this operational training as well as maintaining pressure upon the enemy.

The Nationalists' Situation

At Changchun, defended by Cheng Tung-kuo's 1st Army (6 divisions), the siege lines steadily tightened and crept over the airport. Supplies were now parachuted in but three days of sorties were required to provide a single day's rations. The garrison's situation was made even more perilous in August when the Communists brought in two regiments of anti-aircraft guns, probably with Soviet advisers, which forced aircraft to such heights that accurate resupply was impossible.

Air transport, which was expensive, was now also the only means of supplying Mukden after the PEINING Railway was cut. The Nationalists were able to replace their losses in manpower and even expanded their strength until Wei Li-huang had some 430,000 men but Cheng's 1st Army was isolated, Fan Han-chieh's 6th Army (which had absorbed the

Hopeh–Jehol Border Army) was 200 kilometres away at Chinchou with 14 divisions leaving Wei controlling the 8th (Chou Fu-cheng) and 9th (Liao Yao-hsiang) Armies (21 divisions) together with seven divisions guarding the western rail system.

During the summer the tide of fortune flowed against the Nationalists. Yenan had been lost, Fu Tso-yi was being pressed ever harder while between the Yellow River and the Yangtze the Communists secured Shantung and were tightening their grip on the plains provinces.

In Manchuria defeat and inactivity sapped morale which was further eroded by rampant corruption within a supply organisation incapable even of providing adequate winter clothing. Air support was also at a premium for, when the Communist offensive opened, only 50 aircraft were available in Manchuria. The failure to reinforce the CAF in Manchuria suggests the Nationalist high command had written off the region, and certainly no allocations were requested during discussions on distributing the US$125 million military aid programme.

Communist planning for the offensive began in April and a series of conferences gradually hammered out the details. It was decided to use the trusted 'mousetrap' tactic and much time was spent considering where to build the perfect mousetrap. Mao suggested Changchun but Lin Piao rejected this on the grounds it was too tough a nut to crack, too far away to attract an enemy relief operation and might actually allow the enemy to escape from Mukden. Instead Lin decided to strike the Nationalist left at Chinchou which was a major port and lay on the PEINING Railway. It was a tremendous gamble for he would be exposing his own supply lines to converging attacks by Wei and Fu but Lin was confident the enemy were too timid to attempt such a move.

The Liao-Shen Campaign: First Phase

With the ground drying the first phase of the Liao-Shen (Liaoning–Shenyang) operation began on the night of 11–12 September with eight Second Army divisions making a forced march to Ihsien reinforcing four divisions already besieging the town. Their task was to open the railway to Chinchou for the Communist forces and to prevent intervention from Chengte. The following night diversionary attacks began at Changchun and in the LIAOSI Corridor where another seven Second Army divisions struck in an attempt to isolate the battlefield.

On the same night sealed trains carrying an 80,000 man task force (five divisions) under Han Hsien-chu rolled westward from Ssuping then south to Ihsien arriving on 15 September. There it relieved the Fourth Column which marched westward to isolate Chinchou. Rolling along the line behind the first task force came a second one with 150,000 men (12 divisions) which travelled to Hsinlitun to prevent any relief operation from Mukden. These moves went smoothly and the Communists began exploiting their success. In the LIAOSI Corridor the Fourth Column isolated Chinchou from the south while on 24 September Han Hsien-chu's task force assaulted Ihsien supported by Chu Jui's guns. The town fell on 1 October but the triumph was marred by Chu's death on a land mine.

When Ihsien open, Lin Piao quickly created an outer siege wall of 23 divisions as Chinchou was invested by eight divisions with 100 guns, 400 mortars and 15 tanks. Had Fan Han-chieh's 6th Army been at full strength he might have resisted longer but several divisions had been transferred to the LIAOSI Corridor leaving him only 118,000 men, many of them recruits or administrative personnel. There was little ammunition and half of his eight divisions were Yunnanese formations whose commanders ignored him. Another 5,400 men were flown in from Mukden before the airport was closed by artillery fire on 29 September. The CAF could parachute in only 100 tonnes a day and Fan pleaded for help.

The Siege of Chinchou

Chiang himself recognised that Chinchou was the Communist objective and on 26 September he ordered Wei Li-huang to relieve the city. But Wei still feared an attack on Mukden and believed the forces in the LIAOSI Corridor, part of Fan's command, were better placed to carry out the relief. Even the despatch of Ku Chu-tung, Chief of the General Staff, failed to change his mind and on 1 October a furious Chiang flew to Mukden himself.[7] By the time he arrived a relief force, the Eastern Strike Force (five corps) had been created in the LIAOSI Corridor and as they advanced Chiang perceived an opportunity to envelop Lin Piao.

Under his none too gentle prodding, Wei stripped the Mukden garrison to create, under Liao Yao-hsiang, the Western Strike Force with 90,000 men (11 divisions). On 5 October this began probing westwards from Mukden while 52nd Corps staged a surprise attack southwards to clear the Mukden–Yingkou railway, recapturing Yingkou on 11 October. By then Liao had been advancing upon Changwu for two days on a broad front using the PEINING Railway as the axis. Changwu lay on Lin Piao's supply line and was defended by a dozen divisions but the Nationalists took the town on 10 October. Simultaneously Taian, to the south, also fell to give the Nationalists control of the road network between Mukden and Chinchou. However, Liao was concerned about the potential threat from Hsinlitun and rather than pressing on towards Chinchou diverted troops to secure his flank.

Yet Wei Li-huang's forces were on the verge of the decisive victory they had sought for two years. If Wei pressed home his advantage he could drive Lin Piao's forces out of Manchuria or even destroy them. But time was running out, for the Communist grip upon Chinchou was tightening and by 8 October the defenders had been driven to the city walls. Lin also faced new pressure from the LIAOSI Corridor as the Eastern Strike Force advanced. The Fourth Column, under Wu Ko-hua, was given the task of holding back the enemy and fought an epic defensive battle around Tashan (some 40 kilometres south of Chinchou) until Chinchou was stormed. So important was the column to Lin that he gave it priority from his rapidly diminishing stocks of supplies.

At Chinchou the Communists poured through gaps which the gunners had blasted in the city walls. They pushed the defenders deeper into the blazing city and cornered the survivors in the railway station which surrendered on 15 October. Of the 122,000 garrison some 34,000 had been killed but 88,000 including General Fan were taken prisoner. The same day the bloodied Fourth Column launched a counter-offensive which drove back the Eastern Strike Force.

The Nationalist Collapse

With news of Chinchou's fall, Liao Yao-hsiang reined in the Western Strike Force and pondered his next move. Morale, already reeling, was dealt another blow from Changchun where Lin Piao had secretly been cultivating Tseng Tse-sheng, commander of 60th Corps, who was seeking the best possible terms for himself and his men. The fall of Chinchou proved the catalyst for, on 17 October, Wei Li-huang ordered 1st Army to fight their way to him while most of the Communist forces were committed to western Manchuria. This gave Tseng the bargaining edge he needed with the Communists. Agreement was quickly reached and Tseng's defection, on 19 October, forced most of the 80,000 garrison to surrender. Cheng Tung-kuo, with two battalions of bodyguards, held out in the Central Bank but the following night they were blasted into submission. After a few months' political indoctrination and retraining, Tseng's men were incorporated into the PLA as the Fiftieth Corps.[8]

The Nationalist position in Manchuria was now desperate. The bulk of Wei Li-huang's troops were with the Western Strike Force, leaving eight formations around Mukden and the 52nd Corps holding the railway to Yingkou. It was an opportunity Lin Piao did not miss and while his columns marched eastwards the official news agency published a statement indicating their objective was northern China. Regional forces around the LIAOSI Corridor made appropriate demonstrations and convinced an initially sceptical Chiang who ordered Liao Yao-hsiang to strike the Communist rear. Lin Piao's only fear was of the enemy marching directly to Chinchou and to prevent this he moved the reinforced Tenth Column (Wen Nien-sheng) into a blocking position between hills and marshes at Heishan, some 100 kilometres north east of Chinchou.

The move was timely for on 23 October five Nationalist divisions attacked Heishan where a bitter battle was fought during the next two days and nights, as the temperature dropped. The struggle cost the Communists some 10,000 casualties but enmeshed much of the Western Strike Force, gaining time for a score of Lin's divisions to envelop the enemy after forced marches of up to 50 kilometres a night. Liao Yao-hsiang recognised the danger and decided to retreat to Mukden, but it was too late. As he withdrew, eight Communist divisions marched at a blistering pace to link up on 26 October on the Jao Yang River, some 30 kilometres east of Heishan, and from rudimentary defences they held back the enemy. Once reinforced they attacked and overran the strike force's forward headquarters killing Liao. Trapped and leaderless his troops surrendered in the early hours of 28 October to provide the enemy with 38,000 prisoners, 22 tanks, 150 guns, 600 vehicles and 6,000 horses.

Chiang had Wei Li-huang flown from Mukden to Hulutao, where he had earlier established a command post, leaving his garrison under the command of Chou Fu-cheng's 8th Army. Wei's flight was interpreted as desertion, especially as the Eastern Strike Force was now under the capable command of Tu Yu-ming. When the First Army attacked Mukden on 1 November, few defenders showed any desire to sacrifice their lives for a lost cause. By the late afternoon Mukden had fallen forcing the 52nd Corps to retreat into Yingkou from where it was evacuated to join the Eastern Strike Force in Hulutao. This operation was completed on 5 November to bring the Hulutao garrison to 137,000 men, but almost immediately this port was also evacuated and within four days the last troops sailed out with some 2,000 tonnes of supplies. Significantly, only 3,000 civilians accompanied them.

The loss of Manchuria with its economic resources was a disaster which, even in Chiang's view, overshadowed the loss of more than 300,000 men including 246,000 prisoners or defectors. Almost immediately, Wei was imprisoned on charges of corruption. He was released the following April after Li Tsung-jen became president but retired to Hong Kong. In March 1955 he entered the People's Republic where he became vice-chairman of the National Defence Council in 1959, but died in office within nine months.

Yet it was Chiang's political blunders rather than Wei's military ones which led to defeat. In his desire to impose central authority he ignored regional aspirations and alienated the population. This made them more susceptible to Communist influence and made it difficult to find recruits for the Nationalist army. Lin Piao and the Northeast Bureau also made mistakes but were quicker to learn and to apply the lessons. The final campaign probably cost Lin some 75,000 casualties but these could be replaced while much booty has been taken including 76 tanks, 2,000 vehicles and heavy artillery. The fate of Manchuria was never a foregone conclusion, it had been won by Lin's calculating and decisive leadership both in the field and in the countryside.

5

From the Mountains to the Sea: Northern China

IN CONTRAST to Manchuria, the northern and western theatre from the Great Wall southwards was dominated by brooding hills and mountains, their bare slopes riven by deep gullies. Most agriculture was confined to the major river valleys, such as the Wei, or the broad Hopeh plain with its numerous rivers and streams including the great Yellow River (Huang Ho).

The Yellow River marked the theatre's southern boundary and also bisected the western side, dividing Shensi from Shansi. Within the high ground the wild, young river was deep but it slowly matured to reach its dotage near the Hopeh–Shantung border where it meanders across the vast plain supported by great dikes. Between July and September the moist winds from the south bring the blessing of monsoon rain and the curse of flooding which covers the plain with turgid yellow water. Otherwise the weather is cool but dry, the wind coming predominantly from the west to bring loess, dust from the Gobi desert, in the early part of the year.

The prime lateral railway is the PINGSUI line from Paotao to Tientsin through Kalgan and Peiping, while the longitudinal lines from west to east are the TUNGPU, the PINGHAN and the TSINPU. The TUNGPU (Tatung–Fenglingtu) Railway divides Shansi and runs through Taiyuan along the Fen River valley through Linfen and Houma. In the summer of 1946 the heights east of this line were held by the Communists who restricted the enemy grasp on the PINGHAN and TSINPU lines to the northern sections as far as Shihchiachuang and Tsanghsien respectively. The Nationalists also held the branch

103

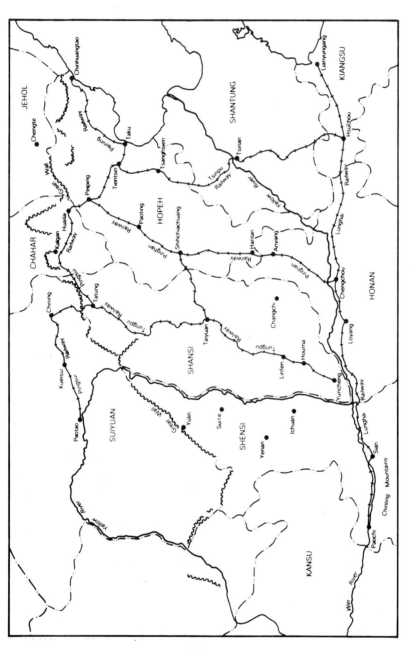

The Northern Theatre

line from Shihchiachuang to Taiyuan. In Shensi the Nationalists held the Wei valley through which ran the LUNGHAI railway. This line, whose western terminus was Lanchou, the capital of Kansu province, ran through Paochi and Sian to link Shensi with Honan.

The Communist Commanders

To the north the Communist capital of Yenan was protected by the Northwest Field Army under 48-year-old Peng Te-huai, the son of a poor Hunan peasant. Five years in a coal mine left him with a slightly crooked back yet he was able to join the Hunan Army in 1916. Even implication in a landowner's murder could not prevent him rising from the ranks and he became a regimental commander in the NRA.

Early in early 1928 he was 'admitted to school' (i.e. he joined the Party) and subsequently distinguished himself in operations against the Nationalists, disdaining guerilla warfare in favour of conventional operations. An ambitious, hot-tempered, foul-mouthed man with beetle brows, Peng distrusted political interference in military operations and was an advocate, against Mao's wishes, of the abortive Hundred Regiments' Offensive. Subsequently he was recalled to Yenan where he studied Russian and Chinese field manuals, although he was never to be noted for profound military thought.

Distrusted by both the Central Committee and Mao his current appointment exploited his undoubted talents while keeping him under the committee's gaze. Significantly the army had been drained of men and equipment to support Lin Piao, becoming the PLA's smallest with a strength of only 70,000. Its former commander, Ho Lung, retained command of the Shensi-Suiyuan (known by its Chinese acronym of CHINSUI) MR's field forces with four columns, leaving Peng directly controlling only three. Ho Lung, a tailor's son, was a fifty-year-old former warlord general and like Peng was also a native of Hunan. As a bandit he proved so successful that the governor persuaded him to join his army. Like Peng he had a hot temper and a foul mouth but he was also a flamboyant character who wore the moustaches associated with the rural elite as an egalitarian gesture.

Eastern Shansi, Chahar and Hopeh were the responsibility of

the Shansi–Chahar–Hopeh (CHINCHACI) Field Army of Nieh Jung-chen. With his delicate features Nieh, aged 47, was the antithesis of Peng both physically and socially, for he was the son of a wealthy Szechwan landowner. He had had a good Chinese education, one of his classmates being Teng Hsiao-ping who was later Liu Po-cheng's political officer. In 1920 he went to France to study engineering and met Chou En-lai through whom he joined the Communist Party. Despite graduating from the Red Army Military College in Moscow and distinguishing himself in military technology at Whampoa (in the 1950s he was to lead China's nuclear arms programme) his military career was initially confined to the political field. His talent, and friendship with Mao, brought him military command after the Long March and during the war against the Japanese he developed a reputation for sudden attacks and elusiveness.

The Siege of Tatung

The military operations in this theatre are best understood if they are considered on a geographic basis. Effectively the theatre consisted of three fronts whose actions were essentially autonomous, although occasionally they were interdependent. These fronts were the Hopeh-PINGUSI Railway, Shensi and Shansi and they will be examined in this order.

In the summer of 1946 Nieh had eight columns with about 100,000 men and his prime concern was the security of the Manchurian corridor running through northern Shansi and southern Chahar. To the east, in northern Hopeh, lay the Nationalist 11th War Zone of Sun Lien-chung, a 53-year-old native of Hopeh. Sun, who had an excellent field record against the Japanese, had held his command for just over a year and had 18 formations with some 160,000 men. To the west lay the Nationalist 12th War Zone of Fu Tso-yi who came from Shansi and was two years Sun's junior. Fu, governor of Suiyuan, also had a distinguished combat record, against the Japanese. He was a rugged austere man with a reputation not only for efficiency but also concern for his men's welfare which ensured they followed him loyally. It was this reputation, rather than the 13 formations (180,000 men) he commanded, which concerned Nieh.

Nieh Jung-chen's attention focused upon Tatung, which lay

between the Inner and Outer Great Walls at the junction of the PINGSUI and TUNGPU lines. The city was part of Fu Tso-yi's command but the presence of the 'Model Governor's' 13 formations in Shansi meant it could become a springboard for an offensive. By advancing towards the Peiping enclave, some 250 kilometres away, Fu could dam the flow of men flowing into Manchuria. By pre-empting such a move the Communists could secure the PINGSUI railway to the east and gain greater 'operational' mobility. Politically such an attack was unwise for it was a flagrant violation of the ceasefire which Marshall had secured. However, the Nationalists were already violating the agreement and Yenan authorised Nieh to proceed.

He assigned the task to Yao Che who had two columns and some 30,000 regional and local forces. The city was defended by 10,000 men, half of them dismounted cavalry, under Ma Chin-shan who were isolated in early August. But they had the protection of extensive fortifications and were supplied by air. Sheer weight of numbers carried the attackers forward but at high cost and only after Ho Lung arrived with reinforcements was the city's eastern gate stormed on 28 August.

However, by concentrating the Communist forces the siege exposed them to a counter-stroke although Fu Tso-yi's initial concept was purely tactical. He planned to re-open the Chining-Tatung railway, lost six months earlier, and after a careful reconnaisance he attacked on 1 September with four divisions supported by some 15,000 cavalry. Within a week they reached the western suburbs of Chining which fell on 14 September despite the arrival of Communist reinforcements.

The PINGSUI Railway Campaigns

While cavalry protected their flanks and outflanked the enemy, the Nationalist infantry marched along the railway and by 19 September were only 40 kilometres north of Tatung at the Outer Great Wall. Their advance had spurred a frenzied attack upon Tatung but the only success was to take the northern gate and even this exhausted the Communists. When the enemy reached the Great Wall, Ho Lung reluctantly decided to break off the attack which had cost him some 10,000 men but he was able to retreat in good order.

The Nationalists, who lost 5,000, claimed they inflicted 35,000 casualties but took only 30 prisoners. Tatung was a severe defeat for the Communists and one in which mounted cavalry, for the last time in military history, were able to perform most of their traditional roles. Cavalry were used later in the Civil War but essentially their role was that of mounted infantry.

As the Communists reeled back, Fu Tso-yi instinctively recognised that he could exploit his success 'operationally' to reopen the PINGSUI Railway. He struck on 20 September, as Tatung was relieved, giving the Communists no time to recover and such was his determination that he committed seven divisions; half his strength, Nieh Jung-chen faced a double threat to the corridor for Sun Lien-chung committed Li Wen's 34th Army (eight divisions) which advanced from Peiping. Nieh left Cheng Wei-shan's column to hold Fu while he assembled 50,000 men to meet the 34th Army in a defensive position around Huailei, southeast of Kalgan. Sun's forces, of similar strength, blundered into these defences on 29 September and for a fortnight tried to smash their way through in a series of uncoordinated frontal attacks. Only when they attempted to outflank the enemy from the north did they overcome resistance.

Meanwhile Fu Tso-yi's forces, with cavalry protecting their left, advanced steadily along the railway towards Kalgan. The city, with a population of 200,000, was occupied by the Communists in 1945 and for both strategic and political reasons the Central Committee wished to retain it. Chou En-lai in Nanking sought, through Marshall, to stem the advance with a mixture of threats and entreaties. Nieh Jung-chen provided more concrete assistance by despatching some 4,000 men from Huailei as others came from neighbouring Jehol; it was hopeless. On 10 October Fu troops entered Kalgan then continued their advance towards Peiping. He failed to trap Nieh, who escaped south into the Wutai Mountains, allowing his enemies to link up on 14 October then reopen the PINGSUI Railway by the end of the month.

For the loss of 4,700 men the Nationalists cut the Manchurian corridor, established control of Jehol and secured vital 'operational' rail communications. They claimed to have inflicted 17,800 casualties and captured 640 prisoners but failed to destroy Nieh Jung-chen's field force which, in the classic guerilla tradition, lived to fight another day. Yet Kalgan was an important victory and Fu was rewarded with the governorship of Chahar, followed in 1947, by supreme military command in northern China.

With Kalgan's fall, Chiang sought to exploit the success by striking south from Peiping to reopen the PINGHAN Railway. But when the conference, chaired by Chen Cheng, was held at Peiping on 19 October none of the northern commanders was enthusiastic. Yet they were reluctant to oppose the Generalissimo's wishes publicly and Sun Lien-chung expressed support for the plan. It was pigeon-holed only after Li Tsung-jen, while expressing willingness to obey the order, pointed out that compliance depended upon reinforcement.

The Hopeh Offensives

The failure to exploit the Battle of Kalgan left the Communists controlling 50 of Hopeh's 130 districts at the beginning of 1947 and in a position to extend their influence. As a result of the autumn defeats, Nieh Jung-chen was unable to provide much support for political activity around the PINGSUI Railway and his fortunes were at their nadir. An abortive morale-boosting attack upon the PINGHAN Railway in January left Nieh depressed until March when Chu Teh and Liu Shao-chi arrived at Hsipaipo, in the Taihang Mountains. They were leading part of the Central Committee who had fled Yenan when the town was attacked by Hu Tsung-nan (see p. 118) and with their arrival Neih's fortunes recovered.

The creation of the Central Work Committee led to a renaissance in the region with Chu Teh helping to plan military operations to support Liu Shao-chi's political work. This involved a bloody period of land reform to reassert wavering Party control in the countryside. Nieh Jung-chen's first attempt to support this process was in April when he invested Shihchiachuang to prevent enemy military interference with political activities in western Hopeh. On 14 May he struck into the centre of the province advancing 250 kilometres to attack the TSINPU Railway within 10 kilometres of Tientsin.

With the summer rains he withdrew into the mountains, leaving behind a Front Committee to supervise operations in central Hopeh while he expanded his columns to corps strength. From September Yang Te-chih's Front Committee steadily extended Communist control in central Hopeh leaving the enemy with a thin ribbon of territory from Paoting to Shihchiachuang.

The Capture of Shihchiachuang

During the summer Lin Piao's attack on Ssuping, and Chen Cheng's subsequent expansion of the Manchuria garrison, drained Hopeh. By August the governor, Sun Lien-chuang, had only 17 formations and in September he lost three when the elite 92nd Corps was ordered to protect the LIAOSI Corridor. With Liu Po-cheng and Chen Yi causing havoc south of the Yellow River, no reinforcements could be expected and consequently Sun became both passive and querulous. Nieh Jung-chen attempted to exploit the situation, initially striking the PINGHAN Railway north of Paoting from 1 October, but at first he had no success.

However, the regional and local forces harassing the railway helped create a major victory for him.[1] They had struck the railway north of Shihchiachuang and to clear the line Sun Lien-chuang ordered the city garrison to despatch the 7th Division. This was the opportunity Nieh had sought all year and, while one column masked the nearby Paoting garrison, Yang Cheng-wu led 50,000 men down the line half way between Paoting and Shihchiachuang.

There he ambushed the enemy on 18 October, annihilated them within 24 hours, then exploited his success by investing Shihchiachuang. This was defended by a single division and an infanty regiment hastily flown in from Paoting but the defenders were demoralised and by 12 November the city, together with large quantities of equipment, was in Communist hands. The supplies gave Nieh the resources to meet the enemy on equal terms and guaranteed his hold on Shihchiachuang from which he could threaten the enemy's north Hopeh enclave.

Following this debacle Chiang Kai-shek appointed Fu Tso-yi commander of the North China Rebellion Suppression Headquarters, but Fu immediately encountered the problems which had plagued his predecessor. In late December, Nieh Jung-chen struck both the PINGHAN and PINGSUI lines close to Peiping but was driven off in early January 1948. Immediately afterwards there was a protracted duel north of Paoting as the Communists sought to isolate enemy formations. On 12 January two columns, led by Cheng Wei-shan, ambushed the 35th Corps' (Lu Ying-lin) headquarters and a division. Some 4,000 men were lost before the survivors fought their way out to the other division which was only three kilometres away yet made no effort to assist. In despair Lu committed suicide.

New Battle around the PINGSUI Railway

Fu Tso-yi had begun 1948 with only 34 formations to protect both the PINGSUI Railway and northern Hopeh yet he could anticipate no reinforcements because of the growing crisis in Manchuria which would also absorb some of his forces. By contrast Nieh Jung-chen had 21 field force divisions in Hopeh and during the 10 weeks following the destruction of 35th Corps he assimilated more recruits and captured equipment. He also acquired six divisions under Hsu Hsiang-chien which had been raised in the Taihang Mountains to reinforce Liu Po-cheng in the Tapieh Mountains. Due to growing enemy pressure upon the latter base it proved impossible to transfer these divisions south and Chu Teh allocated them to Nieh.

In late March Nieh took 18 divisions through the mountains of north Shansi and struck the PINGSUI Railway between Tatung and Kalgan. The raid forced Fu Tso-yi to abandon many small towns around Tatung as Nieh crossed the Great Wall into southern Suiyuan to take Kueisui. His troops continued to operate in northern Shansi and Chahar until mid May wrecking the PINGSUI Railway and giving Fu an excuse to avoid diverting his resources to Manchuria.

Civilian confidence collapsed and during March there was a massive flight of capital, involving CN$20 billion, from the Peiping area to Chungking followed, in May, by another worth CN$7 billion to Shanghai and Hong Kong. The only compensation for Fu Tso-yi was the opportunity to remove Sun Lien-chuang, who had remained governor of Hopeh and become a thorn in his side. Sun was given the sinecures of personal Chief of Staff to the Generalissimo and command of the Nanking garrison.

Despite the setbacks when the US assistant defence attaché, Rigg, visited Fu in May he found him 'full of brusque, smiling confidence'.[2] He wanted his forces to become more mobile and more aggressive but he had lost two good corps, transferred to support Wei Li-huang's defence of Manchuria which he believed was a useless sacrifice. He created two new corps to maintain a strength of 14 corps/reorganised divisions but he was justifiably bitter at Nanking's failure to support him. A US mission which visited him in June reported 11 of his corps/reorganised divisions were poorly armed although the US was unaware Fu was seeking European arms.[3]

Manpower and equipment did not concern the Communists who used the early summer of 1948 to reorganise their forces in northern China. Nieh Jung-chen's Shansi–Chahar–Hopeh (CHINCHACHI) MR was combined with Hsu Hsiang-chien's CHINCHILUYU MR to create the North China MR with 30 field force divisions divided among three army headquarters; Hsu Hsiang-chien's First, Yang Te-chih's Second and Yang Cheng-wu's Third.

The North China Field Army received a baptism of fire from mid July as Nieh Jung-chen struck the enemy throughout his 'operational' depth in support of Liu Po-cheng's operations in Honan. On the PINGHAN Railway, where there had been 11 divisions a few months earlier, there remained only four and the Third Army opened a three-month harassment campaign by destroying one of them. Fu Tso-yi could provide little support because Second Army (nine divisions) was interdicting communications in northern Hopeh and Jehol, briefly cutting the Peiping–Tientsin line before being driven off. In Jehol, where Nieh was joined by two of Lin Piao's columns, Li Wen's slothful 34th Army allowed the enemy to withdraw into his mountain sanctuaries with trifling losses.

The Peiping–Tientsin Campaign: The Situation in November 1948

By the autumn of 1948 Fu Tso-yi was confined to a narrow corridor along the PINGSUI Railway and to the valleys in the mountains of the Hopeh–Jehol border. To defend this enclave he had some 40 divisions with 375,000 men, including support troops, and 98 aircraft. This was inadequate even to meet the threat from Nieh's 130,000 field force troops and Fu correctly anticipated they would soon be augmented by Lin Piao's Northeast Field Army once it completed the conquest of Manchuria. In the cities, especially Peiping, Fu's situation was complicated by thousands of destitute refugees who were reduced to killing stray dogs for food. His only option was to tie down the enemy troops for as long as possible, then escape along the PINGSUI Railway either westwards into the interior or eastwards to the sea. The only optimistic note was the imminent arrival of US arms under the US$125 million military aid package which might help him to prolong the defence.

Nieh Jung-chen recognised the problem but was still not strong enough to meet Fu in a conventional battle. His initial task was to support the Liao-Shen campaign in Manchuria by preventing Fu transferring reinforcements to Manchuria. For this purpose he decided to retake Kalgan, a prize he particularly desired having lost it two years earlier. He ordered Second and Third Armies to march through the mountains and take up a position north of Huailei on the PINGSUI Railway. The two armies arrived by 7 October and were soon harassing the line, nimbly avoiding two corps Fu committed to protect the railway.[4]

Recognising the danger Fu Tso-yi sought to strengthen his hold on the western section of the line by abandoning outposts, including Paoting, on the PINGHAN Railway. The maritime evacuation option was clearly growing large in the Chiang's mind for he was now urging Fu to protect Tientsin and its port of Taku. For this purpose the 17th Army was activated to protect the Peiping–Tientsin corridor, Chengte was abandoned on 14 November and Tientsin was reinforced by a corps from the LIAOSI Corridor.

In Manchuria, after his triumph in mid November, Lin Piao knew Fu Tso-yi would be his next opponent but he had been promised a month's rest to replace casualties and distribute booty. But with Fu strengthening his seaward defences the Communists feared he would escape into central China. On 19 November, Mao sent Lin Piao a telegram asking whether or not his men would prefer to destroy Fu's forces immediately, or rest, allow the enemy to escape, and meet him later. It was a rhetorical question and, although his divisions were under strength and made up of tired veterans and raw recruits Lin quickly reorganised them for an operation which he planned to start within two days!

His staff hastily prepared their plans and on 20 November they began a two-day briefing at Harbin on the 'operational' concept. Recognising that a thrust towards the Peiping–Tientsin corridor would encourage Fu to escape through Kalgan, Lin decided to exploit Nieh Jung-chen's plans for taking the city so that Nieh would act as the anvil to his own hammer.

Three task forces (Route Armies) were created for an operation which involved an assault upon the whole 'operational' depth of Fu Tso-yi's forces. The Second Manchurian Army had already been despatched towards Kalgan where it joined Nieh's two armies to form the largest concentration, the Right Route Army under Cheng Tzu-hua with 26 divisions. Reinforced by 80,000 members of the regional and local forces Cheng was to strike north west of Peiping and entice the largest possible relief column from Peiping while simultaneously preventing Fu's troops from escaping westwards.

The Central Route Army, under Lin Piao's deputy Hsiao Ching-kuang, had 23 divisions[5] and acted as 'operational' reserve but was also to encircle Peiping and prevent the despatch of further relief columns. The weakest force was the Left Route Army under Lin's former Chief of Staff, Liu Ya-lou. He had 20 divisions with which to isolate Taku, dashing enemy hopes of maritime evacuation, then he would storm Tientsin.[6]

The Peiping–Tientsin Campaign: First Phase

On 22 November Lin Piao's troops, some 760,000 strong, began a 650 kilometres march over icy, drift-blocked roads. They reached their staging areas 10 days later but remained concealed until 5 December to prevent the enemy becoming alarmed. Due to the scale of the operation Lin apparently decided not to rely upon the Party organisation for his supplies but instead to use his fleet of captured trucks. But many bridges needed to be repaired, the roads were rough and he failed to create fuel and maintenance facilities so that many trucks broke down. In the end the Party had to rescue him by mobilising 50,000 peasants to repair 290 kilometres of snow-covered road, a task reportedly completed within 36 hours.

The Central Route Army arrived around Chengte followed by Lin Piao who installed his command post at Tsunhua on 5 December after transferring the Party's Northeast Bureau to Kao Kang. Meanwhile the Left Route Army cleared the LIAOSI Corridor, whose Chinhuantao garrison was shipped to Tientsin–Taku.

On the night of 30 November – 1 December Nieh Jung-chen began the initial phase of his offensive by isolating Kalgan with his own two armies. The Third Army struck in the west while the Second Army in the south enticed the two divisions of 35th Corps (Kuo Ching-yun), out of Kalgan[7] then isolated it north-west of Huailei on 6 December. Kuo tried to return to Kalgan but the Communists were too strong and on 9 December he fortified his position. Nearly a fortnight elapsed before the main assault was launched, on 22 December. All co-ordinated resistance ceased during the afternoon, although pockets held out until 24 December when Kuo committed suicide.

Meanwhile the Third Army (Yang Cheng-wu), reinforced by a Manchurian column, attacked Kalgan to prevent the five-division (54,000 men) garrison aiding their comrades. By 22 December the city was isolated and thousands of *min-fu* were brought in to weave a spider's web of trenches around the city. Then Yang learned the garrison intended to break out and, as it was easier to destroy the enemy in the field than in a city, he decided to encourage them by weakening the siege ring in one sector. Beyond sight of the garrison the *min-fu* hastily constructed fortifications to turn the escape route into a killing ground. The plan worked perfectly and within a day of breaking out, on 23 December, the garrison was destroyed permitting the Communists to reoccupy the city.

Another storm grew northeast of Peiping where, on 5 December, the Central Route Army began to march from Chengte. Supported by the Right Route Army's Second Manchurian Army it crossed the Great Wall, destroying the elite 16th Corps in the process, and began isolating Peiping. An American aerial observer later wrote '... the air was filled with the blue haze of burning villages and the flashes of sporadic fighting ... the roads were clogged with motion ...'.[8] By 14 December Peiping's main airport was overrun and seven aircraft captured.

The Siege of Tientsin

While the Communist centre pressed the enemy tighter into their tomb, the Left Route Army began a nine-day campaign on 12 December against slight opposition to isolate Tientsin. A direct assault upon the city was delayed because the Nationalists had the foresight to flood the southern approaches where the numerous submerged canals created additional hazards. This forced Lin Piao to spend a month draining away the flood waters and allowing the ground to dry. The assault was assigned to the Second and Fourth Manchurian Armies with 20 divisions, eight artillery regiments and some armour. The garrison was based upon three corps but even with auxiliary troops it probably had no more than 85,000 men,[9] although the strong field fortifications of the city undoubtedly compensated for numerical weakness.

Pounded by 200 guns the defences quickly crumbled and on 14 January the city was stormed, the struggle dissolving into bloody street battles which lasted until the following day. Within Tientsin the Communists mobilised factory militias to protect utilities and factories and almost immediately after the city's fall, water, telephone, transport and postal services were resumed. No attempt was made by the nearby 17th Army, to the north, to assist either Tientsin or even Taku, which surrendered on 17 January.

The Peiping–Tientsin Campaign: Final Phase

Only Fu Tso-yi's forces with some 240,000 men[10] now remained and they were clearly doomed. Fu was under tremendous pressure from civilian leaders to surrender and protect the treasures of the former imperial capital, but he had no intention of enduring a humiliating capitulation. Disaster dissolved any lingering loyalty to Chiang and he opened negotiations early in December with an offer to surrender, provided his own position and safety were secured and his troops were incorporated into the PLA.

His most powerful weapon was his reputation made during an epic siege near Peiping 21 years earlier when he held out even after exhausting his food. Fu could also count upon the loyalty of his troops for he had also taken great care to provide their families with food and shelter while both sides knew an assault upon Peiping would cost the Communists dear. These were valuable bargaining cards and the talks lasted until 16 January 1949. They ended with Lin Piao presenting an ultimatum that Fu should accept the extremely generous terms offered or suffer the consequences.

Fu's divisions were to be absorbed by the PLA after political re-education while Nationalist officers and their families were to receive the same treatment as those of their PLA counterparts. This offer was made because the Communists were anxious to retain the services of experienced personnel both civilian and military. Those who wished to return home would receive three months' pay, rail tickets together with food and lodging. After four days' consideration Fu accepted.

On 22 January the Nationalists began a phased evacuation and by the beginning of February the Communists were in complete control. On 3 February the PLA held a victory parade led by the Tashan Hero Regiments which marched into Tien-an Men Square to the rapturous cheers of the populace. The troops' behaviour in the city was exemplary, even according to Communists' critics. Most cadres were 'modest and unpretentious' while the soldiers took nothing by force and returned anything they borrowed. They were to maintain their reputation as the People's Army for four decades until they demonstrated in the same square in 1989 that they were really the Party's Army.

Of Fu Tso-yi's troops only those in Suiyuan escaped the net but Governor Tung Chi-wu's son had married Fu's daughter and family ties secured a temporary 'armistice' in mid June 1949. Two months later, on 25 August, the governor formally defected and received a post in the Communist government.

The North Shensi Campaign

At the theatre's other extremity, the Shensi front remained an oasis of peace following the collapse of the ceasefire during the summer of 1946. Perhaps it was this very calm which aroused Communist suspicions of an attack upon Yenan and Chou En-lai warned Marshall that one was imminent. When pressed upon the matter by the US embassy, Nanking categorically denied any such intention but Chiang was certainly seeking to decapitate the Communist leadership.

However, greater priority was assigned the task of opening the TUNGPU Railway in Shansi and it was here that Hu Tsung-nan concentrated during 1946 (see below p. 123). With the end of the campaign Hu had the winter to prepare for the capture of Yenan. Although not a native of the region he had been unofficially dubbed the 'King of the Northwest', a glowing tribute to his undoubted military and administrative talents.

Born in Chekiang in 1895 he was almost rejected for Whampoa because he was so short and thin. He succeeded only through the chief instructor's influence and later became famous for the discipline of his troops. In the war against Japan he distinguished himself in the Battle of Shanghai, then was given command of a northwestern army and made responsible for military training in the region. It was the latter which earned him his 'crown' and so great was his reputation that many senior government officials sent their sons to serve under him, including Chiang's second son Wei-kuo. In 1943 he became commander of the 1st War Zone but the triumph was offset by the death of his family in a Japanese air-raid.

By 1947 he was betrothed to an American-educated university lecturer but he vowed neither to wed nor to cut his hair until he had taken Yenan. For the offensive the 1st War Zone was upgraded to a pacification command, but Hu had only 23 formations and to create the strike force he had to withdraw two reorganised divisions from southern Shansi. He assembled a total of 18 formations and a cavalry brigade for the offensive and divided them into two commands; the 1st Army (Tung Chiao) on the right and the 29th Army (Liu Chin) on the left. In addition he was supported by the Northwest General Head-quarters of Chang Chi-chung who provided a division-size task force for a diversionary operation southwest of Yenan. Altogether some 160,000 men, including support troops, and 75 aircraft were committed to this operation; it had little strategic or 'operational' impact because most of the troops were provided by the 'King' himself.

The Communists could not have been ignorant of the preparations but they appear to have anticipated that the attack would take place in the late spring. They did not expect an attack in the early spring when the ground was covered with 30 centimetres of snow. Consequently Peng Te-huai's three columns were not reinforced, leaving him with 25,000 men to meet the threat.

On 12 March the diversionary attack was launched and the regional forces, in Peng's words, 'did not fight well', suffering 10 per cent losses. He despatched two columns to stiffen resistance leaving him only one column and a training brigade to meet the main attack on 14 March. This forlorn hope could not stop 1st Army but the other two columns were recalled and, under Peng's personal direction, succeeded in delaying 29th Army for a couple of days.

Yenan was doomed and, while the army desperately battled for time, preparations were made to evacuate the town which was in a state of near panic. When the Communist leaders drove out of the town at dusk on 18 March the enemy were only 4 kilometres away and a few hours later Peng's covering forces were withdrawn. The following day the 1st (R) Division entered Yenan by which time the Central Committee were 25 kilometres to the northeast.

The fall of Yenan was the signal for an orgy of Press congratulations and Hu Tsung-nan's betrothed was flown out with a government-supplied trousseau, the wedding taking place after the general had his hair cut! Yet even Hu must have suspected he had won an empty victory for he had taken only 10,000 prisoners, 243 rifles and three machine guns. Many prisoners were clearly innocent civilians and those Communists taken were only small fry., the leadership and their field forces having escaped. Hu's forces had suffered only 1,000 casualties but he had stripped the defences of the 30 most prosperous districts in the province to occupy 45 of the poorest, a dubious bargain at best.

Shensi: The Communist Reaction

Until mid August, the Nationalists tried both to secure the new won territory and to search for the Central Committee whose protection depended very much upon Peng Te-huai's skill. Prescisely why most of the Central Committee remained west of the Yellow River is unclear, for part of it led by Liu Shao-chi and Chu Teh crossed the river to establish a Working Committee at Hsipaipo.

Possibly Mao wished to act as a decoy but such a quixotic gesture was out of character and the key to his decision lay in Shantung. There many cadres had fled to safety when the Nationalist army entered their district and following Chen Yi's I-tsao victory had been ordered to return and fight behind enemy lines. By remaining in Shensi Mao and the Central Committee were setting an example to maintain Party prestige and morale both nationally and provincially. Nevertheless the Party leadership, their secretariat and dependants were forced to play a lethal game of hide and seek in the mountains of northeast Shensi in conditions unpleasantly reminiscent of the Long March's darkest days.

Ironically Mao, the advocate of guerilla warfare by the masses, owed life and liberty to a small professional army fighting a mobile war. Indeed, compared with other provinces, it appears the regional and self-defence force organisation in Shensi was rudimentary to non-existent. The north of the province was sparsely populated and it appears that Peng absorbed the few regional units to augment his own strength.

He exploited the rugged terrain to strike the two pursuing armies at will, simultaneously eroding enemy strength and acquiring desperately needed supplies. His destruction of an enemy regiment a week after Yenan's fall encouraged him to treat the 'King's' army as a cow for milking. In May he destroyed two brigades and took a supply depot whose stocks sustained him throughout the summer and three months later, on 20 August, he destroyed another two brigades.

This success made the 29th Army withdraw to Suite where its communications to Yenan were protected by 76th (R) Division. But after a rapid sweep southwards Peng took the divisional headquarters on 11 October and destroyed another brigade. The new threat to the Wei valley led to the 1st Army being downgraded to the 18th Pacification Area (seven brigades) and it was later reinforced by three brigades from Shansi. To the north, holding Yenan, were eight brigades with the newly created 5th Army (Pei Chang-hui) while the 29th Army 'contained' the Communists.

The weather in north Shensi was now becoming extremely cold and Peng wished to withdraw into winter quarters to rest and rebuild his strength, especially as it was difficult to find recruits in the sparsely populated province. He made an attempt to take Yulin both to secure the area and to protect the Central Committee, but the cold forced him to withdraw in December. Nevertheless he could feel pleased with his work since the fall of Yenan for he had destroyed five enemy brigades or 27 per cent of the 'King's' strike force. The Central Committee established itself in a temporary home at

Yangchiakou where Mao spent three months developing his political philosophy.

An important after-effect of the failure at Yulin was the development of 'pour-out-grievances' meetings. A cadre observed a soldier bemoaning his misfortune and recognised the potential for bringing whole units to new heights of social awareness. As a mental catharsis, units were encouraged publicly to vent their frustrations and anger at the injustice of life under the Kuomintang. This then made them more susceptible to the revolutionary messages of the Party. The process also helped to improve leadership for many of the leading participants were persuaded to become cadres. Peng later observed that if the process, subsequently extended throughout the PLA, had existed earlier it would have been easier to win over enemy prisoners and to expand his forces.

The Communists Retake Yenan

With the New Year of 1948 Peng was still outnumbered, his 12 formations each having only 3,500 to 4,000 men while Hu Tsung-nan had 18 each with some 5,500 men. But the Nationalist formations were scattered over a wide area; the 29th Army in the north, the 5th Army in Yenan and the 18th Pacification Area in the Wei valley. Peng intended to exploit the situation and regain Yenan, but the previous year's fighting had severely reduced the harvest and to ensure his supplies he had first to take the enemy base at Ichuan.

He achieved this with a classic 'mousetrap' ambush using Ichuan as the bait. Four columns (40,000 men) surrounded the town on 15 February 1948 enticing Liu Chin into a relief operation with four of the 29th Army's five brigades. Deep snow confined the Nationalists to a narrow, winding road and they were ambushed at Watzuchieh, west of Ichuan, on 1 March. In a bitter three-day battle the 29th Army was destroyed and Liu was killed. Ichuan fell later and the 5th Army evacuated Yenan which the Communists reoccupied on 15 March. However, the Central Committee did not return but joined Liu Shao-chih in Hopeh. After the Ichuan disaster, the 'King's' chief of staff, Chen Min, reportedly disappeared.[11] The disaster had profound strategic consequences because Hu Tsung-nan demanded replacements and, to the dismay of his US advisors,

Chiang flew four brigades (23,000 men) from Chengchou to the 5th Army. This act of loyalty to a subordinate exposed Loyang in Honan and led to Hu's isolation.

The Wei Valley Campaigns

During April 1948 Peng Te-huai was ordered to support the Central Plains Army's operation around the LUNGHAI Railway in Honan and he responded with a daring sweep with most of the field army into the Wei valley, the heart of Hu's 'kingdom'. Their appearance forced the 'King' to recall troops he had despatched to save Loyang but as they entered the valley from the east, Peng advanced westwards to take Paochi on 25 April. His subordinates were anxious to regain the safety of the mountains for they knew their men were tired and they suspected an imminent counter-strike. But Peng was in an exultant mood, he ignored the danger signals and tongue-lashed anyone who suggested retreat. On 26 April, he suddenly found himself trapped between two brigades from Kansu and the 5th Army (three brigades) from the east. He then compounded his mistake by fighting a conventional battle in which his exhausted men suffered a defeat before he could escape into the mountains.

Between July and November 1948, the two armies contested the foothills north of the Wei which Peng did not secure until 25 November when he took Yungfeng and destroyed its two-division garrison. Then his troops were dispersed for the winter, ostensibly to carry out 'mass work' but probably because food stocks in north Shensi were so low it was impossible to maintain large concentrations of troops.

The South Shensi Campaign

The success of Peng Te-huai and Nieh Jung-chen owed much to the passiveness of Shansi's governor, Yen Hsi-shan, which made his province the eye of the storm. Yen, aged 63, came from a family of minor bankers and merchants but at the turn of the century he opted for a military career. Service in Japan's Imperial Military Academy left him with an admiration for the Japanese army he retained throughout his life and in 1946 he maintained a large force of Japanese mercenaries. A capable, if enigmatic, officer, he could be both witty and charming when he wished and rose swiftly to become military governor of Shansi in the Republic's early days.

He encouraged desire for provincial autonomy by developing both industry and agriculture to establish bonds with his people which earned him the title of the 'Model Governor'. His bid for national leadership was thwarted by the rise of the Kuomintang but he remained a major power broker. During the Japanese invasion his authority was challenged by both the Communists and Nationalists and the strain of fighting his fellow country-men affected his health. He suffered from diabetes, and by 1946 the man who had once sought the mandate of heaven was interested only in controlling a petty fiefdom around Taiyuan, his capital.

In the summer of 1946 Taiyuan still maintained tenuous rail links with Tatung in the north, Shihchiachuang in the east and the Yellow River in the south but the 'Model Governor's' passiveness meant all were severed within a year. In the battle for the TUNGPU Railway in southern Shansi Yen Hsi-shan gave only token support to Hu Tsung-nan's 1st War Zone because it had been Hu who established the Kuomintang presence in Shansi some six years earlier. Hu committed a third of his army to the struggle, which lasted until mid November, but despite the loss of some 17,000 men, the Nationalists failed to control the commanding heights allowing the Communist CHINCHIYU MR to extend its control throughout southern Shansi.

The Communists Take South Shansi

During early 1947 Hu Tsung-nan stripped formations from southern Shansi to attack Yenan and Liu Po-cheng decided to exploit the situation by destroying the remaining enclaves along the TUNGPU Railway. The task was given to Chen Keng who attacked with two columns in April but in mid May he was held at Yuncheng. Hu Tsung-nan's success was temporary and achieved only by withdrawing a reorganised division from the Yenan front. Also in April, Yao Che atoned for his failure to take Tatung by cutting the rail link in eastern Shansi between Taiyuan and Shihchiachuang.

The demands of the Shensi front saw more troops sucked westwards and most of the TUNGPU Railway was abandoned during 1947. By December only Linfen and Yuncheng remained and the latter was taken on 27 December. Linfen survived until the following spring when it was stormed by the whole of Ho Lung's army on 17 May. As a result of these successes, low level guerilla warfare and the 'Model Governor's' timidity, the Communists were able to extend their control throughout eastern and northern Shansi and by the end of 1947 they controlled 11 million of the province's 15 million people.

In June 1948 Ho Lung advanced up the TUNGPU Railway towards Taiyuan using as his spearhead Hsu Hsiang-chien's First Army, borrowed from Nieh Jung-chen. Six of Governor Yen's 13 divisions were destroyed in mid July and he was pushed into the valley around Taiyaun but an impasse was now created. 'The Model Governor' was incapable of taking the mountains while the Communists were too weak to take the valley.

The Siege of Taiyuan

Yen sustained himself throughout the year exporting metal goods, chemicals and cement while importing oil, cotton and tobacco through an airlift involving 36 aircraft based in Tientsin (450 kilometres away) and Peiping (400 kilometres). As the Communists seized more and more territory these flights, made with few navigation aids, became longer and more dangerous.

The Communists did not attempt to storm the city during the summer and autumn of 1948 for they had more important work elsewhere. Peng Te-huai was struggling to prevent the enemy breaking out of the Wei valley, Nieh Jung-chen was tightening his grip on Hopeh, Liu Po-cheng and Chen Yi were preparing to assault the Hsuchou salient and Lin Piao was on the verge of clearing the enemy from Manchuria. Taiyuan itself was too formidable an obstacle to take easily. Around the city were extensive trench systems with barbed wire and stone pillboxes, together with a railway upon which ran an armoured train. The city itself was surrounded by a wall 12 metres thick and 27 metres tall while the garrison had 100,000 men supported by 700 guns and mortars.

Ho Lung's forces were transferred to Shensi leaving Hsu Hsiang-chien's First Army with 12 divisions, together with some

100,000 regional and local troops, to watch the city. The Peiping–Tientsin campaign saw the loss of Governor Yen's two air bases and although an alternative was found at Tsingtao, aircraft payloads were reduced to a minimum. With the end of this campaign it was clear the time had come to settle accounts with the 'Model Governor'.

During March Nieh Jung-chen's three armies concentrated around Taiyuan bringing with them a formidable battering train including one of Lin Piao's artillery divisions and five artillery regiments which, Nationalist historians claim, were formerly Fu Tso-yi's units. By the end of the month 36 divisions and 288,000 men had been assembled around the city with logistic and engineering support supplied by a million *min-fu*. They began a classic siege operation by digging concentric lines of trenches both to imprison the defenders and to assist the assault.

They were directed by Peng Te-huai who had gone to Hopeh in February to attend a Central Committee meeting and then been ordered to Taiyuan by Mao. On 9 April some 3,000 guns and mortars began pounding the defences and five days later the infantry attacked. They infiltrated the wrecked defences with great skill but six days elapsed before they reached the shattered walls through which they poured in great numbers. The defenders fought doggedly in the now blazing city and were not overcome until the evening of 25 April. Bizarrely the last act of this epic siege was the mass suicide of Acting Governor Liang Tun-hu and 500 provincial officials and gentry using cyanide phials.

Governor Yen was not present having flown out before the assault following a summons to a conference in Nanking. The loss of Taiyuan left only a few small towns under Nationalist control north of the Yangtze and during the following month all of them surrendered rather than face the terrible fate of Shansi's capital.

6

The Killing Ground: Central China

THE CIVIL WAR was decided between the Yellow River and the Yangtze where the Nationalist Army gained more territory and people than on any other front. Yet the absence of any positive social and economic action squandered this success, allowing cadres to fan the sparks of resentment into a conflagration which ultimately engulfed the Nationalists. The culmination of their efforts was the Huai-Hai Campaign of 1948 but the rolling plains and mountains were always a killing ground of Nationalist formations.

The theatre's northern boundary was the broad Yellow River which had, since 1853, flowed across north Shantung to the Gulf of Chili. Its course across the Honan–Shantung plains is confined by great earthen dikes but in 1938 the southern banks were breached between Chengchou and Kaifeng to stop the advancing Japanese. This action diverted much of the water southeastwards through Honan and Anhwei where the waters swelled those of the River Huai which ran west to east into Kiangsu. While action to repair the dikes began in 1945 throughout the civil war there remained between the two rivers a 25 to 30 kilometre-broad crescent-shaped area of water and marshes which was dubbed the Flooded Area. The breached dikes lowered the level of the Yellow River below Kaifeng making it relatively easy during the drier winter months for light infantry to cross.

The other major water obstacle in this region of rolling plains was the Grand Canal (Yun Ho) which runs from the Yellow River through west Shantung before curving around Hsuchou

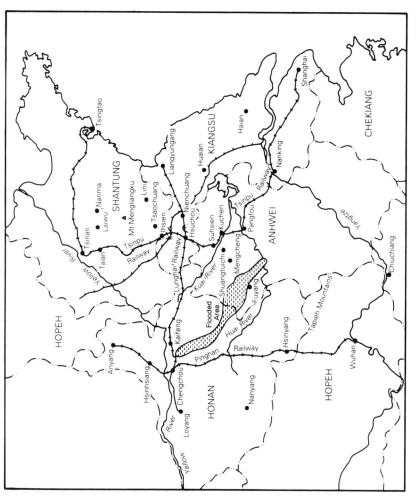

The Central Theatre

then flowing through the wetlands of western Kiangsu into the broad Yangtze river, whose course marked the theatre's southern boundary. The rivers and canals divided the theatre's heartland while on the peripheries were dramatic mountain ranges in western Honan, in southern Anhwei (the Tapieh Mountains or Tapieh Shan) and in Shantung (especially the central mountain massif).

The railways were major axes of operations because of their importance to Nationalist 'operational' movement. The prime lateral system is the LUNGHAI Railway running westwards from the sea Shensi through Hsuchou, Kaifeng, Chengchou and Loyang. At Chengchou and Hsuchou it crosses the PINGHAN and TSINPU Railways respectively; the former bisecting Honan from Anyang (north of the Yellow River) through Hsinhsiang to Hankou. The TSINPU Railway winds from Tsinan through the Shantung mountains before snaking across the Anhwei plain through Suhsien and Pangfou to Nanking. With Shantung, there is a lateral railway which curves through the mountains from Tsinan then crosses the central plain to the port of Tsingtao.

Breakout from the Tapieh Mountains

The summer rains in 1946 restricted operations but the triple threat to the Nationalists' system from the Tapieh Mountains, eastern Kiangsu and the Shantung mountains was too great for them to ignore. Here was their largest concentration of forces; 123 formations and a million men, divided into three commands. In the west, defending the PINGHAN Railway, was Liu Chih's Chengchou Pacification Command (39 formations) supported by the Hupeh-based Wuhan Provisional Headquarters under Chen Cheng (8 formations). To the east, defending the TSINPU Railway and Shantung, lay the Hsuchou Pacification Command under Ku Chu-tung with 76 formations, half of them on garrison duty.

With the ceasefire collapsing, Liu Chih decided to attack the enemy redoubt in the Tapieh Mountains defended by some 40,000 men of the Central Plains MR under Li Hsien-nien. Li was a 40-year-old former apprentice carpenter from Hupeh who had worked in the mountains, near the industrial proletariat of Wuhan, since the 1930s.[1] In June, faced with a concentration of 16 brigades, Li decided to abandon the base. He first dispersed the regional forces then broke out to the west with the field forces on the night of 29–30 June 1946. The Communists sought the safety of the south Shensi mountains and while they usually avoided the enemy army they suffered severely from air attacks. In late July the survivors reached Shensi, crossed the River Wei west of Paochi on 21 August, and by the end of the month had reached Yenan.

Although lasting only two months, this journey proved as great an epic as the Long March and just as bloody with 20,000 casualties. The Nationalists suffered only 1,200 casualites and captured 3,700 rifles together with 28 guns and mortars. The Communist survivors were transferred to Shantung and later became Chen Yi's Thirteenth Column while Li, feted as a hero, was transferred to political duties and never again commanded field forces.

The Kiangsu Campaign

Li's neighbour in Kiangsu, Chen Yi, was the next to feel the Nationalist wrath. Chen, aged 45, was a stocky man whose mean features belied a lively sense of humour. The son of a Szechwan landlord he received a university education in China then studied in France for two years with Chou En-lai and Nieh Jung-chen until he was deported for political activities. He joined the Party in 1923 and served first in the NRA then in the Red Army. By inclination he preferred conventional operations but chance had given him considerable experience in guerilla warfare.

Injury caused him to be left behind when the Long March began and only by adopting guerilla tactics did he and a few others live to see the post-Sian rapprochement. The survivors became part of the New Fourth Army which Chen commanded from February 1941. In 1945 he transferred several thousand men to Manchuria but received replacements from southern China and by the summer of 1946 this self-confident, analytical, leader was harassing the TSINPU Railway south of Hsuchou.

His Central China Field Army probably had about 110,000 men in Kiangsu but they were outnumbered 2:1 and were assaulted from all sides.[2] A simultaneous attack would have destroyed them but the Nationalists struck in sequence; 12 formations from the west on 10 July, six from the south a week later and nine from the north on 12 August, Chen personally led 40,000 men against the southern thrust conducted by Li Mo's 1st Pacification District, leaving his deputy Chang Ting-cheng to deal with the others.[3]

Initially Chen Yi gave ground and for three weeks lulled Li Mo into a false sense of security with low level operations. Then he struck as one formation relieved another on the night of 10–11 August and the Nationalist line collapsed. For a month the battle raged across southern Kiangsu but the need to besiege the town of Haian robbed his advance of impetus. The siege absorbed an ever greater share of his resources and with enemy pressure growing to the north he abandoned the attack during the second week of September. Li Mo was relieved by Tang En-po but this could not conceal the scale of a defeat which cost the Nationalists some 25,000 casualties, 4,900 rifles, 600 machine guns and some 320 guns and mortars. Yet Chen did not escape lightly, losing some 21,000 men including nearly 800 prisoners.

Chang Ting-cheng was far less successful for he tried to fight a conventional battle which led to the collapse of both the western and northern Kiangsu fronts. In the west the Nationalists employed crack US-trained formations which advanced on a 160 kilometre front and ground Chang's regiments to dust. It was the worst defeat in Chen Yi's career, his regiments lost some 36,000 men and much equipment while two years elapsed before he regained the territory. As Chen Yi marched up from the south, Chang now faced the 74th (R) Division, a formation a Communist commander later described as '... bold, aggressive, flexible, hard-hitting ...'.[4] Chang threw in divisions piecemeal to protect Huaian, the Central China Field Army headquarters, but it fell on 21 September after a night-long battle. Chang's lacklustre performance caused great suffering for his men, 2,000 of whom surrendered while the Nationalist army gave a rare demonstration of its potential. For 5,700 casualties the Nationalists gained control of 29 districts and forced Chen Yi to retreat southwards into marshes in central Kiangsu.

The Central China Field Army was now in a desperate position confined into a narrow pocket of marsh land with half its original strength. Chen Yi decided to move north into Shantung leaving resistance to the regional forces. His men travelled in small groups at night and were able to reach Shantung unscathed in early December because the enemy was also transferring troops into the province. Nationalist garrisons were left only in Kiangsu's largest towns, which were easily bypassed, and while peasant support for the Communists understandably cooled, few guerillas were betrayed. The savagery of the returning landlords aroused resentment among the peasantry but they bided their time and awaited an opportunity for revenge. In central Kiangsu regional forces received sufficient support to begin harassing enemy communications and by April 1947 only the roads within a kilometre of the larger towns were safe. The Communists steadily regained ground here and later in the year created a field force column.

Liu Po-cheng's Relief Operations

Chen Yi's survival was also assisted by the Shansi–Hopeh–Shantung–Honan (CHINCHILUYU) Field Army under Liu Po-cheng who now had seven corps-strength columns. From mid August onwards Liu's aggressive probing towards the LUNGHAI Railway eased pressure upon Chen and earned Liu, aged 54, a formidable reputation. The son of a poor Szechwan scholar, Liu was one of the oldest generals in the PLA. Denied the opportunity to sit the civil service examinations he joined a warlord army and in succeeding years he lost an eye, earning the nickname the 'One-eyed Dragon', and once fought Chu Teh. He joined the Party in 1926 and two years later went to the Soviet Union to improve his military education. He returned to China in 1931 and towards the end of the Long March became chief of staff of the Red Army but as a leading participant in the Hundred Regiments' Offensive he was later transferred to the CHINCHILUYU army.

Liu believed conventional mobile forces were the decisive factor in any conflict and this philosophy was constantly expressed upon the battlefield where he relegated guerilla operations to a supportive role. Yet for a general he retained many scholarly features; his spectacles giving him an owlish appearance, and he frequently used poetry to express tactical and 'operational' thought. Whenever possible he encouraged his small staff to study for a couple of hours a day.

Ironically his first diversionary operation which lasted for a week following 10 August, saw guerilla tactics feature prominently. To divert the enemy from Kiangsu, Liu struck the

LUNGHAI Railway east of Hsuchou and systematically wrecked it. Five formations were needed to push him northwards in a confused series of small actions. For once the Nationalists attempted psychological warfare offering an amnesty to those who surrendered weapons. This led to the surrender of 1,000 firearms but the experiment was never repeated.

Success encouraged 'Little Tiger' Hsueh Yueh of the Hsuchou Pacification Command to clear the western plain of Shantung to the Yellow River and in open terrain Wang Ching-chiu's 32nd Army (six formations) took the key towns and 1,400 prisoners by 20 September for the loss of only 200 men. Yet the Nationalists were unable to force a crossing across the Yellow River whose willow-lined banks provided Liu with sanctuary.

The Central Shantung Campaign

They were also unsuccessful in central Shantung which was defended by Chang Yun-yi's Shantung Field Army with 70,000 men.[5] Chang, aged 54, came from a middle class family on Hainan Island yet his education was exclusively military and he graduated from the Paoting Military Academy. Persuaded to join the Party by Chou En-lai he held senior military positions before the war, acting as Liu Po-cheng's planning chief during the latter stages of the Long March then as chief of staff of the Military Affairs Committee.

In 1937 he joined the New Fourth Army and in 1941 became its deputy commander. In August 1945 he was in Shantung but lost many men to Manchuria and had to rebuild the Shantung Field Army from a core of veterans and upgraded regional regiments. In northern Shantung he had only 40,000 men facing 15 divisions (125,000 men) in enclaves at Tsinan and Tsingtao, yet it was not until 23 June that the Nationalists sought to challenge him.

Timorously the two garrisons reached out along the line to meet on 5 July but the railway was never secure. For example during the first 41 days of 1947 there were 24 attacks during which five bridges were destroyed together with 99 rails and 431 sleepers. However, this did not prevent the Nationalists later extending their control northwards to the coast and occupying district capitals and the main ports.

The I-tsao Campaign

In the south the Nationalists entered the massif in August 1946, having secured the Grand Canal, and by early October established a bridgehead along a branch line of the TSINPU Railway running from Ihsien to Tsaochuang. A further advance was prevented by Liu Po-cheng who thrice struck the Anyang salient and the west Shantung plains between late October 1946 and mid January 1947 destroying three brigades and inflicting some 16,000 casualties. These operations provided recruits and booty to strengthen Liu's forces as well as gaining time for Chen Yi to reach south Shantung where he blocked further enemy progress.

For a fortnight, as in south Kiangsu, he remained passive allowing enemy complacency to be honed into a deadly weapon of self destruction. On the night of 2–3 January, the eve of the Lunar New Year holiday, he struck the eastern part of the bridgehead then rolled up the enemy positions. The defence, hampered by torrential rain and the unauthorised absence of a key commander, collapsed and Chen's troops crushed enemy strongpoints at their leisure, the last falling on 19 January. The I-tsao (Ihsien–Tsaochuang) Battle was a stunning victory in which Chen's lightly armed columns boldly attacked a force superior in both numbers and firepower. Nine brigades were destroyed, 40,000 casualties inflicted and a colossal amount of booty taken including 25 tanks, 26 howitzers and 2,200 rifles. It was the biggest Communist victory in the 'defensive phase' from July 1946 to June 1947 and was to remain unrivalled until the autumn.

It proved an important morale booster for the Communist cause because in the preceding months they had lost 19 of 35 district capitals in Shantung, cracking the confidence of many cadres who fled to safety. With the enemy army now in disarray the Hopeh–Shantung–Honan District ordered these cadres back to their districts to reopen guerilla warfare and to challenge Kuomintang authority. While this policy was to be handicapped by the PLA's habit of absorbing regional units into the field forces, it slowly eroded Nationalist control of the countryside.

The Nationalists Drive into Shantung

A fortnight elapsed before the Hsuchou Pacification Command organised a new attempt to take the massif, but six months and three campaigns (Laiwu, Mengliangku, Nanma) were to pass before the Communist field forces were driven out, and then only temporarily. Like a tide, the Nationalist advance lapped deeper into the mountains but the waves ebbed and flowed. Their forces (between 17 and 49 formations) lumbered into the rugged terrain like oxen dragging the impedimenta of a modern army behind them. Inevitably road-bound, they squandered time and resources repairing and securing communications which robbed the advance of impetus. Co-ordination between the columns was often poor and little effort was made to patrol the mountain slopes. This exposed many formations to enemy attack (11 were lost) in campaigns which cost some 107,000 casualties.

Chen Yi's forces exploited the enemy weaknesses mercilessly as the Communist general satisfied to the full his penchant for bold manoeuvre. His columns criss-crossed the mountains with impunity and, during the Mengliangku and Nanma Campaigns, infiltrated through the lines of the advancing enemy. This tactic dubbed 'You come to my house, I move to your house', allowed him to attack enemy communications. The CAF, which committed up to 64 aircraft, proved of limited value in detecting the Communists because of the volatile local weather system which (as the US Marines discovered the previous autumn) could decimate formations. Few peasants volunteered information about the Communists, but many passed information to them, allowing the PLA divisions to march along roads as if on parade, confident they would not be surprised. When field forces retreated, the regional and self-defence forces gathered intelligence and sabotaged communications. The railways proved especially vulnerable and in Shantung the Communists not only tore up the road bed but also levelled embankments then encouraged peasants to plant crops on the newy created field.

The Laiwu and Mengliangku Campaigns

In the Laiwu Campaign (30 January–24 February) the Nationalists attempted a double envelopment from Tsinan in the north and from the south. Lini was taken but the northern column (six brigades) was ambushed in a narrow valley on 21 February and only 3,000 of the 40,000 men escaped. Many surrendered, the majority newly arrived troops from southern China who were formed into the Kwangtung–Kwangsi Column with former guerillas transferred to Shantung when Mao abandoned the southern bases in 1945. This policy of combining men from the same region into homogeneous columns reduced confusion caused by regional dialects and occurred as the two Communist armies in Shantung were merged into the East China Field Army under Chen Yi.

The scapegoat for two disasters in as many months was Hsueh Yueh, who was relieved from a command he had held for only five months. He was replaced by his predecessor, Ku Chu-tung, who had been transferred to Chengchou. Ku was the 54-year-old son of Kiangsu gentry who had joined the Imperial Army in 1908 and later graduated from the Paoting Military Academy. Loyal to Chiang he had acted as a trouble shooter before the war and played a major part in persuading the Sian plotters to compromise. In the war against Japan he became 3rd War Zone commander and participated in the New Fourth Army Incident in 1941.

He committed 49 formations to the Mengliangku Campaign (11–16 May) which proved of only limited success. The plan was for a broad sweep eastwards from the TSINPU Railway but Chen Yi staged a pre-emptive assault on Taian to cut the railway. When the Nationalist offensive was resumed Chen staged a bold attack along a boundary between two armies to isolate the crack 74th (R) Division. Its quixotic commander, Chang Ling-fu, tried to redeem himself by drawing the enemy to the barren slopes of Mengliangku, 50 kilometres north east of Lini, where they might be enveloped by his colleagues. But Chen's divisions prevented relief and it was the 74th Division which was destroyed, the staff killing themselves in the command post with grenades. The 5,000 survivors joined the PLA but most returned to the Nationalist Army at the first opportunity.

The Nanma Campaign

The only redeeming feature of the campaign was that it established the Nationalists firmly in the western part of the massif and they exploited this success in the Nanma Campaign

(27 June – 1 August). On this occasion reorganised divisions, like errant children, were paired for their march through the mountains to prevent each other falling into danger.

The advance began in heavy rain which impeded movement, then a diversion drew away 14 of the 25 formations as Chen Yi's 13 divisions stalked their prey like wolves. But his plans misfired; twice he struck but enemy firepower and prompt responses to calls for assistance denied him victory. Worse still the constant marching and counter-marching strained the Communist supply network, draining many districts of supplies. While the Nationalists suffered some 40,000 casualties during this period the Communists paid a similar price and morale plummeted so low that 11,900 men surrendered or deserted.

By late July Chen recognised he had lost central Shantung but, aware of Liu Po-cheng's imminent offensive in the west Shantung plain, he decided to split his command to support his colleague. One column remained in the massif while five under Su Yu marched eastwards across the Tsinan–Tsingtao Railway to enter the Chiaotung Peninsula mountains. With the remainder Chen marched westwards, crossed the TSINPU Railway and picked up a column in the mountains west of the line. Then he swooped onto the plain and in July annihilated 2nd Army (see p. 138) before withdrawing across the Yellow River.

The Communists Gain the Initiative

For the next four months Chen Yi used this sanctuary to chisel at Nationalist authority upon the plain and in the surrounding provinces. Only once, in early September, was he seriously challenged but he still destroyed two brigades. His columns ranged far south of the Yellow River, tearing out a 150 kilometre stretch of the LUNGHAI railway and even raiding the TSINPU Railway south of Hsuchou. Nationalist historians gloss over the events of the latter part of the year but their forces were clearly losing the initiative as well as control of a vital 'operational' region.

In eastern Shantung, too, the Nationalist cause was steadily weakened during the latter part of 1947. From September, 13 brigades attempted to clear Su Yu from the mountains of the Chiaotung Peninsula but Su responded aggressively. By early December the Nationalists had lost some 20,000 men and the

54th (R) Division was trapped at Haiyang some 100 kilometres up the coast frm Tsingtao. The Navy was forced to evacuate it, initially to Tsingtao and ultimately to Manchuria, leaving the peninsula in Communist hands.

By the end of 1947 the Communists had secured their sanctuaries and could begin to expand the East China Field Army which, by spring 1948, had some 400,000 men. Their prospects of regaining Shantung were excellent for many heavy weapons had been taken and, with the growing trend towards conventional warfare, the winter was spent training gunners, observers and signallers. Elsewhere there was encouraging news; Lin Piao was slowly driving the enemy into Manchuria's cities while Nieh Jung-chen had taken Shihchiachuang in Hopeh.

Communist Probes in North Honan

But the most dramatic operation of 1947 was conducted by Liu Po-cheng. The 'Dragon's' first sorties from his Taihang Mountains lair in February saw the enemy display a gratifying reluctance to leave the safety of their fortifications. This response may well have planted in the mind of Liu, and of his political officer Teng Hsiao-ping, the seeds of a plan to re-open the Tapieh Mountains base abandoned the previous year. The evolution of this plan remains obscure but the sequence of events suggest it was an instinctive reaction to a perceived opportunity rather than a response to orders from the Military Affairs Committee. Fan Han-chin's Chengchou Pacification Command, which was responsible for defending Honan, had been steadily stripped and in the six months ending in March 1947 its strength dropped from 39 to 19 formations. This might have been justified on the grounds that the Yellow River shielded Fan's troops from the 'Dragon's' fury but it was still a gamble.

Between March and May 1947 this gamble appeared justified. As the Nationalists penetrated the Shensi sanctuary and took Yenan, the 'Dragon' tried to divert the enemy. He struck the Yellow River rail bridge leading into the Anyang salient and then the salient itself. The bridge remained in Nationalist hands but Liu isolated Hsinhsiang and Anyang, although they did not surrender until 7 May 1949. With his rear secure Liu heard the siren call of the Tapieh Mountains grow louder and he recognised a decision could not be long prolonged. Repairs on the Yellow River dikes, under United Nations auspices, brought the prospect of the river returning to its pre-war level to impede Communist 'operational' movement. Having persuaded Chu Teh, Liu planned to cross the river east of Kaifeng then march south exploiting the boundary between the Chengchou and Hsuchou Pacification Commands but shielded from their combined wrath by the Flooded Area. To protect his former base he left three newly raised columns under Yang Yung who would stage a diversion near Kaifeng.

The Crossing of the Yellow River

The crossing was planned on a grand scale with four columns secretly assembling near Puyang. Once across they were to advance through the west Shantung plain while two under Chen Keng conducted a secondary crossing west of Chengchou. As usual the Party organisation provided efficient support, maintaining security, supplying intelligence, supplies and all-important ferrymen.

On the night of 30 June – 1 July the columns began crossing the river but it was not until 5 July that they completed their assembly on the far bank. With 95,000 men Liu now began to march south across the plain while simultaneously Chen Yi's columns swept out of the mountains in support. The enemy garrisons cowered behind their ramparts and were bypassed but two, which threatened the line-of-march, were stormed on 12 July and four brigades were destroyed.

To protect the threatened LUNGHAI Railway the Nationalists hastily assembled the 2nd and 4th Armies with six reorganised divisions, the Chengchou Pacification Command being stripped of half its formations. The 2nd Army had the misfortune to meet Chen Yi first and in a fierce battle during the second half of July the Communists ambushed and destroyed three reorganised divisions. Meanwhile the 4th Army worked its way between the 'Dragon' and his lair, but this opened the way for Liu Po-cheng to cross the LUNGHAI Railway on 8 August having inflicted, with Chen Yi's help, some 100,000 casualties.

The Advance to the Tapieh Mountains

Once across the railway the Communists marched rapidly, sometimes making 48 kilometres a night. The few maps available were used to plan a general line-of-march which exploited the Flooded Area where regional units from the Tapieh Mountains had established themselves in the previous year. The Party organisation they had created provided Liu Po-cheng's troops with food, shelter and guides. Staff officers at control points, and notices posted on walls, ensured columns and divisions moved in the right direction. At the end of the night's march there was hot food and the men would disperse to prearranged bivouacs.

These arrangements gave the march a rhythm which boosted morale by giving the men a sense of purpose. Only on 24 August did three reorganised divisions catch Liu's forces at the River Jun but after a bloody battle the Communists escaped and during the last week in August crossed the River Huai, the last barrier before the Tapieh Mountains whose shelter was quickly reached.

It quickly became apparent that the mountain population had been devastated physically and morally by 10 years of war and required extensive political work. Liu Po-cheng, like Li Hsien-nien the previous year, had to face the fact that the sanctuary was untenable in the short term and could not sustain a large army. His political officer, Teng Hsiao-ping, organised a meeting in late September when it was decided to retain some units for mobile operations while others were effectively down-graded to regional status to protect the rural revolution. While the new military and political web was woven Liu sent a detachment under Wei Chieh back north to obtain recruits during the winter. Wei was successful but the reinforcements were diverted to Nieh Jung-chen (see previous chapter p. 111).

The Nationalists Invest Liu Po-cheng's Base

With great difficulty the newly named Central Plains Field Army expanded its base. It was especially successful in the west, controlling all the approach routes from Wuhan, and the south where some 160 kilometres of the northern bank of the Yangtze came under Communist authority. Initial resistance was weak for there were few formations and Communist strength was underestimated so the reaction was piecemeal. Only when the scale of the threat was appreciated were reinforcements brought in, some from as far afield as Shantung. Yet it was not until 20 November that a unified command for the region was created at Chiuchiang under Pai Chung-hsi whose strike force totalled 27 brigades (225,000 men). For Pai it was the first operational command of the war, having been Minister of National Defence since June 1946. On 29 November his troops closed in from all sides and to gain room for manoeuvre Liu Po-cheng despatched half of his six columns from the base, one column marching back to west Shantung.

As Nationalist formations set off in pursuit, pressure on Liu's perimeter was further eased by attacks from Chen Keng's west Honan base and from Chen Yi in Shantung, both of which were met by formations milked from the Chiuchiang Command. The 'Dragon' then resumed mobile operations with his three remaining columns crossing and re-crossing the mountains until the winter snows paralysed all movement. By spring 1948 the exhausted Chiuchiang Command was in no shape to resume the offensive, although in early April it was able to thwart Liu's attempt to take Fuyang, which controlled the road network across the Flooded Area into Anhwei.

The Communists Retake Shantung

Pai Chung-hsi was unable to resume the offensive partly due to Communist pressure in Shantung where Chen Yi tightened his grip during the spring of 1948. In central Shantung Hu Shih-yu's East Front Army (three columns and 40,000 guerillas) on the night of 9–10 March began a campaign which rapidly captured the Tsinan–Tsingtao Railway. Enemy garrisons were too dispersed to offer effective resistance and had been cowed by constant pressure from the regional forces.

The campaign was completed on 14 April when the last stronghold, Weihsien, fell after an 18-day siege. While regional forces blockaded Tsingtao, the victorious field forces marched westward and from 30 May to 13 July cleared the TSINPU Railway south of Tsinan. Preoccupied by the struggle for Kaifeng (see below pp. 141–142) the Nationalists made no attempt to regain the lost towns from the south while a half-hearted relief operation by the Tsinan garrison ended in disaster when the rearguard was ambushed and destroyed on the night of 15–16 July.

The Tsinan garrison, some 86,000 men of Wang Yao-wu's 2nd Pacification Area, was contained by 70,000 regional troops while Chen Yi's field forces supported the 'Dragon' during the summer. Chen desired the city because it controlled the eastern rail network but he recognised its reduction would involve considerable resources and these became available only in late August when Su Yu was given seven columns and 300,000 *min-fu*. Su quickly completed his preparations and the first attack, on 14 September, overran the airfield, thwarting Nationalist plans to fly in a division. On the night of 19–20 September the 84th (R) Division under Wu Hua-wen defected opening a huge gap in the western defences and the defenders fled to the city walls.[6] But the Communists, supported by tanks, fought their way in and took the city four days later capturing Wang and 64,000 of his men. Apart from the Tsingtao bridgehead (evacuated on 2 June 1949), the Communists had regained Shantung as far south as Tsaochuang and Lini after two long years. This secured supplies and recruits for the East China Field Army which was also able to import equipment across the Gulf of Chihli from Manchuria now that Lin Piao controlled most of the region. With the sinews of war strengthened all was ready in the east for the capture of Hsuchou.

The Kaifeng Campaign

In the west too the Communists rapidly extended their control during 1948 with the initial objective of cutting the LUNGHAI Railway. To this end Chen Yi and Liu Po-cheng collaborated skilfully to confuse and disperse the enemy whom they could then defeat in detail. On 26 May Chen Yi used Chen Shih-chu (nine divisions) to feint from west Shantung towards Hsuchou in order to draw the 5th Army (Chu Shou-nien) away from Honan's capital, Kaifeng. Simultaneously Liu marched north to Kaifeng with six divisions and with Chen's help isolated the city on 16 June. To defend the city, Li Chung-hsin had only five brigades (two peace preservation) with 35,000 men and the defence was hamstrung by his dispute with Liu Mao-en, the provincial governor. By 22 June the Communists had taken the city and while Governor Liu escaped the mortally wounded General Li remained to commit suicide.

The 5th Army, and the remaining six brigades of the 4th (Kaifeng) Pacification Area, were held back until the Communists chose to abandon the city after a four-day occupation. On a map the Nationalist net appeared to be closing on Liu from all sides; the 5th Army (six brigades) from the north, Chiu Ching-chuan's 2nd Army from the east and Huang Pai-tao's 7th Army (three brigades) from the southeast.[7] The 'Dragon' ignored the map, allowed the 2nd and 5th Armies to approach within 10 kilometres of each other, then surrounded 7th Army and contained 2nd Army while Chen Shih-chou enveloped the 5th Army. Half of 5th Army was destroyed during the next four days but Chiu, absorbed with his own survival, made no attempt to help. Eventually he fought his way eastwards, and, by accident rather than design, relieved Huang's army on 6 July. In this campaign the PLA inflicted some 65,000 casualties and demonstrated that no city was safe, indeed Kaifeng was soon reoccupied to confirm Communist control of eastern Honan.

The Loyang Campaign

Further west Chen Keng was also consolidating his position. He had crossed the Yellow River in August 1947 with 60,000 men and established a base in the mountains southwest of Loyang. He attacked the city in mid October but was driven off by Hu Tsung-nan, ever sensitive to any move which would isolate Shensi. Hu was unable to do anything about Chen's base, which threatened all of western Honan, because of Peng Te-huai's activities and Chen tightened his grip upon the region during the winter of 1947–48 aided by two of Liu's columns from the Tapieh Mountains.

On 17 March 1948, sheltered from air attack by torrential rain, Chen Keng took Loyang after a 10-day siege but promptly abandoned it as relief forces came along the LUNGHAI Railway. The Nationalists did not hold the city long. Peng Te-huai's victories in Shensi drew away four brigades while other units were sucked eastwards to meet Liu Po-cheng's attack upon Fuyang (see above p. 140) leaving only a regiment in Loyang. Chen struck again on 5 April and the Red Flag flew permanently over Loyang. During May he completed the conquest of western

Honan in a lightning campaign and three months later the Communists drove a corridor across the PINGHAN Railway to pass men and supplies from Shansi to the Tapieh Mountains. Throughout Honan the Party hastily created an organisation to mobilise the masses while Chen's forces, now the Second Central Army, cleared Honan to the Flooded Area.

Preparations for the Huai-Hai Campaign

As the autumn of 1948 approached, the Nationalists were confined into a hammer-like salient at whose head lay Hsuchou. To the north, in Shantung, lay Chen Yi and the East China Field Army with 420,000 men while in Honan and the Tapieh Mountains lay Liu Po-cheng's Central Plains Field Army with 130,000 men. The destruction of the last concentration of enemy forces, some 450,000 strong, north of the Yangtze preoccupied the minds of the Communist command from the summer and to control operations between the River Huai and the sea (*hai*) the General Huai-Hai Front Committee was created under Teng Hsiao-ping.

Because his forces were less heavily engaged Liu, assisted by Chen's deputy Su Yu, pondered the problem from late July. He appears to have anticipated a campaign lasting a year in which the Hsuchou salient would be reduced in stages; first (November – December 1948) isolating it from the sea then eliminating it in a second stage (March – July 1949). This strategy may well have been influenced by a temporary Nationalist success in Kiangsu during the summer when a sweep drove out the field forces and disrupted the Party organisation. Yet it is hard to imagine that Liu intended to remain entirely passive for he was aware that the 'shaft' of the salient contained only a third of the garrison while the majority, 280,000 strong, were in the 'head'.

Nevertheless the original order transmitted by the Central Committee on 11 October 1948, called only for the enemy to be cleared from south Shantung and north Kiangsu. This was to be achieved through the envelopment and destruction of Huang Pai-tao's 7th Army which had a quarter of the divisions in the 'head'. Such a move would prevent the evacuation of the salient by sea and allow Chen's forces to re-enter Kiangsu and reoccupy Huaian, his headquarters in 1946, a task which was to be completed in December.

The pivot of this operation was the Second Eastern Army (15 divisions) north of Hsuchou which was to contain the majority of the Hsuchou garrison with the support of Liu's 21 divisions in the west. The main strike force in southeast Shantung consisted of Chen's First, Third and Fourth Eastern Armies with some 30 divisions, supported by the tanks and artillery of the Special Column and three regional divisions south of the LUNGHAI Railway. They were to cut the railway, envelop the 7th Army east of Hsuchou and complete the occupation of northern Kiangsu as far as Lake Hungtse. Chen was given a month to prepare for the offensive and in late October senior military and political officers organised briefings down to battalion level, thus demonstrating their confidence in both the loyalty and ability of their men. During the first week of November the troops moved out of training camps towards their jump-off positions fully briefed, fully equipped, and with a secure supply system all of which inspired confidence.

Nationalist Defences

The Nationalist high command, by contrast, could be confident of nothing save the imminence of battle. The Generalissimo had reinforced the salient with 24 divisions (12th, 13th, 16th Armies) but he regarded it as a breakwater to prevent the full force of the Communist flood smashing into the Yangtze valley. Even as the Communists moved into position the Nationalist defence remained in a state of flux with dispositions incomplete and no agreement on the overall defensive concept. Many wished to abandon Hsuchou and fight in the more advantageous terrain around the River Huai.

But Chiang, having earlier abandoned both Chengchou and Kaifeng, refused to give the enemy so valuable a strategic prize as the LUNGHAI Railway. No longer confident of his subordinates, he planned to direct the battle personally through the Ministry of National Defence in Nanking and for this reason the Hsuchou Rebellion Suppression Headquarters was assigned the mediocre Liu Chih.[8] The Generalissimo also hoped to bring to bear his superior firepower (including 166 aircraft) which would be boosted by the imminent arrival of US arms under the US$125 million arms package. Yet he was to receive no succour from this source, for the Communist Party cell in the Shanghai

Customs Bureau began a go-slow in November which disrupted all imports.

Against this background the Nationalist Army reorganised the Hsuchou garrison. West of the city in mid October were Chiu Ching-chuan's 2nd Army (14 divisions, one cavalry brigade) and Liu Ju-ming's 4th Pacification Area (six divisions). Around the city was Li Mi's 13th Army (six divisions) and protecting the eastern approaches, its left flank shielded by the Grand Canal, was Huang Pai-tao's 7th Army (10 divisions) which was later reinforced by three divisions from the LUNGHAI Railway. On Huang's left, astride the TSINPU Railway and along the canal was the autonomous 3rd Pacification Area (four divisions) of Feng Chih-an.

With 39 divisions in the 'head', Nationalist leaders were concerned about the vulnerability of their long rail link to Nanking. This was shielded to the west by Sun Yuan-liang's 16th Army (four divisions), but more troops were brought in. On 5 November the 4th Pacification District was transferred from the LUNGHAI Railway to Kuchen renamed 8th Army and made responsible for the central sector of line. The southern sector was the responsibility of the newly created 6th Army at Pangfou to which were transferred six divisions from Shantung. Belatedly it was recognised that the western approaches of the railway needed further protection and the 12th Army (10 divisions), which had been engaging Liu Po-cheng in Honan, began marching eastwards through Fuyang to establish its head-quarters in Shuangtuichi south of Suhsien.

The Huai-Hai Campaign: First Phase

As the defenders moved, the offensive began on the night of 7–8 November. The transfer of 4th Pacification Area exposed 2nd Army and when he became aware of this Liu Po-cheng quickly exploited the situation. Previously he was to act as the anvil for Chen's hammer but now he received permission to cut the TSINPU Railway south of Hsuchou at Suhsien. The assault drove 2nd Army into the western and southern suburbs of Hsuchou as Chen Yi's strike force swept into Kiangsu. While the First Eastern Army pinned down most of Huang Pai-tao's over-extended 7th Army along the Grand Canal, the Third and Fourth Eastern Armies began to envelop him from the south after crossing first the LUNGHAI Railway then the Grand Canal. The defection of 3rd Pacification Area on 9 November permitted a double envelopment which isolated Huang and 10 divisions around Nienchuang.

As the Communists strengthened the siege wall, Chiang ordered 2nd and 13th Armies to relieve Huang but they ran into fierce resistance and could advance no more than 13 kilometres in 10 days despite support from 100 tanks under the Generalissimo's youngest son Chiang Wei-kuo. The situation of the Nienchuang pocket was now desperate and on the night of 19–20 November a general assault began from the east. By dawn Huang Pai-tao's headquarters had been overrun and many tried in vain to break out towards Hsuchou. Of 70,000 men only 3,000 succeeded, Huang himself being killed in an ambush on 22 November.

This defeat was nothing compared to the catastrophe emerging south of Hsuchou where a column from each Communist field army drove a wedge between 2nd and 8th Armies. On 11 November the 2nd Army was driven northwards from Suhsien allowing Liu and Chen to meet then drive 8th Army southwards. When it became clear reinforcements were needed to reopen the TSINPU Railway, Chiang moved 16th Army south of Hsuchou on 13 November and for three days this army ineptly attempted to retake Suhsien. Chen Yi's forces, reinforced by divisions from the Nienchuang pocket, not only held back 16th Army in the north but also pushed the 8th Army south to the River Kuai. The Hsuchou garrison was now isolated while the decision to withdraw 16th Army from Mengcheng, which controlled the road network west of the TSINPU Railway, exposed the left of Huang Wei's 12th Army as it marched towards Suhsien.

The Huai-Hai Campaign: Second Phase

A moment of 'operational' decision was approaching, one which could save the PLA six months, and a conference was hastily convened under Su Yu to decide the course of action. Rather than storm Hsuchou, the Huai-Hai Front Committee decided to encourage an enemy break out to the south to destroy them in the open. Simultaneously Chiang ordered the Hsuchou garrison to break out as the 6th, 8th and 12th Armies pushed north. With hope borne out of desperation he envisaged the Communists becoming paralysed by a two-front attack allowing him to salvage divisions to defend the Yangtze. As a bonus he hoped also to inflict heavy casualties upon the enemy but cold reality was soon to triumph over warm illusion.

Meanwhile Liu Po-cheng enticed a reluctant 12th Army northwards by abandoning Mengcheng, Huang Wei proceeding only at Chiang's insistence. He rightly suspected a trap and on 25 November the First and Second Central Armies (21 divisions), after being relieved by Chen Yi, surrounded him at Shuangtuichi. Huang managed to break out to the southeast and advanced 32 kilometres towards Pangfu but the Nationalist garrison was too cowed to assist him and a counter-attack by Second Central Army (Chen Keng) drove Huang's men back to their start line. A second break out planned for 28 November was foiled when the vanguard division under Liao Yun-chou a participant in the Sian Incident, defected forcing Huang to remain on the defensive until the 210,000-strong Hsuchou garrison could relieve him.

On the day Liao Yun-chou's division defected, Liu Chih, and Chang Wei-kuo (commander, 13th Army) flew to Pangfou as preparations for the break-out from Hsuchou got underway. The garrison, under Tu Yu-ming, and thousands of civilians streamed out of the city between 30 November and 1 December. There were ugly scenes at airports as panic-stricken soldiers fought their way onto aircraft which used their propellors as fans to blow them away. Chen Yi promptly occupied the city while the Second and Fourth Eastern Armies pursued the garrison whose progress was impeded by long lines of vehicles which jammed the roads.

Guerillas harassed the columns slowing progress and gaining time for the field forces to surround the garrison on 4 December. Thousands of *min-fu* arrived to establish fortified rings 5 kilometres deep around the pocket. Villages were turned into mutually-supporting strongpoints, linked by trench systems, each of which required exhausting assaults to overcome. Once one ring was penetrated the attackers found another behind it and all the time the pockets were under artillery bombardment.

The Huai-Hai Campaign: Final Phase

The first pocket to be reduced was that of 12th Army which was now surrounded by 33 divisions. As food supplies were exhausted and the temperature dropped below freezing, morale collapsed. All but five divisions defected on 8 December but the remainder, including the US trained 18th Corps, fought on for a week until their ammunition was exhausted. On the night of 15–16 December they were overwhelmed and Huang Wei attempted to escape in a tank. He was soon captured and spent the next 27 years of his life in Communist prisons.

To the north an assault on the main pocket by Chen Yi temporarily isolated 13th Army, now under Li Mi. When he rejoined the main force Li discovered the 16th Army had been destroyed attempting a breakout which had already been cancelled. Supported by airlifts the 2nd and 13th Armies crawled towards 12th Army some 50 kilometres away frequently fighting hand-to-hand but by 10 December they were exhausted.

On the night of 12–13 December the 8th Army retreated to Pangfou, arriving on 25 December having ignored Tu Yu-ming's radio pleas for assistance. On 19 December rain and snow prevented further air supply while the Communists began a psychological warfare bombardment as their troops were given a fortnight's rest. Liu Po-cheng and Chen Yi flew north to Hsipaipao to discuss the forthcoming south China campaign with Mao and Chu Teh. By Christmas Day Tu Yu-ming reported his men were eating tree bark and grass while to keep warm they were burning houses, clothes and furniture, yet only 10,000 of the 130,000 men defected.[9]

Improved weather on 29 December led to renewed supply drops, some as low as 600 metres, but strong winds often blew the loads into the enemy lines.[10] The two armies were compressed into a small perimeter around Chinglungchi and Chiang offered to fly Tu Yu-ming out of the pocket but he refused to leave his men. On the afternoon of 6 January 1949 the final Communist offensive began and quickly dissolved into ferocious hand-to-hand fighting. A despairing Tu Yu-ming left his subordinates to their own devices and formations were destroyed piecemeal. By 12 January only 2nd Army was left as an amorphous mass of company and battalion sized units which were themselves quickly overwhelmed. Their disappearance made the River Huai defence line untenable and on 15 January it was abandoned together with all of China north of the Yangtze.

The Huai-Hai Campaign was a textbook example of a battle of encirclement, yet one achieved by accident rather than design. The original objective was to isolate the salient by destroying a single army. The concept was changed even as it was executed as PLA leaders ruthlessly and speedily exploited enemy weaknesses to eliminate a force with a combined strength of 528,000 men, of whom 304,700 (57 per cent) were killed or captured. By contrast the Nationalist generals lost control from the moment the battle began, indecision and dissension hamstringing all their responses.

The Communist success was also due to the efforts of the Party's East, Central and North China Bureaux who not only inspired the troops and the supporting peasantry but distributed food and ammunition to support the army's manoeuvres. Some 2 million peasants served as *min-fu* and without their contribution the Communists would have been defeated. As Whitson[11] has observed while the Huai-Hai Campaign was, at one level, a conventional battle at another it represented the ultimate example of 'people's war' in which mass will compensated the PLA for it's technological deficiencies.

7

Collapse in the South 1949–50

BY THE spring of 1949 Communist forces held most of the northern bank of the Yangtze from the Tapieh Mountains to the coast. Their enemies held only a few bridgeheads, the largest around Nanking, yet to foreign observers it appeared the great river would remain the boundary between Communist and Nationalist China for many years.

The Communists faced formidable problems with a war-ravaged economy and revolutionary work barely begun in many areas. To the south lay an army of some 400,000 men supported by 60 aircraft nominally under a new leader, Acting President Li Tsung-jen, long associated with the southern provinces' struggle for autonomy. Between them lay the great river patrolled by the Nationalist navy and considered an obstacle too formidable for the PLA to attempt. Indeed Wedemeyer told the new US Secretary of State Dean Acheson, the Nationalists could defend the Yantze with broom sticks if they so wished. It was a view Stalin evidently shared and he suggested the Communist leadership concentrate upon consolidating their position in the north and leave the south to the enemy.

Nationalist Divisions

The proposal was indignantly rejected by his Chinese comrades who recognised, through instinct or obstinacy, that a paper tiger lay on the far bank. The defence was utterly compromised by profound divisions begun when Chiang made provincial leaders responsible for their own defence on 16 January. As for Li,

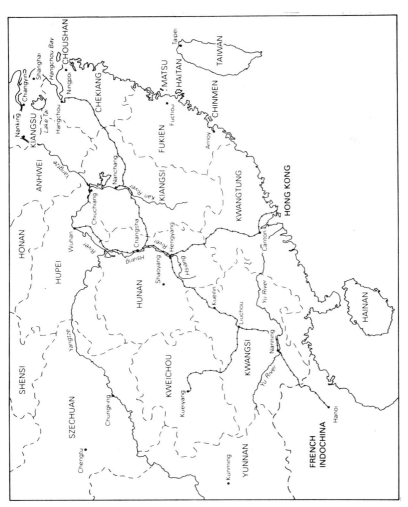

The Southern Theatre

through a combination of inexperience and political naivety he rapidly alienated foreign and domestic supporters alike. In return for Soviet assistance with negotiations he offered Nanking's strict neutrality in the event of a superpower conflict, then he sought US approval! Stalin's lack of influence together with provincial pressure to negotiate a settlement forced Li to accept the Communists' eight-point peace plan as a basis of negotiation but this offended the Cabinet (Executive Yuan). In a fit of pique the Cabinet led by Premier Dr Sun Fo decamped to Canton early in February accusing Li of exceeding his authority and thus shattered the President's hopes of maintaining a facade of unity.

Such hopes were illusory while Chiang, ostensibly a private citizen, still controlled all aspects of government through loyal subordinates. Poor Acting President Li drank the cup of bitterness to its dregs as Chiang's cronies openly and contemptuously flouted his authority. One was Tang En-po, commanding the armies at the mouth of the Yangtze, who channelled men (including the 'Young Marshal') and material to the Generalissimo's redoubt on Taiwan. Another was the Governor of the Central Bank of China, O. K. Yui, who transferred to Taiwan by 20 February the national gold reserve, 14 tonnes worth some US$300–335 million. This sabotage accelerated the decline of the Gold Yuan and by early May one US dollar was worth GY10 million.

It was Chiang, not Li, whom Tang En-po consulted in February when approached by Chekiang's Governor Chen I, a former patron, and offered a large bribe in return for his defection. Tang subsequently arrested Chen and took him to Taiwan where he was tried and executed for treason in June 1950. The acting president first learned of the arrest in the newspapers.

To resolve the political crisis Li asked Chiang either to resume office or to stop interfering. But the Generalissimo saw no reason to assist a man who had challenged his authority in the past, and negotiated with the hated Communists. Instead he left Li in limbo and allowed the Communists to play cat-and-mouse with him. The Party's Central Committee had moved, on 25 March, to Peiping – which had become capital of the Communist-held north.[1] They now proposed holding talks here on 1 April using their own plan as the basis.

But in Peiping Li's delegation found no room for manoeuvre

and the Communists, realising they were prevaricating, presented an ultimatum demanding either Nanking accept their conditions by 12 April or the PLA would cross the Yangtze. The deadline was later extended to 20 April as Li desperately sought support, even asking Washington for a statement to deter the Communists from crossing the Yangtze. The US rejection, on 21 April, was academic for that morning the Communists began their crossing.

Situation on the Yangtze

The defence's prospects were dismal for the three northern catastrophes had wiped 135 divisions off the order-of-battle and cost 1.1 million of the Nationalist army's best men with all their equipment.[2] Before 'withdrawing', the Generalissimo had planned to replace the lost legions by recruiting 2.5 million men for 400 new divisions. To this end 15 training commands were created on the mainland and Taiwan with 41 corps. Yet there was a desperate shortage of equipment and even if all the US$125 million of the US military aid programme had reached the mainland it would have been inadequate.[3] In fact Chiang had been diverting shipments to his Taiwan redoubt since the previous autumn.

Aware of his military weakness, President Li tried to prolong negotiations with the Communists in a forlorn hope of buying at least three months to prepare his defences. He and his friend Pai Chung-hsi planned to defend southern China for at least a year, during which time they hoped a significant change in the international situation would bring US support. While Chiang also anticipated such a change he believed the mainland would be lost first and for this reason continued to strengthen Taiwan

As Li negotiated and Chiang plotted, the Communists prepared to cross the Yangtze with their three best field armies (34 corps); from west to east Liu Po-cheng's Second, Lin Piao's Fourth and Chen Yi's Third. Peng Te-huai's First Field Army (seven corps) was to contain Hu Tsung-nan in Shensi but well-founded concern about Peng's abilities led Chu Teh to allocate him half of Nieh Jung-chen's 11 corps once the siege of Taiyuan was successfully completed. A further four corps, all former Nationalist units, were undergoing indoctrination pending their use for internal security.

The Nationalists had 22 corps along the 1,200 kilometres of the lower Yangtze while Central China Military and Administrative Commissioner Pai Chung-hsi had 19 corps around Wuhan. Hu Tsung-nan's Sian Pacification Area had 11 corps in Shensi and there were 10 corps/reorganised divisions in the Northwest. In the southern provinces were 13 corps, some fighting guerillas who reappeared in their mountain bases during 1947. However, while Communist corps strength was 20,000 to 25,000 most Nationalist corps had only 7,000 to 15,000 men while the PLA had most of its enemy's equipment.[4]

Communist Plans

The initial Communist objective was to occupy the Nationalist heartland; Nanking and China's commercial centre of Shanghai, by means of a double envelopment. The task was facilitated by the enemy's dumbell-like dispositions with Pai Chung-hsi at Wuhan, Tang En-po along the Nanking-Shanghai Railway and a token force in between. Chen Yi's Third Field Army was to strike first, at the Yangtze's broadest point, in an operation whose audacity would convince the enemy it was the main blow. Chen would sail across 3 kilometres of water to land near the fortress of Chiangyin and act as an anvil for the hammer blow delivered by Lin Piao. His Fourth Field Army would cross in the centre, where the river was narrower, shielded by Liu Po-cheng who would swing southwards after crossing to block any attack northwards by Pai Chung-hsi.

Following the Huai-Hai Campaign the field armies engaged in hectic activity; reorganising, absorbing replacements and training with newly-captured equipment some of which was used to create more artillery divisions. The conventional nature of the offensive led to an expansion of schools to provide gunners, radio operators, mechanics and drivers. Logistic and engineering support was provided by some 3 million *min-fu*, many brought by the Party from the northern provinces, to dig trenches, assemble boats and collect food at 100 supply centres.[5]

All ranks regarded the crossing apprehensively. While numerous boatmen were persuaded to participate in the operation, many troops had to row themselves across the great river and others were given cumbersome straw lifebelts to help them swim across. Boat drills and river crossing tactics were constantly practised but Liu Po-cheng and Lin Piao were both handicapped by the lack of suitable exercise sites. The numerous rivers and lakes of Kiangsu gave Chen Yi a much needed advantage for in early exercises some divisions took as long as three days to cross a lake.

Not only were the Communists active behind their own lines but also behind the enemy's. As early as August 1948, at a meeting of the Sixth All-China Labour Conference, a representative of the Communist underground organisation in Shanghai publicly pledged to protect all the factories, warehouses and public utilities in the city. From January 1949 the Communists began to make good that pledge stockpiling food in case of a prolonged siege and organising factory protection teams. They hindered all efforts to export war material to Taiwan and also contacted key military and political leaders to organise defections.

Nationalist Defences

The facade of a defence had some 325,000 men of whom 16 corps held an extended right-angled line along the river to Chiuchiang, the boundary with Pai's command, with only five in reserve. Of these 22 corps all but eight were between Nanking and Shanghai clearly demonstrating Tang En-po's ultimate intention of conducting an evacuation. Allowing for service and support troops, average corps' strength was about 10,300 men, with corresponding shortages of equipment. Firepower was augmented by some 200 tanks, 150 guns and 58 aircraft while there was a substantial naval presence of 27 warships. But the defection, on 2 March, of the cruiser Chungking raised justified concern about the navy's reliability which was not allayed even with the sinking of the cruiser in Shantung a fortnight later.

In the short term Acting President Li and Pai Chung-hsi hoped to defend the Yangtze or at least the rich lowlands of Hupeh, Hunan and Kiangsi. If this proved impossible they could fall back to their personal heartland in the rich provinces of Kwangtung and Kwangsi which were sheltered by the mountains of southern Hunan and southern Kiangsi. They had hoped to stage a double envelopment of the enemy on the Yangtze front using Pai's force in the west and Tang En-po's in the east, but Tang refused even to consider the idea and a passive defence was the only alternative.

Loyalty to the old regime was the 49-year-old Tang's strongest characteristic although his career began with an act of rebellion when he threw a stone at a magistrate. He later joined the army and during the Sino–Japanese War his reputation reached its zenith as the architect of the spectacular victory at Taierhchuan in 1938. Six years later it reached its nadir when his forces in Honan collapsed and he was given only minor field commands until 1949 when he became responsible for the lower Yangtze.

On 23 March the Communists began to eliminate most of the northern bridgeheads while establishing their own on the south bank. Meanwhile all cadres from division level upwards were assembled at Peiping for a week's briefing on the political and military problems they would encounter in southern China. These briefings included cadres who had operated secretly south of the Yangtze and who were able to provide eye-witness accounts on the terrain, customs and social conditions in an area with numerous ethnic minorities.

Assault across the Yangtze

During the night of 20–21 April a myriad small boats carried half-a-dozen corps, drawn from Chen Yi's Ninth and Tenth Armies, across the mouth of the Yangtze. Here the river was covered by 30 guns of Chiangyin fortress but the defection of the garrison meant not a single shell was fired at the Communists. Earlier Li Tsung-jen had warned Tang En-po this would happen but was ignored. Now the unopposed Communists established beachheads which threatened the Nanking–Shanghai Railway while Chiangyin protected their eastern flank.[6]

Defection took place on the opposite flank too, involving the upstream naval task force and part of the 88th Corps opposite a Third Army bridgehead. Liu Po-cheng quickly exploited the situation, and drove from the bridgehead to pursue the remaining defenders as they retreated down river. Simultaneously his Fourth and Fifth Armies crossed and began advancing up river towards Nanchang capital of Kiangsi. The following night, after several hours' artillery preparation, Lin Piao's men struck a defence growing more confused and weaker with every hour.

Within two days Lin split the defenders in half and the exposed capital was abandoned to both the Communists and the diplomatic corps on the night of 23–24 April. Any apprehension which the United States might have felt at the take-over proved unfounded, although their staff were placed under house arrest. Surprisingly the Soviet envoy was one of the few who did not remain, choosing instead to join the Nationalist government in Canton.

Meanwhile, the Nationalist Army disintegrated under the pressure of retreat. The northernmost corps fled to Shanghai but were battered as they ran the gauntlet of Chen Yi's troops. Those corps in the south had great difficulty breaking contact and five were destroyed by the Third Army as it marched on Hangchou capital of Chekiang, which fell on 3 May. Chen Yi broke out of his bridgehead and advanced upon Shanghai but on 24 April was stopped by the 123rd Corps and held at bay for 17 days. This success was achieved by exploiting Lake Tai (Tai Hu) as a breakwater to channel the advance into easily defended terrain criss-crossed by rivers and canals. However, it only delayed the inevitable for the defence of the Yangtze had cost the Nationalists 180,000 men, more than half their strength, and even with reinforcements there were only 150,000 men to hold the unfortified port.

The civilian population, swollen by a million refugees, sought an end to their sufferings because the loss of raw materials had brought stagnation to the city's industrial and commercial life. The Chinese business community, unlike the Europeans, recognised a Communist take-over would deal a mortal blow to Shanghai's commerce and were leaving in droves, many transferring their families and capital to Hong Kong. Thousands of poorer citizens also sought flight while Nationalist security forces rounded up and executed suspects in droves.

During early May the Eighth, Ninth and Tenth Armies worked their way around 123rd Corps' southern flank and by 13 May were only 30 kilometres from the city centre closing in from both sides. Chiang came to the city to supervise the evacuation and the port was kept open by transferring a corps into the eastern suburbs where it held out for a fortnight until overwhelmed by the newly arrived Seventh Army. On 23 May the PLA broke the defensive perimeter and reached the city centre as the defences dissolved into a panic-stricken mob clawing a way to the last ships before they sailed on the evening of 25 May. The following day the Communists completed their occupation having inflicted 95,000 casualties upon the defenders (nearly two-thirds of their strength) and taken a vast amount of booty.

The final phase of the battle was fought in heavy rain which caused severe flooding within the Yangtze watershed as well as the provinces to the north. Despite the rain the Third Field Army cleared Chekiang and Chen Yi assigned the Tenth Army (four corps) the task of occupying Fukien, which it entered late in July. The province was defended by four corps of 6th Army with only 40,000 men and by mid August the Communists were closing on Fuchou. To entice the defenders out of the city the PLA ostensibly left a clear exit to the south but when 6th Army took the bait it was ambushed on 17 August and only 12,000 escaped to Amoy (Hsiamen).

The American Reaction

The Communist capture of the Yangtze estuary created a dilemma for US Secretary of State Acheson who inherited the reappraisal of Sino–American policy begun by Marshall. The Communist successes in 1948 confirmed the US Administration's view that the Nationalists were doomed yet the only positive decision was to avoid further involvement in the civil war. The US State Department hoped either for an accommodation which protected US interests or for a Tito–like schism with the Soviet Union. The alternative of a virulently anti–US government proved too unpleasant to contemplate, especially early in 1949 when nobody anticipated an early collapse of the Nationalists, and consequently progress towards recognising a Communist government proceeded at a snail's pace.

The first stage involved the US Administration removing the Nationalist albatross. On 14 April 1949 it divided European Recovery Program funding from that of China in return for spending the China Aid Act's remaining US$54 million after the Act's expiration date. Exactly a week later, as the Communists stormed across the Yangtze, the Senate created a bi-partisan committee to investigate US policy in the Far East. The fall of Nanking stunned Chiang's American friends but as the Communists advanced on Shanghai in early May they rallied and pressed for a new military aid programme. However, in June Acheson told a private session of the House Committee on Foreign Affairs he would not support such a plan because it was militarily unsound.

A further complication in Sino-American relations was Canton's announcement of 20 June of an air and naval blockade of the Communist coast which was to take effect six days later. In fact a British merchantman was attacked on 21 June and further attacks followed upon both British and US ships, yet the United States stood by Acheson's declaration of 29 June which refused to recognise the blockade. Fear of involvement in the civil war prevented either London or Washington providing naval escorts for their ships which were soon forced to avoid Communist waters. The blockade proved especially severe for Shanghai which also had to endure air attacks, the first of which inflicted 550 casualties on 29 June.[7]

There was tacit US support for these attacks as Washington feared a growth of Soviet influence in Asia if southern China fell into Communist hands. Indeed during June 1949 the National Security Council issued directive NSC 48/1 calling for the United States to contain Soviet power and influence in the Far East. Anxiety increased following the publication, on 1 July 1949 of Mao's foreign policy statement 'On People's Democratic Dictatorship' which declared China must ally itself with the Soviet Union. In September the Communists began to export food to the Soviet Union in return for economic and military aid, some 15 million tonnes being despatched in the first year alone. The declaration dashed US hopes of breaking with the Nationalists and obtaining a rapprochement with the Communists. On 16 July US Deputy Undersecretary for State Dean Rusk wrote to Acheson calling for an action programme which would include aid for non-Communist groups in China and two days later Acheson requested a draft programme.

Proclamation of the PRC

Meanwhile, following the capture of Nanking, the Communists began to seek US diplomatic recognition but the State Department response was hamstrung by fears of Congressional reaction. The US Congress was angry both at the Communist refusal to recognise financial agreements signed by the Nationalists during the civil war and by their seizure of foreign commercial and business enterprises. Consequently, Ambassador Stuart returned a noncommittal answer when approached on 2 August and relations between the two countries rapidly deteriorated, exacerbated by harassment of Americans. Eventually the arrest of the US vice-consul in Shanghai led to the embassy's transfer to Canton on 17 August.

The Communists ignored this rebuff and on 1 October 1949 Mao proclaimed the establishment of the People's Republic of China then requested international recognition. The Soviet Union and her satellites promptly responded the next day while India became the first non-Communist country to follow suit on 30 December. Apart from France most European countries followed the example of the British who recognised the régime on 5 January 1950. France's refusal occurred because Peking recognised Ho Chi-minh's government in Indochina on 18 January 1950 when France was supporting the cause of Emperor Bao Dai. The Communist seizure of US Government property on 14 January 1950 finally ruptured Sino-American relations and Washington's remaining diplomatic missions were withdrawn from northern China. In the aftermath of international recognition Peking demanded the Nationalists' seat on the U.N. Security Council on 8 January 1950 and was supported by the Soviets. The US was not unwilling but the Council itself rejected the request on 13 January leading to a Soviet boycott which continued until the Korean War began during the summer.

Pai Chung-hsi Prepares His Defences

In China itself the summer rains of 1949 provided Pai Chung-hsi with a welcome respite as he prepared to defend the south. Pai was 56-years-old and highly regarded both as tactician and strategist. He and Acting President Li had been school friends, and later forming part of a southern triumvirate which advocated provincial rights and opposed Chiang before the Sino-Japanese War. Reinstatement during the war did not mean Pai was trusted and his appointment as Minister of National Defence in 1946 was essentially a sinecure. He exchanged his ministry for a field command in 1948 after quarrelling with the Generalissimo over the need for a unified command between the Yellow River and the Yangtze. Their relations were further strained at the end of 1948 when Pai spearheaded the provincial demand for negotiations with the Communists.

His defence of southern China was undermined by the unreliability of the Generalissimo's followers and by the failure of Chiang to provide supplies. On paper, Pai had 17 corps, with another 20 being created, while half-a-dozen were on internal security duties in his rear. Yet his average corps strength was only 7,000 men. Despite the loss of Shanghai he still hoped to hold the rich lowlands around Wuhan, Nanchang and Changsha but if driven out he knew there were plenty of defendable lines in the mountains to protect his Kwangtung–Kwangsi heartland. The rugged mountain ranges of Fukien, eastern Kiangsi and Szechwan secured his flanks leaving only two approach routes to Kwangtung from the north; the eastern one along the River Kan (Kan Chiang) valley from Nanchang to Kanchou while the western one followed the River Hsiang (Hsiang Chiang).

The main railway in southern China runs from Wuhan across the plain and up the Hsiang valley through Changsha to Hengyang where it follows the valley of the River Lei (Lei Shui) across the mountains and down to Canton. At Henyang another line branches southwestwards along the Hsiang valley, across the mountains and into Kwangsi at Kueilin. From there it runs through Nanning to Hanoi, then in French Indochina. In 1944 these rail routes had been the axes of the Japanese Ichigo Offensive in which the Nationalist defence of Henyang in particular had aroused the world's admiration and Pai hoped to emulate this success.

Guerillas in Kiangsi, Kwangtung, Fukien and Hunan conducted 'sparrow tactics' with 15,000 men from seven small bases in remote mountain regions but the campaigns which followed were essentially conventional struggles. The defenders were usually restricted to the railways and main roads allowing the revolutionary forces to exploit the mountains in broad enveloping movements from which the enemy instinctively recoiled. The speed of the advance meant there was little time for cadres to mobilise the masses behind the enemy lines, although they were able to find guides and porters. Indeed it appears the deciding factor in winning popular support was the army's reputation for good conduct. Ironically these were the very same features which gave the Nationalists victory in the same region during the Northern Expedition a quarter of a century earlier.

The defeat of Tang En-po's forces on the lower Yangtze allowed Liu Po-cheng's Fourth and Fifth Armies to sweep along the river's southern bank and take Nanchang on 22 May but by committing the 4th, 10th and 12th Armies, mostly raw troops, Pai Chung-hsi was able to hold the enemy south of the city. Simultaneously Lin Piao's Sixteenth and Seventeenth Armies began energetic probing attacks north of Wuhan encouraging one corps to defect and forcing the abandonment of the triple city on 15 May. Following this withdrawal Pai's men held a long concave line covering the eastern approaches to Chungking and the northern approaches to Changsha a city famous as a bastion of resistance against the Japanese a decade earlier.

Two of Lin Piao's corps probed these defences in the north but his long supply line, further strained by flooding, forced him to leave the Sixteenth and Seventeenth Armies (100,000 men) north of the Yangtze both to secure the revolution and to carry out construction work. Operational reasons also influenced the decision for both armies were made up of regional force divisions and the new campaigns required experienced field force formations. During June Lin gradually ferried to the southern bank of the Yangtze the Twelfth, Thirteenth, and Fifteenth Armies, the last being attached to Liu Po-cheng's Second Field Army, bringing Communist strength to some 15 corps with which they resumed their advance on 28 June.

The Loss of Changsha

Pai tried to tempt his opponent into over-extending himself but the key position, the hills north of Changsha, were held by the 1st Army under Chen Ming-jen, the hero of Ssuping in 1947. He remained aggrieved at his subsequent dismissal while Hunan's governor, Cheng Chien, sought accommodation with the nation's new rulers. Their intentions were no secret but no steps were taken to prevent their defection which occurred on 3 July and forced the abandonment of Changsha and a retreat to an S-shaped position in the mountains west and south of the city.

The new line was some 750 kilometres long and to protect it against 300,000 well-trained, well-equipped enemy troops Pai had 14 corps with five in reserve yet even with support troops they had less than 95,000 poorly equipped men, many of them raw recruits. A Nationalist spoiling attack west of Changsha on 11 July succeeded in mauling an enemy corps but on Chiang Kai-shek's orders the troops in the Yangtze valley withdrew towards Chungking dashing Pai's hopes of a large-scale offensive.

In mid July Liu Po-cheng's Fifth Army staged their own attack up the Kan valley to take the mountains northwest of Kanchou ready to strike at Henyang.

The Henyang Campaign

The PLA now occupied a line which roughly followed the course of the Long March's first weeks. The summer rains, which paralysed the battlefield for two months, gave Communist military leaders time to reflect upon this and upon their next moves. The initial objective was to take Kwangtung and Kwangsi in the south, followed by the capture of the mountainous eastern provinces of Kweichow and Szechwan, but the provinces were difficult to attack because of the terrain, well-watered plains and densely wooded slopes, and the weather. The region is semi-tropical and tropical with high rainfalls which could mire any advance. The driest period of the year is between autumn and spring and Chu Teh recognised he had only a small window of opportunity.

He decided to advance southwestwards and westwards in rapid succession so his forces would swing around like a door hinged upon the Yangtze. In the summer of 1949, Lin Piao was responsible for the PLA right while Liu Po-cheng held the left, but Chu realised Liu was not strong enough to drive into the southwest and decided to reverse their roles with an 'operational' sleight of hand. The 'Dragon' was now to strike westwards into Szechwan from Hunan and two of his armies were to be transferred from the Hunan–Kiangsi border and replaced by Lin Piao's corps. Initially the Third Army in Hunan was relieved by the Twelfth and Thirteenth Armies (see p. 168) as the Fifteenth Army joined the Fifth Army between the Hsiang and the Kan valleys. Liu's Fifth Army would now join the opening stages of the advance upon Canton but then would be withdrawn northwards.

The Communists now had some 350,000 men and they were determined to smite the enemy hip and thigh. Once again a double envelopment concept was selected using the Twelfth and Thirteenth Armies from west of the River Hsiang while the Fifteenth Army and Liu Po-cheng's Fifth Army struck east of the river. The attack began on 19 September and within a week the Nationalist line west of the Hsiang was on the verge of collapse. Pai demanded a counter-offensive along the whole front on 28 September but most commanders used their discretion and the piecemeal assault by the faithful merely accelerated defeat. The fall of Shaoyang and the towns to the west followed on 2 October to open the road to Kwangsi.

There was also disaster east of the River Hsiang where the Fifteenth Army struck westwards through the mountains towards Hengyang while the Fourth and Fifth Armies rolled south to Kanchou. The town fell on 20 September and within three days Liu Po-cheng's troops entered Kwangtung to threaten the Henyang–Canton Railway, Pai's escape route to the south. This was cut on 4 October and as the Fifth Army was now withdrawn Lin Piao became responsible for exploiting the victory. His double envelopment of Pai's corps failed and they escaped south along the railway to Kueilin but the rearguard was caught and surrendered on 16 October.

The Kwangtung Campaign

While Lin Piao prepared to follow the enemy to Kueilin, the Fourth Army (reinforced by the Kwangtung–Kwangsi Column) swept down on Canton. The Nationalist capital was protected only by a handful of guard units and peace preservation regiments of Yu Han-mou's Kwangtung Pacification Area Command. They were reinforced by the 4th and 12th Armies which the enemy assault had cleaved away from Pai Chung-hsi's right flank but together they had only 10,000 men. Harassed by guerillas the weary Nationalist troops attempted a stand 60 kilometres north of Canton but on 14 October the Fourth Army enveloped the 12th Army and pulverised the 4th Army then marched into Canton the following day. Politicians and officials had already flown to Chungking, which once again became the capital, but thousands fled south on foot to the nearby British colony of Hong Kong whose garrison was substantially increased.[8] Fears that the Communists would take the colony at bayonet point kept tension high for several months but it eased when Britain recognised the People's Republic. As for Canton's defenders the remnants of 4th Army fled westwards to the Leichou Peninsula (Leichou Pan-tao) harassed by defecting militias. A few thousand arrived in late October by which time the Communists had occupied Hunan, Kiangsi and almost all of Kwangtung.

The Defence of Kwangsi

In Kwangsi, Pai Chung-hsi rallied his mauled army then prepared to defend his native province. He had 12 corps deployed in an arc covering the approaches to Kueilin and they faced Lin Piao's Twelfth and Thirteenth Armies. Pai had some 100,000 men whom he was paying a silver dollar a month together with a meagre rice ration. There was no money for new recruits, no reserve of supplies and only limited stocks of arms and ammunition. Chiang ignored him and a request to the US for light weapons fell on deaf ears, although the CIA was sympathetic. With the loss of Kwangtung, Pai was in a dilemma; withdrawal from Kueilin would open Kwangsi to invasion from the north but he needed to maintain his communications to the sea. He attempted both by maintaining the shield and simultaneously despatching his five reserve corps southwards to the Leichou Peninsula. It was a fatal mistake for it stretched his resources to breaking point.

His only alternative was to withdraw to Liuchou then march northwest and use Kueiyang, the capital of Kweichow Province, as a redoubt, but Lin Piao had anticipated such a move. In late October he despatched Thirteenth Army through the torrential rain to Kueiyang while to the north the Third and Fifth Armies' advanced into Szechwan. Desperately Pai stripped one flank to hold open the route to Kueiyang but it was too late for, with the flight of the provincial corps, the city fell on 14 November. Simultaneously Lin's Twelfth Army began to envelop first Kueilin (which was hastily abandoned) then Liuchou which fell on 26 November shattering Pai Chung-hsi's shield. On his right the Fourth and Fifteenth Armies marched westwards across Kwangtung and on 27 November they smashed Pai's corps north of the Leichou Peninsula. A few survivors reached the 4th Army on the peninsula before it was evacuated to Hainan Island on 7 December.

Caught between Liu Po-cheng in the north and Lin Piao in the east, Pai's remaining troops were pushed westwards towards the mountains along the Indochina border and ordered to conduct what was euphemistically described as 'guerilla warfare'. The 10th and 17th Armies succeeded in reaching the River Yu (Yu Chiang) valley but on 13 December the spirited pursuit drove the 1st Army, with elements of 11th Army, over the Indochina border where the 18,000 men were disarmed by the French.

During the winter of 1949–50, probably with French encouragement, the 4,000 men of the 17th Army harassed the Viet Minh near Cao Bang in Indochina.[9] But they stirred a hornet's nest and half were lost on 7 February 1950 when they were caught between Chinese and Vietnamese Communist forces. The survivors struggled in Kwangsi a few months longer under mounting pressure, some of the PLA units being commanded by the defector Chen Ming-jen, but in May they opted for internment by the French.[10]

The Tide of War in Shensi

By late 1949 Szechwan and Yunnan faced threats not only from the south but also from the north, although the year in Shensi began brightly for the Nationalists. While Peng Te-huai attended a Central Committee meeting in Hopeh a new advance was made up the Wei valley only to be smashed by a lightning counter-attack which took 1,000 prisoners on 8 March.[11] Peng returned in May to command a renewed effort using his First and Second Armies (five corps) while the Eighteenth and Nineteenth Armies (six corps) were earmarked to reinforce him. Impulsively he decided to attack immediately and initially the gamble seemed successful for it forced Hu Tsung-nan to abandon the eastern half of the valley, including Sian itself on 17 May.

But Peng was walking into a trap because Hu had assembled three corps around Paochi and another five in the Chinling Mountains (Chinling Shanmo) south of the Wei. Meanwhile Northwest Military and Administrative Commissioner 'Big Horse' Ma Pu-fang, despatched five corps supported by cavalry and militia from Kansu. These troops filtered into the mountains north of the Wei and on 10 June ambushed Second Army. The Communists were driven back in a retreat which came close to a rout until they rallied west of Sian having lost 10,000 men or 10 per cent of their strength.[12] With the arrival of the Eighteenth and Nineteenth Armies Ma withdrew to protect Kansu leaving the outnumbered and exhausted Hu to face the enemy wrath. Early in July some 200,000 Communist troops swept westwards and brushed Hu out of his Wei valley 'kingdom', taking Paochi on 14 July.

The Kansu Campaign

Hu retreated south into the Chinling Mountains followed by the Eighteenth Army as the remaining Communist armies marched into Kansu on a broad front. Only the 'Big Horse', who commanded 50,000 well-armed troops, could stop them and to this end he proposed a grand encirclement of the advancing enemy. He would attack from the west supported by the Governor of Ninghsia, Ma Hung-kuei, in the north and Hu in the south. Governor Ma was willing but Hu was not for relations between the Moslems and the Han Chinese had been strained by the 'Big Horse's' withdrawal two months earlier.

Unable to win support from Li Tsung-jen or Chiang, Ma Pu-fang launched a desperate attack on 18 August as the Second and Nineteenth Armies closed in on Lanchou. His allies did nothing, pleas for air support were ignored and he was utterly defeated. Two days later the Second Army attacked Lanchou where the defenders, according to the Communists, 'fought like devils'. But the odds were too great and on 25 August Ma abandoned the city and retreated into Chinghai Province. The army evaporated and the 'Big Horse' flew to safety on 28 August, having seized gold bullion worth US$1.5 million. In Canton he sought President Li's forgiveness, in Mecca he sought God's then he emigrated to California to breed horses.

His cousin surrendered Chinghai on 5 September and became its new vice-governor. The remaining Nationalist garrisons in Kansu and Ninghsia, 150,000 strong, quickly sued for favourable terms which were granted on 20 September. This opened the way to Sinkiang Province whose governor, Tao Chih-yueh, also declared for the Communists in a move which exposed the pro-Soviet Eastern Turkestan People's Army whom he had been fighting. Stalin ordered its leaders to ally themselves with Mao but all died when their aeroplane crashed en-route to Peking.

The Szechwan Campaign

By the autumn of 1949 the mountains of Szechwan and Yunnan offered the Nationalists a last mainland redoubt, and one which had proved impregnable during the war against Japan. With Hu Tsung-nan's forces on the Szechwan border, the province's capture was a formidable challenge to the Communists who decided to rely upon guile rather than brute force. The Eighteenth Army was ordered to create a diversion in Shensi's Chinling Mountains while the main blow came from the southeast through Kweichow.

The first phase began in September when the Eighteenth Army probed gently into the mountains with orders not to alarm Hu. Meanwhile Liu Po-cheng's Third Army was withdrawn from Hunan ostensibly to reinforce the Shensi thrust. It crossed the Yangtze and took train for Chengchou where its arrival was greeted by a well-publicised ceremony. When the Communists attacked Hengyang in September, the Third Army secretly returned down the PINGHAN Railway and returned to western Hunan. There it was joined in October by the Fifth Army which had been secretly withdrawn from Kiangsi.

On 14 October, as the defenders of Canton were overwhelmed, the advance upon Szechwan began; the two armies swept into Kweichow and southern Szechwan. Facing them in Kweichow was the 19th Army and in Szechwan the 14th Army, but the latter disintegrated under the strain of a month-long retreat which ended in the outskirts of Chungking. Briefly the Generalissimo flew in to direct a token defence then he departed, pausing only to order the execution of 'Old Yang', the 'Young Marshal's' co-conspirator at Sian. After a three-day battle China's wartime capital fell on 30 November.

The government moved northwest to Chengtu, which was surrounded by vast abandoned air bases built in 1944 for Superfortress bombers. Hu Tsung-nan was slow to recognise his mistake and only in mid November did he abandon Shensi and withdraw his seven corps into northern Szechwan. The Eighteenth Army, now under Ho Lung's command, harassed the retreating columns to prevent them fortifying Chengtu. Pressure came too from the south where the Third and Fifth Armies marched up from Chungking during early December destroying two corps of the newly created 22nd Army, whose commander and third corps defected.

On 9 December the Generalissimo assigned Hu the forlorn task of defending Chengtu which faced double envelopment from north and south. On paper he had five armies with 22 corps yet even with support troops there were no more than 165,000 men to hold the city. They faced three-well-equipped armies who, despite the casualties of the past six weeks, could put as many men into the firing line. The defensive perimeter was relentlessly compressed and on 23 December the battle rolled into the city suburbs. The 16th Army opposite Ho Lung now defected to be followed by most of the remaining armies during the next four days. Only Li Wen's 5th Army fought on, its three corps being fortunate to escape when the PLA command halted the Third and Fifth Armies to give Ho Lung the accolade of taking the city.

Some 20,000 men escaped the debacle and reached Sikang Province where Hu attempted to rally support for the Generalissimo early in 1950. He assembled 35,000 men but early in March they were dispersed by a 130,000-strong Communist expeditionary force. From Sikang five PLA divisions were despatched into Tibet where they annihilated the ramshackle Tibetan army at Changtu in October but the capital, Lhasa, was not occupied until March 1951.

The Fall of Yunnan

Yunnan fell at the same time as Szechwan in circumstances of low intrigue and high drama. On 9 December with the Communists on his borders, Governor Lu Han defected and arrested three loyal corps commanders in Kunming but he had failed to allow for their soldiers' loyalty. The corps promptly marched on the city to rescue the generals and after securing their release retreated westwards towards Burma and Indochina pursued by the Thirteenth Army.

Some 3,000 men were forced to surrender to the French on 18 January 1950 but another 2,000 reached Burma where they were regrouped and re-equipped with CIA assistance. Li Mi led them in a couple of abortive cross-border operations in 1950 and during the summer of 1952 the airline CAT flew in reinforcements from Taiwan to bring Li Mi's total strength to 8,000.[13] But they were more interested in controlling the drug trade in the Golden Triangle than fighting the Communists. Eventually Chiang abandoned the struggle and flew some 5,500 troops back to Taiwan.

The Coastal Campaigns

As the mainland was cleared, fighting flared along the coast as the Communists strove to break the Nationalist blockade although handicapped by Chiang's transfer of most warships and landing craft to Taiwan.[14] Nevertheless, relying upon junks, sampans and even rafts the PLA took Miao Island in the Gulf of Chilhi on 14 August 1949 and within a month a daring attack by Chu Shao-ching's Twenty-eighth Corps took Haitan Island off Fukien in the teeth of a typhoon.

This success encouraged Chen Yi's political officer, Jao Shu-shih, to demand a similar attack by the Tenth Army upon Chinmen Island (Chinmen Tao) also known as Quemoy, which blocked the entrance to the port of Amoy. The landing, supported by 50 guns, was made on 17 October but the defenders (directed by Tang En-po and a Japanese adviser Lieutenant General Hiroshi Nemoto) confined the Communists to a beachhead. When Nationalist reinforcements arrived on 25 October the beachheads were crushed, the Communists losing 8,000 men (including 6,000 prisoners) and much equipment.

Hainan Island, of Kwangsi, should have been a stronger nut for it had a garrison of five corps under the 'Little Tiger', Hsueh Yueh, with adequate air and naval support. Teng Hiua's Fifteenth Army had no such support for its attack but could count upon 3,000 guerillas under Feng Pai-chou who had lived in the island's mountainous interior for 15 years. Two attempts at amphibious assault in mid March and mid April proved bloody failures with only 3,000 men reaching the island to join Feng in the mountains. He saved the situation by attacking the demoralised garrison which was hastily evacuated by the end of April. Appropriately Feng raised the Red Flag over the capital of Haikou on May Day.

Only the Choushan (or Tinghai) Islands off Hangchou Bay (Hangchou Wan) remained and from there 27 warships and 40 aircraft blockaded Shanghai. Their bases were protected by Shih Chueh's Choushan Defence Command with 15 divisions and 125,000 men. Soon after the fall of Shanghai in 1949 the Communists had probed the islands and during the spring of 1950 they prepared to launch a major assault from Ningpo with five corps and 9,500 vessels. More ominously a Soviet air detachment of some 100 aircraft including a regiment of the latest MiG 15 jet fighters was deployed around Shanghai ostensibly to protect the city from air attack.[15] The Soviets began to harass air traffic around the islands and during April destroyed three aircraft, one falling to the MiGs. With air superiority compromised, Taiwan decided on 10 May to withdraw the Choushan garrison and despatched a convoy of 16 freighters. Amid some confusion the evacuation was successfully completed on 17 May with most of the war material being returned to Taiwan.[16]

The final expulsion of the Nationalists from the mainland probably cost the Communists about 150,000 men to the end of 1949 and some 135,000 the following year but it was a price well worth paying.[17] The succession of failures left Li Tsung-jen a completely defeated man plagued with ulcers and as the enemy closed on Chungking he flew to Hong Kong on 20 November 1949. He remained in the British colony for a fortnight before departing to seek medical treatment in the United States.

Chiang Returns to Power

Meanwhile Chiang Kai-shek, gradually returned to public life. Following the fall of Shanghai, and ever-sensitive to Washington's changes of mood, he visited a number of neighbouring states during the summer of 1949 seeking an alliance of anti-Communist states. One visit, in early August, was to South Korea where he discreetly arranged asylum with President Syngman Rhee in the event of Taiwan being overrun. With Li Tsung-jen's departure, Chiang formally grasped the levers of power although a decent interval elapsed before he resumed the presidency on 1 March 1950 by which time the capital had been transferred to Taipei on Taiwan.[18]

In the United States the frustration and the bewilderment of many Americans at the collapse of an ally expressed itself in the paranoic belief that the failure was due to a conspiracy within the US State Department. The issue was first raised by Hurley in 1945 but it was not until 1949 that the loathsome Senator Joseph McCarthy stumbled upon the issue. His investigation into 'Un-American activities' began a witch-hunt which poisoned Sino-American relations for two decades.

Sino-Soviet relations, on the other hand, naturally warmed, and on 14 February 1950 the two nations signed a Mutual Assistance Treaty by which the Soviet Union agreed to provide economic and military aid.[19] During the first half of 1950 some US$30 million worth of Soviet military equipment was imported and while little appears to have been used during the civil war its appearance seemed to herald the fall of Taiwan. Washington publicly refused to intervene and the extinction of Nationalist China appeared only a matter of time.

8

Full Circle: The Aftermath of the Civil War

THE FALL of Hainan cast a pall over Taiwan and at Pacific air bases the Americans prepared aircraft to evacuate the Generalissimo and his family should the need arise.

Publicly and privately Washington had made it clear it would do nothing to prevent the Communists taking over the island. Nevertheless the strategic importance of the island was formally recognised by the Joint Chiefs of Staff as early as November 1948. In January 1949 the National Security Council considered the question and produced two options; US occupation or support for an island administration which would provide base rights.

The US and Taiwan

With the Cold War entering a glacial era and US resources strained to the limit, the Joint Chiefs of Staff were reluctant to sanction any further unilateral military commitments as they made clear in February and March 1949 to Secretary of Defense James V. Forrestal and the National Security Council. On 22 August 1949, while again conceding the strategic importance of the island, they stated their military value did not justify occupation. A month later, in a politically-inspired move, they even advised the new Secretary of Defense, Louis A. Johnson, it was not worth despatching a military mission.

During the autumn, the collapse of Nationalist power in southern China brought the prospect of a Communist takeover of Taiwan ever nearer and, shortly before the fall of Canton in early October, the Joint Chiefs of Staff proposed economic aid for Taiwan and the re-establishment of the military advisory group which had quit China some nine months earlier. Two months later, on 8 December, Taiwan's relevance to the overall policy of containing Communism was discussed by the National Security Council. Again the Joint Chiefs of Staff endorsed the State Department's policy rejecting the use of US forces to defend the island. But when asked to provide a purely military recommendation, they proposed despatching a fact-finding mission and some military assistance.[1]

The Republicans were already pressing for a more positive US policy towards Taiwan including the use of the navy to defend the island. Anxious to encourage a Sino-Soviet schism and to avoid anything which might compromise such an objective both Acheson and Truman decided in January to define publicly the Administration's policy towards Taiwan. In a press statement on 5 January 1950, Truman repeated that the United States would not become involved in the civil war, that it had no ulterior motives with regard to Taiwan and would not provide the island with military assistance. A week later Acheson sought to underscore this statement when he addressed the National Press Club on 12 January. He placed the blame for the Communist victories entirely upon Chiang and the Kuomintang and defined the United States' essential line of defence as running from the Aleutians, through Japan, the Ryukyus and the Philippines. By deliberately excluding both Korea and Taiwan, as one observer[2] has pointed out, Acheson was giving hostages to fortune.[3]

General Douglas MacArthur, the Supreme Commander for the Allied Powers (SCAP) in Japan and virtual viceroy in that country, did not agree. After the war Japan retained strong links with Taiwan, its former colony, and these ensured MacArthur was well informed about events on the island. This allowed him to press for US commitment to prevent it falling into Communist hands. Discreetly he also provided assistance and in June 1947 had despatched Japanese advisers, one of whom participated in the defence of Chinmen Island (Quemoy). Through them he also maintained contact with Sun Li-jen, the US-trained general who now commanded the army on Taiwan.

The appearance of Soviet jets in Kiangsu, and the subsequent Nationalist evacuation of the Choushan Islands, provided further ammunition in MacArthur's battle to save Taiwan from the Communists. In a memorandum of 29 May he raised the spectre of Soviet aircraft using the island's airfields to neutralise the USA's chain of island bases. The Joint Chiefs of Staff were also growing concerned about such a possibility and now urged action to neutralise Taiwan, while during early June even the US State Department began to review its policy towards the island.

Soviet military assistance effectively ended both the Nationalist naval blockade and their air attacks upon Shanghai and Nanking. Yet it could not help the Communists take Taiwan which was saved by a mixture of foresight and fortune. The foresight was the decision to remove almost all the Chinese Navy's seagoing fleet, including landing craft, to Taiwan early in 1949. Mao discovered that the few warships which had fallen into his hands were in no condition to give battle and that his Soviet allies could not replace them. Nor could they quickly create a new Chinese air force to match the CAF with its first-line strength of 250 aircraft. The Nationalist Army had 31 divisions (280,000 men) whom the mighty PLA was confident it could destroy, if it reached Taiwan. It was still pondering how to pass over the Straits of Taiwan when fortune smiled upon the Nationalists.

The Korean War Breaks Out

On 25 June 1950 four years of bitter feuding on the Korean peninsula came to a head when the Democratic People's Republic invaded the south. This event brought about the change in the international situation which the Nationalists had been anticipating for a year, although it proved too late to save the mainland. Nevertheless, with the Third World War seemingly a heartbeat away, the war in Korea led to a reappraisal of US strategic interests in the Far East and acted as a catalyst in the policy review of Taiwan.

In a statement of 27 June, Truman said the new war raised the menace of wider aggression and that he would not permit the Communists to occupy Taiwan and so threaten peace in the Pacific. He therefore imposed 'neutrality' upon the island and ordered the 7th Fleet both to prevent an attack upon it and to prevent Nationalist air and naval attacks upon the mainland.

The island's future status, he said, would await '. . . the restoration of security in the Pacific. . . .'[4] In protecting Taiwan, therefore, Truman was also restricting the future options of the Nationalist government.

The 7th Fleet, already heavily committed to Korea, had to divert a cruiser and four destroyers to impose the blockade. As reinforcements arrived Task Group 77.3 was created on 1 August based upon a couple of cruisers, four destroyers and an oiler, together with land-based maritime reconnaissance aircraft. The fleet's presence only confirmed the end of the Nationalist blockade which the Soviet presence had broken three months earlier. But it was this presence which led the US to resume military and economic aid to Taiwan in 1950. The following year a US Army mission was established on the island whose air bases were soon used by the US Air Force. When they decided to intervene, neither Truman nor Acheson envisaged any major change in the United States' relationship with Nationalist China. Yet their actions were to guarantee its security for the Generalissimo's lifetime and compromised efforts to seek a rapprochement with Peking.

Taiwan and Korea were also to prove Truman's downfall, the former indirectly and the latter directly. During the early autumn of 1950 the largely-US United Nations' forces defeated the North Koreans and advanced into the Democratic People's Republic. Communist China had not been involved in the Korean War until then, indeed despite commercial agreements there were no formal diplomatic relations between Peking and Pyongyang until August, but this situation was soon to change. The prospect of US troops on the Manchurian border alarmed Peking and when diplomatic action failed to restrain the advance, the PLA was committed.[5]

In the battles which followed, thousands of Chinese prisoners were taken and their repatriation became a major bone of contention between the negotiators seeking to end the war. With the reappearance of the 'Left Tendency' and moves against both rich and middle peasants, many of the prisoners had no desire to return to China and preferred to go to Taiwan. The US was implacably opposed to Communist demands for forcible repatriation and advocated voluntary repatriation instead. The issue is said to have added a year to the war, whose bloody futility was a major issue in Dwight D. Eisenhower's successful presidential campaign during 1952.

Under Eisenhower relations between the United States and Nationalist China became closer with Washington recognising the Republic of China in Taiwan, rather than the People's Republic of China in Peking, as the legitimate government of China. Under the Eisenhower Administration the 7th Fleet abandoned neutrality and began to assume a more supportive role for the forces of Taiwan with whom the United States signed a Mutual Defense Treaty on 2 December 1954. In 1955 the 7th Fleet helped to evacuate the Tachen Islands and on 24 January Eisenhower asked US Congress for emergency powers to permit the use of US forces in protecting both Taiwan and the Pescadores Islands. Throughout the 1950s, hostilities between the two Chinas continued at a low but bloody level, involving raids upon coastal installations, naval skirmishes (which cost each side approximately a dozen ships) and air battles.

The Quemoy Crisis

Mao Tse-tung still sought to settle accounts with Taiwan but even with Soviet aid this was not feasible. In the summer of 1958 Peking decided to remove the irritant of the Nationalist island bases of Chinmen (Quemoy) and Matsu using the threat of Soviet intervention to neutralise the US. In August massive artillery bombardments of both islands began to soften up the defences in anticipation of invasion. The United States promptly deployed land, sea and air forces to Taiwan to display its determination. Washington implied that an invasion would be met with nuclear weapons and it had nuclear-tipped Matador cruise missiles permanently based on the island.

This alarmed the blustering Soviet leader Nikita Khruschev, who was only too aware of his own country's nuclear weakness. Not only did the Soviet Union refuse to provide China with a nuclear shield but also it reneged on an agreement to provide the Chinese with blueprints for a nuclear weapon. The Quemoy Crisis continued for two months but there was only aerial combat and during October the bombardments gradually declined in scale then ceased. Effectively the crisis marked the end of the civil war and the beginning of the split between the Soviet Union and China.

Peking's Isolation

Between 1964 and 1974 tensions between the two nations erupted into border incidents and the Soviet Union increased its Far Eastern garrison to bring the threat of invasion, especially after China exploded its own nuclear weapon in October 1964.[6] By then Peking faced a threat not only from the north but increasingly from the south from a former friend. Peking had quickly recognised Ho Chi-Minh's Communist government in Indochina and in 1953 provided the weapons which helped bring about the victory at Dienbienphu. But the Chinese were Vietnam's traditional enemies and Hanoi turned increasingly towards the Soviets, especially when its ambitions brought it into conflict with the United States in the 1960s.

The use of military force to settle a dispute on the Tibetan border in 1962 alienated India, an early friend, so that as war with the Soviet Union seemed imminent during the late 1960s Peking was isolated internationally. Simultaneously the nation was weakened by the turmoil of the Cultural Revolution which cost many civil war heroes their liberty and three of them, Chen Yi, Ho Lung, and Peng Te-huai, their lives. In its aftermath a fourth, Lin Piao, was killed in mysterious circumstances apparently after plotting a *coup d'etat* against Mao.

Peking's only route from isolationism led to the United States which, under President Richard M. Nixon and Secretary of State Henry Kissinger, now recognised that the bi-polarisation of the post-war world was fragmenting into multiple power groupings of which China was one. From Nixon's visit to Peking in February 1972 relations between the two nations steadily assumed a more formal footing although it was not until after Mao's death (September 1976) that formal diplomatic links were restored on 1 January 1979.

This action ended the diplomatic recognition which Washington had hitherto accorded to the Republic of China and also meant the abrogation of the Mutual Defense Treaty. However, it did not bring about the collapse of the Nationalist regime on the island. This had undergone a renaissance since its arrival in 1949 when the prospect of obliteration had wonderfully concentrated the corporate mind.

The Nationalist Renaissance

After Chen Cheng was appointed governor he instituted a three-stage land reform programme which proved more effective and infinitely less disruptive than the Communists'. In the first stage, rents and interests were reduced in line with existing Kuomintang regulations, regulations the Communists enforced throughout the war against Japan. The second stage, in June 1951, involved selling former Japanese land to establish thousands of new farms while the third stage, launched in January 1953, saw the compulsory sale of all other land to the government which then sold or rented it to farmers.

This last measure, executed with US assistance, not only increased production substantially but also brought prosperity to rural areas. Former landowners usually invested the money they received in commerce and industry which were stimulated by the government five-year plans and US economic assistance. By these means the gross national product rose from US$1.2 billion in 1952 to US$9.39 billion in 1973, further encouraged by the reduction in government expenditure from 63 per cent of GNP in 1955 to 35 per cent in 1985.

Chiang died in April 1975 but he had lived to see Taiwan become a significant economic power capable of existing without US aid. During the 1980s the island began to re-establish circuitous trade links with the mainland and by the end of the decade was exporting billions of dollars worth of goods. Those who had fled the mainland decades earlier were often able to return and visit relatives while Peking began to make encouraging noises about the possibility of reconciliation. With the massacre at Tien-an-Men Square in June 1989, (Tiananmen Square in Pingyin transliteration) these noises have ceased for the time being.

The reforms which brought Taiwan financial prosperity and social stability were authorised by Chiang, but the wonder is that he did not introduce them earlier. He and his circle were fully aware of the corruption and the incompetence of Nationalist China, indeed he publicly acknowledged that these were the prime cause for his defeat. Yet it was only after being defeated on the mainland that he attempted the social and economic reforms which firmly established the Republic of China.

The key to success was the absence of interests on Taiwan which would prevent him enforcing his will. On the mainland, before the Japanese invasion, there was a strong political element within the Kuomintang to press for reform but Chiang knew any attempt to impose his will on distant provinces would lead to exhausting confrontations which might weaken his national authority. After Japan's defeat the politicians had been discredited, while Chiang was too engrossed in the struggle with the Communists to bother with reforms which he appeared to believe were the responsibility of others in the Kuomintang.

For the rural population after 1945 the Nationalists had nothing to offer except exploitation by the 'big trees' and pauperisation through insupportable economic burdens. There appears to have been a growing awareness in both central and provincial government that some policy to improve rural life was essential. But there was no agreement as to the form that policy should take while existing government regulations, which offered a means of generating rural support, were constantly flouted. It was the Communists who filled the vacuum.

Revolutionary War

From them there came no rhetoric of a golden tomorrow, rather there was a golden today. They recognised that the peasants were extremely pragmatic and interested primarily in material benefits. Land reform, the act of rural revolution, brought those benefits and gave those who participated a stake in the new society which the Communists sought to create. Benefits such as agricultural implements might seem paltry but to the peasant family, especially poor peasant families, they were symbols which turned outcasts into people of sustance. They also made them willing to take up arms in the Communist cause or to support it in other ways.

The aim of revolutionary war is to give people a social, economic and political stake in a society which they will then be willing to defend. Mobilising the masses is difficult enough for a politician in peace time but for an insurgent it is both difficult and perilous for it is a two-edged weapon capable of being used as either sword or shield. As a sword, revolutionaries can persuade people to sweep away an established order yet as a shield the established order can, with intelligent execution, turn the masses against revolutionary movements often with dramatic effect. This is important to remember in a world where guerilla warfare, the armed struggle element of people's war, is becoming the prime method of conflict encouraged by the Communist victory in China. The Viet Minh success soon afterwards in Indochina served as further encouragement to revolutionaries and produced a rash of insurgencies in Africa, Latin America as well as in Asia.

The 'European' and 'Asian' models continue to be used, the former in the Americas, the Middle East and in Europe, the latter mainly in Asia while both are found in Africa. The Palestinian Liberation Organisation may be regarded as the most famous contemporary example of the 'European' style of insurgency. Its attempts to establish a military presence in Israel having been thwarted it resorted to terrorist tactics and in 1981–82 attempted to create a conventional military presence in the Lebanon before being driven out in the Israeli attack of 1982. Although the PLO undoubtedly has the support of the overwhelming majority of Palestinians there appears to have been little effort at political organisation within Israel. Deprived of both military and political power the PLO is now dependent upon the uncertain forces of world opinion to achieve its goals.[7]

It is interesting to compare this failure with two contemporary insurgencies which succeeded. In Algeria the FLN based their struggle upon the 'European' model but established an extensive political network. This continued to control the Arab population even when the military structure was shattered making the country ungovernable and forcing the French to withdraw. In Rhodesia/Zimbabwe both models were used; Joshua Nkomo's ZAPU adopted the 'European' approach and made little headway while Robert Mugabe's ZANU were advised by Mozambique rebels to adopt the 'Asian' model. They followed this advice and within six years controlled most of the countryside and were steadily isolating the white-dominated cities.

Counter-insurgency Successes

In the aftermath of the First Indochina War (1945–1954) there was a tremendous surge of interest among military thinkers into guerilla warfare and this led to numerous books and articles. The majority focused upon the tactical features of guerilla warfare and few considered the 'operational' implications of people's war. This is because military society is essentially monastic and, while there is increasing integration into civilian life, their philosophies are frequently contradictory. Military society accepts that civilians are their paymasters but resents their interference in its affairs and traditionally has avoided the civilian prerogatives of political, social and economic affairs. While senior military leaders must act politically to achieve their ends, they avoid social and economic affairs. Yet in facing insurgency, military leaders must take into account these very factors which are as important as political grievances in generating support for the guerilla.

The Philippine leader Ramon Magsaysay recognised this when fighting the Hukbalahap rebels (1946–1954) as did Sir Harold Briggs and Sir Gerald Templer, key figures in shaping the British response during the Malayan Emergency (1948–1960). In Malaya, people's war was turned against the Communists by giving the landless Chinese their own farms, better living conditions and security in protected villages. Above all the people were made to feel they would no longer be neglected and that they were part of the nation. The insurgents did not formally surrender until 1989 but for the last three decades they were impotent and based in a remote part of Thailand. It is no coincidence that the same counter-insurgency techniques were practised successfully in Thailand during the 1980s. Yet when the USA came to consider counter-insurgency concepts for South Vietnam they dismissed the British experience for reasons both irrelevant and inaccurate. It was irrelevant that the Chinese were a minority among the Malays because their numbers were rapidly approaching those of the indigenous inhabitants of peninsula. It was inaccurate to say the concept worked simply because Malaya was a British colony when most of the states were actually protectorates with considerable autonomy in their internal affairs.

The US forces in Vietnam

Consequently US ground forces entered Vietnam in 1965 devoid of a cohesive counter-insurgency doctrine for which they substituted airmobile tactics. This fundamental error was compounded by their refusal to create a unified and integrated command structure with the Vietnamese. The *coup de grace* to

US efforts was the decision to focus the US military effort upon the Communist main force (the Vietnamese equivalent of the PLA's mobile field forces).

The US rationale for this decision is that the war increasingly assumed a conventional aspect during the late 1960s. While this argument has a considerable degree of weight it also displays an ignorance of the differences between conventional war and guerilla war, where military and political activities are closely related. In Vietnam, as in China, Communist military action was designed to support the political infrastructure through which they control the population. Militarily this organisation provided food, finance, recruits, labour, shelter and intelligence as well as providing the Communist forces tactical and 'operational' mobility.[8]

The vital task of destroying the infrastructure was assigned only to the inept attentions of US civilian agencies and the South Vietnamese whose activities may be likened to weeding a garden with a plough. The emphasis was upon the sword rather than the shield and while the Communist organisation was dented there was little attempt to replace it with a friendly one. Above all the military forces failed to provide real security for the villagers, with the conspicuous exception of the United States Marine Corps. The military expression of Communist political control was the harassment of communications and installations by local forces (the equivalent of PLA regional force) together with devastating ambushes, frequently involving fortified villages.

The implications do not appear to have been recognised in senior US military echelons whose decisions created a dichotomy of effort against both the main forces and the infrastructure. The failure to eliminate the infrastructure meant overstretched US units effectively faced a two-front war, against the main forces and their logistics network, when their resources were inadequate for one. The apparent immolation of the Viet Cong infrastructure merely confirmed the opinion that the war had become quasi-conventional and 'possees' of US units continued to strive to catch the 'bad guys'. The main forces, increasingly supplied by the North Vietnamese Army, continued their mission of diverting the enemy army from the population and weakening it while the political web was rewoven. The ultimate objective, achieved after the US withdrawal, was to create a situation in which the enemy army was so over-stretched it could be destroyed in a conventional final phase. The tasks were facilitated by the creation of infrastructures in Laos and Cambodia although these appear to have been purely for logistical support. Nevertheless their existence must have eased considerably Hanoi's burden of maintaining the Ho Chi-minh Trail and building up the main force.[9]

The spectres of Vietnam and Afghanistan continue to haunt armies who ignore the insurgencies which have been defeated in such diverse places as Malaya and Oman. Here were victories torn from the jaws of defeat and they were achieved by using people's war as a shield to protect the government rather than as a sword to destroy it. These are lessons which must be recognised for despite the Kuwait crisis, insurgency is likely to be encountered more frequently if the western world continues to maintain rapid deployment forces.

Their development has been in response to perceptions of a conventional threat but it is far more likely that they will be deployed for counter-insurgency. Most armies have relegated this field to the special forces who provide advisors but this is essentially a tactical solution for an 'operational' problem.

Insurgency and its Problems

It reflects the dichotomy of thought between armed forces and governments on counter-insurgency with the former essentially seeking a military solution while the latter seek a political one. If a rapid deployment force were involved in an insurgency situation it would focus upon destroying the enemy forces and leave the host country to destroy the infrastructure. But unless the host country is willing to concede major political and social reforms it is unlikely to achieve much progress, and the very existence of the insurgency makes such concessions unlikely, as Washington discovered with Chiang Kai-shek. In the 1940s and 1960s Washington discovered that once a major commitment is made it creates a political dilemma. Withdrawal without victory will lose international prestige while the reforms needed to achieve victory may have to be imposed and thereby create resentment which will ultimately compromise the intervention.

In considering their response to insurgency, therefore, foreign governments must first produce an essential package of reforms which will erode popular support for the insurgent. That such foresight has still to be shown was demonstrated by the US response to Colombia's request for aid to fight the Medelin drugs cartel. While willing to provide advisors and equipment to fight the cartel's gangs and destroy their crops Washington has not indicated any willingness to compensate the farmers for the inevitable drop in their living standards which this will produce. Consequently the cartel will continue to receive a considerable degree of public support in what is essentially a people's war scenario, indeed it is no coincidence that drugs and insurgency have become so intermingled in South America and the Middle East.[10]

The importance of the infrastructure created by people's war is highlighted by the increasing sophistication of guerilla weaponry and communications. In Afghanistan the *mujahedeen* used Stinger surface-to-air missiles to protect themselves from air attack, Milan anti-armour missiles to destroy fortifications and hand-held radios to co-ordinate attacks. This will make the traditional counter-insurgency tactics, little more than bandit hunting, increasingly difficult, for the guerilla will be on more equal terms with the government's forces. Here is an added incentive for armies to become more involved in destroying the infrastructure for by this means it is possible also to destroy his capability for transporting and storing sophisticated weaponry.[11]

The Nationalists made no such effort between 1945 and 1949, instead they sent their armies to hunt 'bandits' whose military skills proved far superior to theirs. The Chinese civil war was not the guerilla war of popular imagination, one based upon part-time guerillas. They existed and played a useful role but the decision was forced by a professional military body in the form of the PLA. They fought a war which ultimately developed a conventional aspect but one which was deeply influenced by the tactics and philosophy of guerilla warfare. From first to last it depended upon the infrastructure which the Communist Party created and without people's war the Red Flag would never have flown over China.

Notes

Chapter 1
The Rude Awakening: China 1936–45

1. China's imperial capital, Peking ('Northern Capital') was renamed Peiping ('Northern City') when the Nationalists captured it in 1928. After the Communists captured the city and made it their capital they gave it back its old name (Beijing in Pingyin transliteration) on 27 September 1949.
2. Kataoka, *Resistance and Revolution in China*, p. 1.
3. This caused much confusion during land reform when the Communists attempted to categorise the peasants using Soviet models.
4. During the 18th century in northern China the average family farm was 70–80 *mou* (4.48–5.12 hectacres), a century later 30 *mou* (1.92 hectacres) and by the 1930s only 20 *mou* (1.28 hectacres). Myers, *The Chinese Peasant Economy*, pp. 137–141.
5. The problem with village-level officials was endemic and even affected Communist controlled villages.
6. Levine, *Anvil of Victory* (hereafter Levine) p. 219.
7. The two armies should be strictly called the Eighth Route Corps and the New Fourth Corps but in this case the new army designation is more apt. The official Eighteenth Army (or Group Army) designation for all Communist forces under Nationalist command was not widely used.
8. Levine, p. 30.
9. Crozier, *The Man Who Lost China*, p. 88.
10. The US called this project the Cannon Project after Colonel Andrew Cannon, the C-54 wing commander. The US tactical transport squadrons and the Chinese themselves appear to have flown in a further 30,000 personnel. See Tunner, *Over the Hump* and Chassin, *The Communist Conquest of China* (hereafter Chassin).
11. Tseng Ko-lin subsequently commanded the Third Column and ended the war as deputy political officer of the Sixteenth Army.
12. There were 730,000 Japanese troops north of the Yangtze including 330,000 with 13th Corps in the Yangtze estuary but the number of puppet troops is unclear. Chinese sources variously claim between 350,000 and 650,000 but the latter appears to include airmen, sailors, police and militias. The figure of 275,000 which I have arrived at is based upon wartime intelligence estimates kindly provided by Mr Lee Ness, with allowances for service troops.
13. The IIIrd Amphibious Corps consisted of the 1st and 6th Marine Divisions and the 1st Marine Aircraft Wing with 16 squadrons. Shaw, *The US Marines in North China 1945–1949*.

14. The 1st Marine Division was landed in Hopeh from 30 September with Marine Air Groups (MAG) 12 and 24 while the 6th Marine Division with MAG 25 and 32 went to Tsingtao in Shantung arriving from 9 October. Ibid Shaw.
15. Mukden, the capital of Manchuria, is also known as Shenyang. During the civil war the former name was more commonly used by English-language sources.
16. Its despatch was delayed by the shortage of shipping and by Wedemeyer's insistence upon adequate preparation, including inoculations, and the supply of warm clothing which was flown from Alaska. See also Hooper, Allard and Fitzgerald. *The United States Navy and the Vietnam Conflict: Volume 1*, (hereafter Hooper et. al.) pp. 104–110, 116.
17. The cost to China including the provision of replacements and production losses was estimated by the Americans at US$2 billion, but the actual value of the looted material was equivalent to US$895 million, although the Russians later claimed its real value was US$95 million.

    The Manchuria war booty was required because hopes of looting the industry of fascist Europe was thwarted by western strategic bombing. The sale of destruction made the Russians acutely aware of the impact of air power and led them both to strengthen their air defences and to deny the Americans access to Manchuria. See Levine and Zaloga, *Soviet Air Defence Missiles*.
18. Russian freedom of action may well have been handicapped by Stalin's demobilisation programme for the Red Army. Of the 60 divisions which entered Manchuria in August 1945, Malinovsky appears to have had only half-a-dozen by the New Year of 1946 and none of these were at full strength.
19. In 1935 Great Britain provided 12.65 per cent of China's imports but took 25 per cent of her exports while US figures were 18.96 and 23.71 per cent respectively. In 1946 the United States provided 57 per cent of China's imports compared with 5 per cent for Britain. Although 39 per cent of China's exports were to the United States the British Empire took some 30 per cent, mostly through Hong Kong. *China Year Book 1936* p. 131–2, *China Year Book 1950* p. 502–4.
20. As Pickler (United States Aid to the Chinese Nationalist Air Force 1931–49, p. 293) observes, China actually received only 400 of the 1,149 combat aircraft allocated under Lend-Lease and 31 of these crashed en route. By December 1945 China received US$407 million worth of equipment. Quantities are not available but the scale can be gauged by comparing the wartime allocation and the amount required to equip 39 divisions:

	Guns*	Mortars	Machine-guns*	Rifles	Sub Machine-guns
Lend-Lease	2,529	5,770	25,517	299,711	63,251
39 divisions	1,404	7,722	54,132	214,929	41,145

* Guns include anti-tank guns. Machine-guns in Lend-Lease exclude aircraft and anti-aircraft weapons.
Figures based upon Harry H. Collier *et. al. Organizational Changes in the Chinese Army 1895–1950* and Theodore E. Whiting, *US Army in World War II: Lend-Lease Statistics*.

21. By mid April 1946 the Central Government booty included 291 serviceable aircraft, 383 tanks, 151 armoured vehicles, 12,446 artillery pieces (including

mortars), 29,822 machine-guns, 685,897 rifles and some 150,000 tonnes of ammunition. Hsu Long-hsuen and Chang Ming-kai, *History of the Sino-Japanese War*, p. 569.

22. Hurley returned with Wedemeyer. While in Washington the Ambassador began to hint that ill-health might prevent him returning to China. He proposed Wedemeyer as his replacement.

Chapter 2
A Lifetime of Regret: The Politics of Defeat 1946–49

1. The CC Clique was named after the brothers Chen Li-fu and Chen Kuo-fu who were its leaders. The Chen brothers were adopted as nephews by Chiang Kai-shek after their father, a close friend of the future Generalissimo, was murdered. The strength of the clique lay in its control of the Kuomintang's Organisation Department which controlled appointments.

2. The Military Advisory Group in China, MAGIC, replaced the US Army's China Theater on 2 April 1946. Afterwards Wedemeyer returned home hoping to return as ambassador upon Marshall's recommendation: Wedemeyer, *Wedemeyer Reports!* pp. 364–5.

3. A year earlier a coal shortage hindered the build-up for the Manchurian offensive forcing Stalin to authorise use of emergency stocks. Shtemenko, *The Soviet General Staff* at War, p. 343.

4. The Russians captured 686 tanks, 1,836 guns, 13,099 machine guns, and 700,000 rifles in Manchuria, North Korea and Sakhailan Island. In 1967 they claimed it was all given to the Chinese who admit receiving only 369 tanks, 1,226 guns, 4,836 machine guns, and 300,000 rifles:
Ustinov, *Geschichte des Zweiten Weltkrieges Volume 11* p. 223;
Thornton, *China a Political History*, pp. 220, 251, 467 f/n 105/6;
Wetzell, *From the Jaws of Defeat*, pp. 160–186.

5. Given Chiang Kai-shek's obsession with a man who had defeated the Taiping it is curious that Chiang Kai-shek should select as the capital of Nationalist China the city of Nanking, which was also the Taiping capital. On 5 May 1946 Chiang's government formally returned to the city.

6. Morwood, *Duel for the Middle Kingdom*, p. 341.

7. Mao Tse-tung, *Selected Works (herefter Selected Works) Volume 4*, pp. 89–95 'Smash Chiang Kai-shek's offensive by a war of self defence'.

8. The arms embargo came into effect on 29 July 1946 in the United States and in mid-August in the Pacific. The United Kindom imposed an arms embargo upon China in October 1946 but permitted Hong Kong to be used for European arms shipments. UK Foreign Office files F 494, 1993, 5240, 5278.

9. Included in the war-surplus material agreement, which covered property in China, India and 17 Pacific islands was the sale of small craft, construction and communications equipment, spares and ground support equipment for aircraft all of material benefit to the Nationalist forces. It also covered fixed installations, tools, industrial, electrical and medical equipment. Department of State, *United States Relations with China with Special Reference to the Period 1944–1949* (hereafter China White Paper) pp. 227–8.

10. The Committee met after the Wedemeyer Mission visited China in the summer of 1947. During the meeting the CC Clique insisted upon the banning of the Democratic League, the Kuomintang's main non-Communist opponents. This forced many opposition groups to collaborate with the Communists. Tang Tsou *America's Failure in China* (hereafter Tang), pp. 461–2.

Notes

11. Pickler, *United States Aid to the Chinese Nationalist Air Force 1931–1949* (hereafter Pickler), pp. 349, 377, 388–9.
12. These were post-war prices, the wartime value of the equipment was US$4 billion.
13. The China Aid Act, passed by the US Congress in April 1948, allocated 10 per cent of its economic aid package for agrarian reform. However, it was not until May 1949 that a Joint Commission on Rural Reconstruction for Western China was set up to buy land from the landlords and distribute it to the peasants. Landlords could then invest their money in commerce and industry. The Communist victory curtailed its activities on the mainland but the work continued successfully on Taiwan. Eastman, *Seeds of Destruction*: (hereafter Eastman), p. 84; Melby, *Mandate of Heaven*, p. 255; Tang p. 170.
13. Crozier, *The Man Who Lost China*, pp. 304–5 f/n.
14. The Communists based their classification of rural society upon the economic exploitation of people. Landlords relied upon exploitation for their income and did little or no work while rich peasants worked but received a substantial amount of their income from exploitation. Middle peasants worked their land but were neither exploiters nor exploited, poor peasants owned little land and were exploited by others while workers lived by selling their labour. Pepper, *Civil War in China*, (hereafter Pepper), p. 235.
15. Pepper, p. 209.
16. *Selected Works Volume 4*, pp. 157–176.
17. Chiang, in his speech, used the word withdraw rather than retire.
18. Chen I is transliterated in this way to distinguish him from the Communist general Chen Yi.

Chapter 3
From the Barrel of a Gun: The Armies and the War 1946–49

1. Provincial units were more likely to defect than those of the Central Army, partly because they bore the brunt of demobilisation. This led at least two corps, 38th in Honan and 100th in Kiangsu, to defect in the first half of 1946. The 38th Corps served with distinction as a semi-autonomous element of Liu Po-cheng's command under Chen Keng. Eastman, pp. 164–5; Whitson, *The Chinese High Command* (hereafter Whitson), Chart C.
2. Chao Chia-hsiang, chief of staff of the North East Rebellion Suppression Command quoted by Levine, p. 137.
3. So named after the NRA's military academy which was established in Whampoa, Kwangtung Province. The academy was renamed the Central Military and Political Academy in 1926 and later moved to Nanking. Many of the students distinguish themselves on both sides during the civil war. The Whampoa Clique was itself divided between earlier and later graduates of the academy. See Jordan, *The Northern Expedition*, p. 31 and Liu, *A Military History of Modern China 1924–1949*, pp. 256, 262.
4. Also known as the Central Bureau of Investigation and Statistics.
5. Pepper, p. 47 f/n 8.
6. Whitson, pp. 75–82, 84–85.
7. *Selected Works Volume 2* pp. 83–87, 103–106.
8. Op. cit pp. 136–145.
9. The term 'operational', sometimes called 'grand tactics', refers to military activities at army to army group level. Tactics refers to military activity below this level while strategy is above this level.
10. By contrast the Soviet Union, with a population of 193 million, had some 8

million facing the Germans and Japanese in December 1944 and several million more in the various military districts.

11. *China White Paper*, pp. 313–8.
12. The Soviet observer Vladimirov believed the Eighteenth Army had only 410,000 men in the summer of 1945. The PLA strength figures refer only to the mobile field and the regional forces. The field force element steadily increased over the years from 612,000 in June 1946 to a million a year later, 1.49 million in June 1948 and 2.1 million in February 1949. Gittings, *The Role of the Chinese Army*, pp. 2, 304; Vladimirov, *China's Special Area*, pp. 486–7.
13. B. Crozier, *The Man Who Lost China*, pp. 304–5 f/n.
14. The Northeast Democratic United Army was apparently renamed in the summer of 1946. By the winter of 1946–47 the SHENKANNING and CHINSUI Armies were combined as the Northwest Field Army.
15. They bore a bewildering series of titles in succession. These included general headquarters, commands of the general headquarters army, pacification commands and, in 1948, rebellion suppression commands.
16. To avoid confusion reorganised divisions are referred to in the text as (R) divisions e.g. 54th (R) Division. The term 'formation' used below refers to combinations of reorganised brigades and unreorganised divisions. This paragraph is based upon Collier and Lai's *Organizational Changes in the Chinese Army 1895–1950* (hereafter Collier) and data supplied by Major General Chang Chao-jen, Director of the Military History and Compilation Bureau, Ministry of National Defence, Taiwan.
17. A Chinese division in 1945 was supposed to have 18 doctors and 205 nurses together with a field hospital. In practice the whole army had only 1,922 doctors and 384 nurses together with 13,945 'unqualified medical personnel'. Similarly there were a large number of specialised trades such as farriers and blacksmiths on the establishment which could not be met without draining the entire economy. *China Handbook 1950*, p. 700; Collier pp. 222–240.
18. The need for personal influence within the supply system was not confined to the army. Of the two Chinese fighter groups equipped with the P–51 Mustang fighter, the 3rd Group suffered a 'critical' lack of spares until the summer of 1946 while the 5th Group appeared to have no problems at all: Pickler, pp. 350–1.
19. Calculations based upon incomplete data in Office, Chief of Military History, (US) Department of the Army, *Civil War in China* (hereafter Civil War).
20. Some idea of the amounts of equipment available may be gauged from *Zhongguo Renman Jiefang Zhanzheng Sinian Zhanji* p. 5 which lists the booty taken by the PLA. This included 587 howitzers, 681 field guns. 2,187 mountain guns, 1,305 anti-tank guns, 431 infantry guns, 12,667 mortars, 199,692 machine-guns, 2,992,258 rifles and 120,017 sub machine-guns. In September 1947 the Nationalist Ministry of National Defence reported that between August 1945 and June 1947 it had transferred to second-line units 17,253 machine-guns and 423,422 rifles: Eastman p. 159.
21. Even in the Korean War, which was a conventional struggle, a PLA soldier consumed only 4.5 kg of supplies per day compared with 27 kg for a US soldier. Griffith, *The Chinese People's Liberation Army*, (hereafter Griffith) p. 157.
22. Even when Communist wartime fortunes were at their nadir following the One Hundred Regiments' Offensive they controlled 25 million people.
23. This, and similar casualty figures, is based upon monthly averages of Communist casualties published in *Zhongguo Renmin Jiefang Zhanzheng Sinian Zhanji* p. 6. The figures may only apply to mobile field and regional forces.
24. From the 53rd Regional Regiment under Wang Chih-tao, deputy commander

Notes

of the CHINCHACHI 14th Military Sub-District. Data from Nationalist inquiry into incident.

25. From 1946 the US Marine presence in China was slowly reduced. The 6th Marine Division at Tsingtao was replaced by the 3rd Marine Brigade on 1 April 1946 and this was absorbed by the 4th Marines on 10 June, the same day the IIIrd Amphibious Corps was disbanded. This reduced the strength of the Marines in China to some 24,000. In April 1947 the 1st Marine Air Wing and the 5th Marines departed and the evacuation of Hopeh was completed when the 1st Marine Division command post closed on 21 June. This left only three Marine battalions and two air squadrons under Fleet Marine Force, Western Pacific which was slowly reduced until the last troops, of the 7th Marines, departed in May 1948: Shaw, *The United States Marines in North China 1945–1949* (hereafter Shaw), pp. 8, 10, 14, 16, 21, 22, 24, 25. There was also a significant reduction in the US naval presence off mainland Asia. On 1 January 1947 the 7th Fleet was downgraded to the US Naval Force, Western Pacific, with barely a dozen cruisers and destroyers. Hooper *et. al*, pp. 66, 76, 382.

26. These accounts of the Anping and Hsin Ho attacks are based upon Frank & Shaw's *History of the US Marine Corps Operations in World War II: Volume V, Victory and Occupation* pp. 610–27; Shaw Pg 17, 21–2; Myers, *The Chinese Peasant Economy* (hereafter Myers), Maps 8 and 10. Through the kindness of Mr Danny J. Crawford, head of the Reference Section of the US Marine Corps History and Museums Division I have acquired a copy of the Nationalist Chinese investigation which is full of detail.

27. The CNAC (China National Aviation Corporation) had 41 aircraft (6 DC–4, 17 DC–3, 18 C–46), the CATC (China Air Transport Corporation) had 32 DC–3 and C–46 while CAT (China Air Transport) had 18 C–46 and C–47: Leary, *The Dragon's Wings*, p. 208.

28. The CAF sought to equip its transport squadrons with the larger C–54 Skymaster but the United States refused to supply them, arguing that the twin-engined C–46 and C–47 transports were adequate for China's needs.

29. Based upon Pickler's figures but adding aircraft of Japanese and Soviet origin which remained in first line service in 1945 and 1946.

30. During 1947 the CAF received 60 AT–6 trainers and 150 C–46 transports, (40 transports were transferred to the airlines). The only combat aircraft received were from a consignment of 250 Mosquito FB Mk 26 light bombers purchased in Canada, of which 129 were assembled in China. For the 12 months from September 1948 the CAF received 483 aircraft from the United States of which 318 were transports or trainers: Pickler pp. 385, 403, 407 and personal research.

31. *Selected Works, Volume 4*, pp. 113–114.

32. Griffith, p. 131.

33. *Selected Works, Volume 4*, pp. 157–173.

34. With the end of the US arms embargo substantial quantities of arms and ammunition reached China.

In the summer of 1947 the US Marine Corps 'abandoned' in Hopeh 6,500 tonnes of stores including 1,500 tonnes of small-arms ammunition, 2,800 tonnes of shells and 300 tonnes of mortar bombs.

In June 1947 some 530 tonnes of 7.92 mm ammunition was bought by China while at the end of the year a contract for 1,200 tonnes of 0.50 calibre ammunition was awarded by Nanking to an American company.

France, Belgium and Czechoslovakia also supplied ammunition with Belgian orders being for some 4,000 tonnes of small-arms ammunition.

Under the US$125 million package China was to receive 1,707 machine-guns, 8,793 Browning Automatic Rifles (BAR), 132,851 rifles and 12,975 sub machine-guns together with 41,000 tonnes of ammunition. Based upon *China White Paper* pp. 952–976; UK Foreign Office files F 494, 1993, 5240, 5278.

Chapter 4
Defeat into Victory: Manchuria

1. Rigg, *Red China's Fighting Horde*, (hereafter Rigg) pp. 202–6; Robinson, *A politico-military biography of Lin Piao*, pp. 157–168.
2. Whitson, p. 207.
3. During this battle C–47 transports were used on a large scale as night bombers.
4. However, it was only in 1949 that most Korean regional divisions were transferred across the Yalu to become the 5th, 6th and 7th North Korean Divisions. See also Bermudez, *North Korean Special Forces*, pp. 16–18.
5. Whitson, p. 310.
6. The New 5th, New 6th and 49th Corps each with three divisions. Many of the New 5th Corps were former Manchukuo troops.
7. Chiang had earlier sought the opinion of Tu Yu-ming who appears to have been given a roaming commission to act as the Generalissimo's eyes.
8. Subsequently the corps served with distinction in Korea. See Spurr, *Enter the Dragon: China at War in Korea.*

Chapter 5
From the Mountains to the Sea: Northern China

1. Railways throughout Hopeh suffered constant attack. During 1947, between Peiping and Tientsin alone there were 522 incidents in which 131 kilometres of track were destroyed and 115 bridges were damaged. During the last quarter of 1947 traffic could use the Peiping–Paoting section of the PINGHAN Railway on only 16 days. Myers p. 286.
2. Rigg p. 262.
3. In May he requested, through the Consul-General in Tientsin, 20,000 machine guns and 100,000 rifles from the United Kingdom and from Belgium 6,000 machine guns, 100,000 rifles and 3,000 sub machine-guns. The British refused to break their own arms embargo but the Belgians may have supplied some arms: UK Foreign Office files F8013, F12240/G.
4. To ensure the 'Model Governor' did not consider coming to Fu's aid the First North China Army (Hsu Hsiang-chien) was to stage a diversionary attack upon Taiyuan.
5. First and Third Manchurian Armies, Seventh North China Column.
6. Fourth Manchurian Army and North China regional divisions.
7. Whitson p. 351 indicates it came from Peiping but *Civil War* p. 140 makes clear it was already in Kalgan.
8. Melby, *The Mandate of Heaven*, p. 293.
9. Whitson p. 321 says 130,000 men; if this is true nearly half the garrison consisted of rear area personnel, para-military units and militias.
10. 4th, 8th, 9th and 17th Armies with 25 divisions together with cavalry units.
11. According to Ezpeleta, *Red Shadows over Shanghai*, p. 142.

Notes

Chapter 6
The Killing Ground: Central China

1. Communist sources say 60,000, Civil War says 50,000 but Whitson's figures for the previous year would suggest a realistic figure for field forces and regional troops of 40,000 with 100,000 self defence troops.
2. Figures in Whitson p. 583 n. 82 would suggest 140,000 men but they appear to be based upon establishment tables which Chen could not meet due to equipment shortages. Interestingly Su Yu, Chen's deputy, stated Chen had only 70,000 men in 1946, article in People's Daily 'Liberation of Taiwan in Sight', quoted by Rigg p. 87. The figure may refer only to field force troops.
3. My estimate based upon Communist order of battle (see Note 2). The Nationalists estimated it at 50,000.
4. Su Yu quoted by Whitson p. 233.
5. Figures based upon Whitson p. 583 n. 82. The Nationalists say 150,000 men.
6. In 1940–1941 Wu commanded a large Nationalist force in Shantung which was collaborating either secretly or openly with the Japanese. See Kataoka, *Resistance and Revolution in China*, p. 288.
7. With five brigades and 1st (R) Cavalry Brigade.
8. Command was first offered to Pai Chung-hsi but when he expressed a desire to fight on the Huai the Generalissimo decided to control the battle himself.
9. See Leary, *Perilous Missions*, p. 52 for Tu Yu-ming's Christmas Day message.
10. Between 23 November and 11 January CAT transported 37,136 troops, 135 tonnes of ammunition and 1,501 tonnes of food. Op. cit. pp. 50–53.
11. Whitson, p. 243.

Chapter 7
Collapse in the South 1949–50

1. The move also re-established the Party as the leader of the urban proletariat at a time when restoring and increasing industrial production was regarded as of paramount importance. Pepper p. 379.
2. The US military attaché calculated the Nationalists lost 230,000 rifles between September and November 1948, 100,000 of them American. By January the figure had increased to 400,000. *China White Paper* p. 375.
3. Between September and December 1948, 112 P–47 Thunderbolt fighter bombers were delivered to Taiwan while 53 P–51D Mustangs were delivered to mainland China. Only the 11th Fighter Group, based in Shensi and later Szechwan, used the Thunderbolt. Of the US$125 million; US$60.9 million was spent in 1948, US$55 million in 1949, US$9 million in 1950 and US$1 million in 1951. Tang pp. 393–4, 481; *China White Paper* p. 945.
4. Based on Chinese data the Americans estimated the Nationalists had 315,000 men at the mouth to the Yangtze, 120,000 around Wuhan, 175,000 in Shensi, 120,000 in the north western provinces and up to 150,000 elsewhere. *China White Paper* p. 323.
5. In Kiangsu 12,000 cadres mobilised a million peasants who built 969 bridges and repaired more than 1,600 kilometres of road. Figures quoted by Rigg p. 289.
6. As the British frigate HMS *Amethyst* sailed up the Yangtze to Nanking on the morning of 20 April she came near Chen's headquarters. His suspicious gunners, believing the ship to be hostile, promptly shelled it and inflicted such damage that it had to be run ashore. There it was trapped for several weeks until it escaped on 30 July. Barber, *The Fall of Shanghai*, pp. 84–92, 170–2, 181–4; Chassin, pp. 218–9. See also *Yangtze Incident* by C. Lucas Philips.

7. Keesing's Contemporary Archives pp. 10189–10190. UK Foreign Office Files F 10547, 10769, 108611.
8. On 25 April the UK Defence Chiefs recommended reinforcing the Hong Kong garrison, which had a brigade and one fighter squadron. Within two months the 40th Infantry Division was created and despatched to Hong Kong in July 1949 with two brigades. The 3rd Commando Brigade also reinforced the Hong Kong garrison together with three RAF squadrons and a naval task force.
   The task force proved of great value during the early days of the Korean War when it reinforced the over-stretched US Navy: Field, *History of United States Naval Operations-Korea*, pp. 55–56; UK Foreign Office file F 6218/G; UK War Office file WO 268/289.
9. During the autumn of 1950 the French Army suffered near Cao Bang its worse colonial defeat since the Battle of Quebec in 1759. See Gras, *Histoire de la Guerre d'Indochine* (hereafter Gras), pp. 323–354.
10. Before the arrival of the Chinese Communists on Indochina's borders in November 1949, Ho Chi-minh's contacts with the Chinese had been confined to the Nationalists. From 1943 they encouraged and supported his efforts to overthrow French rule, indeed the forces of Governor Lung Yun of Yunnan sold their own and Japanese weapons to the Viet Minh after occupying Tonkin in September 1945.
   It was not until 2 April 1949 that the Viet Minh and the PLA (presumably guerillas) established contact but relations did not become closer until the end of the year. In late December 1949 a Vietnamese delegation led by Nguyen Dai Chi visited Peking to seek military aid and the following month Vo Nguyen Giap, the Vietnamese military leader, visited Nanning.
   On 18 January 1950, the day Peking formally recognised Ho Chi-minh's Democratic Republic of Vietnam, the two governments signed a commercial and military aid agreement which was to be implemented through an office established in Nanning on 10 February. Between May and September 1950 some 20,000 Viet Minh field force troops were trained by the Chinese who supplied them with 40,000 US and Japanese rifles, 125 machine-guns and 75 mortars. Gras pp. 286–9, 315: Hooper *et. al.* p. 165; Short, *The Origins of the Vietnam War* (hereafter Short), pp. 25–6, 36–7, 44.
11. It is unclear who was the Communist commander in this defeat.
12. Nationalist estimates.
13. The CIA did not become involved in China until July 1949 when it came into contact with Claire L. Chennault founder of both the famed 'Flying Tigers' and China Air Transport (CAT). The Agency saw the airline as a means of supporting anti-Communist resistance in the Far East and in November agreed to subsidise it in return for covert operation support. Nine months later the Agency purchased the airline which was renamed Air America. Leary, *Perilous Missions*, pp. 70–2, 82, 110–2.
14. The Chinese fleet had the following ships, numbers in parenthesis indicate those which went to Taiwan: 7 destroyers (7), 23 frigates and escorts (15), 61 small warships (47), 98 landing craft (34): Gray, *Conway's All the World's Fighting Ships 1947–1982*, Part II, pp. 327–330.
15. One source states the Communist first line air strength was only 9 P–51 fighters, 15 B–25 bombers and 22 C–46 transports: UK Foreign Office file FC 10338/116.
16. Details of the Soviet presence are based upon UK Foreign Office files FC 10338/107, 124, 125 and 132 together with data supplied by Dr Raymond Cheung.

17. Calculations based upon figures in *Zhongguo Renmin Jiefang Zhanzheng Sinian Zhanji* p. 6 and Rigg pp. 273–4.
18. Li Tsung-jen remained in the United States for more than 15 years before making his peace with the Communists and returning to live in Peking.
19. The figure is based upon data in UK Foreign Office file FC 10338/125 which states that by June 1950 the Soviet Union had supplied China with 50 tanks, 135 guns, 55 anti-aircraft guns, 1,000 machine guns and 15,000 rifles. Most of this material appears to have been used to supplement the equipment the PLA took into Korea during the autumn of 1950. Only in the following year were Chinese formations in Korea completely re-equipped with Soviet equipment. Based on UK Foreign Office files FC 10338/125, 10338/94, 99, 102, 106, 107, 109, 116, 124, 125 and 132. Prices are based upon Rigg p. 285 and *China White Paper*, p. 945.

Chapter 8
Full Circle: The Aftermath of the Civil War

1. The deteriorating situation in mainland China led the Pentagon to reverse the policy of reducing US naval strength in the Pacific. As late as the spring of 1949 it was planned during Financial Year 1950 to reduce the Pacific Fleet by 24 ships (including halving the carrier force to two ships) through transfers and decommissioning.

   The first step to reversing this policy was the creation on 1 August 1949 of the 7th Task Fleet which replaced Naval forces, Western Pacific by the end of the month. However, five months elapsed before the new force was upgraded and it was only with the arrival of an aircraft carrier that the task fleet was renamed the 7th Fleet on 11 February 1950. Hooper *et. al.* pp. 156–7, 159, 382.
2. Lowe, *The Origins of the Korean War*, p. 119.
3. While appearing to abandon northeast Asia, Washington was simultaneously becoming more involved in southeast Asia. In October 1949, following the Republican clamour for military aid for Chiang, a sum of US$75 million was allocated for use at the President's discretion 'in the general area of China'. On 28 December 1949 the Joint Chiefs of Staff recommended this sum should be used as part of an integrated programme of military assistance to French Indochina.

   Two days after China recognised Ho Chi-minh's government the Joint Chiefs recommended on 20 February 1950, that US$15 million worth of aid be despatched to assist the failing French. Truman agreed in principle on 10 March and authorised the despatch of aid on 1 May inaugurating the costly, and ultimately futile US involvement in Indochina. For US policy towards Indochina in this period see Short pp. 69, 74–87; Hooper *et. al.* pp. 167, 170–175.
4. Foreign Relations of the United States 1950, *Volume 7*, p. 203.
5. Initially Chen Yi's Ninth and Lin Piao's Thirteenth Armies were committed to Korea. At its height the PLA commitment consisted of 21 corps (39 divisions), two tank divisions, nine artillery divisions and 18 air divisions (leaving four air divisions).

   The Soviet Union equipped these troops together with others in key areas as well as providing 2,400 aircraft to the Chinese. In addition 'several' fighter divisions of Mig–15 fighters and an anti-aircraft corps with three divisions were transferred to Manchuria. Five divisions in the Soviet Union's Maritime Provinces were earmarked for commitment to Korea if the need arose.

Schmid and Berends, Soviet Military Interventions since 1945, p. 76; Tyushkevich, The Soviet Armed Forces: A history of their organisational development, p. 375, Whitson pp. 93–7 and information from Steven J. Zaloga.

6. The Chinese nuclear weapon programme was directed by Nieh Jung-chen.

7. European 'terrorist' organisations such as the Provisional IRA, the Baader–Meinhof Gang, ETA and the Red Brigades have naturally followed the 'European' style of guerilla warfare. None has made a significant attempt to establish political control over those whom it claims to represent and instead they have sought victory by 'armed struggle'.

Occasionally their activities have forced governments to respond with political concessions and in this respect it might be argued their struggle has been justified. But having failed to mobilise popular support and in the absence of a comprehensive political programme the activities of these groups, while occasionally spectacular, must be regarded as exercises in bloody futility. At best they create a temporary impasse but ultimately the political initiative swings against them so that violence becomes an end in itself, further eroding their limited political support.

8. For US post-war anaysis see *Assessing the Vietnam War*, edited by Lloyd J. Matthews and Dale E. Brown, Pergamon-Brassey's, McLean, Virginia, 1987. For an interesting commentary upon the strength of the Viet Cong infrastructure after the 1973 ceasefire see *Vietnam from Ceasefire to Capitulation by* Colonel William E. Le Gros, US Army Center of Military History, Washington DC, 1985 pp. 65–6.

9. An excellent account of US military activity in South Vietnam is Shelby L. Stanton's *The Rise and Fall of an American Army*, Spa Books Ltd, Stevenage, 1989. See also Douglas Pike, *PAVN (People's Army of Vietnam)*, Brassey's Defence Publishers, London, 1986, pp. 45–9, 58–9 (n. 18).

10. For recent commentaries upon US-trained forces in counter-insurgency and for the relationship between insurgency and drugs see International Defense Review's Internal Security and Co-in Supplement No. 1 (May 1990) with articles by Tammy Arbuckle ('US Co-in: El Salvador's bad example') and Victor Dennison ('Dangerous liaisons: Insurgency and drugs').

11. This was written six months before the US General Accounting Office published its report 'US Weapons: The low-intensity threat is not necessarily a low-technology threat', Washington DC, 1990.

Bibliography

In researching this book many books and articles have been consulted. A bibliography is included below but the reader may find it of greater value if the list is broken down into relevant subjects.

The essential reference work for both the civil war and the preceding decades is Fairbank and Feuerwerker's *The Cambridge History of China: Volume 13*. I also found valuable Hsu's *The Rise of Modern China*, which provided a Chinese perspective, and Rodzinski's *A History of China: Volume 2*, the author being a former Polish Ambassador to Peking. A valuable study of political development is Thornton's *China: A Political History*. *The China Year Books* also provide a valuable source of material on many aspects of the conflict and China's external relations.

For Nationalist China from 1937 onwards, I found Botjer's *A Short History of Nationalist China*, Chi's *Nationalist China at War*, Eastman's *Seeds of Destruction* and Morwood's *Duel for the Middle Kingdom* especially valuable. In addition Melby's *The Mandate of Heaven* provides a viewpoint from an American diplomat. For Nationalist China in the Sino-Japanese War I would recommend Hsu and Chang's *History of the Sino-Japanese War*, which is a compendium of the 100-volume official history. However, it should be read with Romanus and Sunderland's *Time Runs Out for CBI*. For an understanding of the rift which grew between the Communists and the Nationalists I believe Jordan's *The Northern Expedition* is essential reading.

The most important account of the rise of the Chinese Communists is to be found in Harrison's *The Long March to Power*. However, the reader will find it worth his or her while also reading Chen's *Making Revolution*, Kataoka's *Resistance and Revolution in China* which describe and analyse the process by which the Communists gained power in northern China. Mao Tse-tung's *Selected Works* are essential reading but should not always be taken at face value. For the Long March and Mao's return to power Salisbury's *The Long March* is unrivalled.

Much valuable data may be found in Boorman's *Biographical Dictionary of Republican China* where the lives of most of the major figures in the civil war are examined. For Chiang Kai-shek I found Crozier's biography, *The Man Who Lost China*, the best work but I have supplemented it with Furuya's *Chiang Kai-shek*. There are numerous biographies of Mao and I have largely relied upon Wilson's *Mao: The People's Emperor*. An excellent biography of Lin Piao during this period is to be found in Robinson's *A politico-military biography of Lin Piao Part 1* and Li Tsung-jen's memoirs are also valuable.

For the social, economic and political background to the civil war Pepper's *Civil War in China* is essential reading while Eastman's book examines various aspects in greater detail. Further details upon China's agricultural problems are in Buck, *Land Utilisation in China*, Huang *The Peasant Economy and Social Change in North*

China and Myers, *The Chinese Peasant Economy* which should be read in conjunction. Huang and Myers also provide data and insight on some aspects of the 'sparrow war'. Nationalist China's financial collapse is documented in Chou's *The Chinese Inflation* and Feuerwerker's *Economic Trends in the Republic of China*. A valuable insight into Communist 'political struggle' at village level is in Hinton's *Fanshen*.

For the Nationalist Army I found Collier and Lai's *Organizational Changes in the Chinese Army* extremely useful while Dorn's jaundiced views in *The Sino-Japanese War* provide some interesting insight. The Communist Army is better documented with the best works being Whitson's *The Chinese Communist High Command*, Griffith's *The Chinese People's Liberation Army* and Rigg's *Red China's Fighting Hordes*. Whitson's book has an invaluable account of operations while Rigg's account examines numerous aspects. It should be noted that he was Assistant Military Attache in Nanking and was captured by the Communists in 1946, but this should not detract from an extremely illuminating work. Valuable data may also be found in Gittings' *The Role of the Chinese Army* and Price's *Cadres, Commanders and Commissars*. For the Chinese Air Force I can recommend Pickler's dissertation *United States Aid to the Chinese Nationalist Air Force*.

Information on military operations is more difficult to come by. The most comprehensive works, apart from Whitson, are Chassin's *The Communist Conquest of China*, Liu's *A Military History of Modern China*, the Office of the Chief of Military History's *Civil War in China* and Whitson *et. al*'s *Military Campaigns in China*. Chassin was a French Air Force general who wrote in the early 1950s and while this account may have been overtaken by subsequent research it remains a valuable account. Liu is disappointing but has some useful data while *Civil War in China*, a translation of a Nationalist official history, is essential reading. Military Campaigns in China provides useful sketches of some of the campaigns. Daniel and Herbig's *Strategic Military Deception. Zhongguo Renmin Jiefang Zhanzheng Sinian Zhanji* provides statistical data on the PLA while Kalyagin's *Along Alien Roads*, although written about the Sino-Japanese War provides background on Chinese logistics.

In studying the Manchuria campaigns, Levine's *Anvil of Victory* and Wetzell's dissertation *From the Jaws of Defeat* are essential reading. Valuable data is provided by *Liaoshen Zhanyi Qin Liji* Zheng Dongguo's *Du Yuming Jianjun*, accounts by Nationalist officers living in Communist China. Facets of the campaign are examined in Rigg's article *Campaign for the Northeast China Railway System* and in Clubb's two articles *Manchuria in the Balance* and *Military Debacle in Manchuria*.

For operations in northern China, Peng Te-huai's *Memoirs of a Chinese Marshal* together with those of Li Tsung-jen are interesting. It is also worth reading about the US Marines in this theatre in Frank and Shaw's *History of the US Marine Corps Operations in World War II – Volume V* and Shaw's *The United States Marines in North China*. There is little on the central China theatre apart from Belden's *China Shakes the World*.

The fighting south of the Yangtze and in the north east has generally been neglected but Leary's two works on air transport, *The Dragon's Wings* and *Perilous Missions* are worth reading. Barber's *The Fall of Shanghai* and Ezpeleta's *Red Shadows Over Shanghai* are interesting. The best accounts, apart from *Civil War in China*, are those by Liu and Li Tsung-jen.

For the diplomatic background and Sino-US together with Sino-Soviet relations there are several excellent works. Sino-US relations are dealt with in great, but not tedious, detail by Borg and Heinrichs in *Uncertain Years*, Stueck's *The Road to Confrontation* and Tang Tsou's *America's Failure in China*. The China White Paper, more properly the *Department of State's United States Relations with China with special reference to the period 1944–1949* is a vast compendium of data and comment which is essential reading. The memoirs of Truman, *Years of Trial and Hope*, and Wedemeyer, *Wedemeyer Reports!* provide personal accounts by decision makers while Beal's *Marshall in China* is a personal account by Marshall's press officer. For the Sino-Soviet relations Garthoff's *Sino-Soviet Military Relations*, essays in Kurt London's *The Soviet Union in World Politics* and Vladimirov's *China's Special Area* are interesting. Schmid and Berends in *Soviet Military Interventions* since 1945 provide some data on the Soviet military presence in Communist China.

A useful general work is Gittings' *The World and China* while for the relationship between the Chinese Civil War and the conflicts in Korea and Indochina the best accounts are Lowe's *The Origins of the Korean War* and Short's *The Origins of the Vietnam War* respectively. Gras' *Histoire de la guerre d'Indochine* is interesting and various American service histories provide useful data.

Reading List

Books

Barber, Noel, *The Fall of Shanghai*, Macmillan London Ltd, London, 1979.

Beal, John Robinson, *Marshall in China*, Doubleday & Company, Garden City, New York, 1970.

Belden, Jack, *China Shakes the World*, Monthly Review Press, New York, 1970.

Bermudez Jr, Joseph S., *North Korean Special Forces*, Jane's Publishing Company, London, 1985.

Beyer, Siegfried and Meister, Jürgen, *Die Marine der Volksrepublik China*, Bernard und Graefe Verlag, Munich, 1982.

Boorman, Howard L. (editor), *Biographical Dictionary of Republican China*, Four volumes, Columbia University Press, New York, 1967.

Borg, Dorothy and Heinrichs, Waldo (editors), *Uncertain Years: Chinese American relations 1947–1950*, Columbia University Press, New York, 1980.

Botjer, George F., *A Short History of Nationalist China 1919–1949*, G. P. Putnam's Sons, New York, 1979.

Buck, John Lossing, *Land Utilisation in China*, The Commercial Press Ltd, Shanghai, 1937.

Chassin, Lionel Max, *The Communist Conquest of China*, Wiedenfeld & Nicolson, London, 1966.

Chen, Yung-fa, *Making Revolution: The Communist Movement in Eastern and Central China 1937–45*, University of California Press, Berkeley, California, 1986.

Chi, Hsi-sheng, *Nationalist China at war: Military defeats and political collapse*, The University of Michigan Press, Ann Arbor, Michigan, 1982.

China Year Book 1936 (edited by H. G. W. Woodhead), The North China Daily News & Herald Ltd, Shanghai, China 1936.

China Year Book 1950, Rockport Press Inc., New York, 1950.

Chou, Shun-hsin, *The Chinese Inflation 1937–1949*, Columbia University Press, New York, 1970.

Collier, Harry H. and Paul Chin-chih Lai (translators), *Organizational Changes in the Chinese Army 1895–1950*, Office of the Military Historian, Taipei, Taiwan, 1968, (Library of Congress Microfilm 51414).

Crozier, Brian (with Eric Chou), *The Man Who Lost China*, Angus & Robertson, London, 1976.

Daniel, Donald C. and Herbig, Katherine L. (editors), *Strategic Military Deception*, Pergamon Press, New York, 1982.

Reading List

Department of State, *United States Relations with China with special reference to the period 1944–49/The China White Paper*, Stanford University Press, Stanford, California, 1967.

Detwiler, Donald S. and Burdick, Charles B. (editors), *War in Asia and the Pacific 1937–1949*, Garland Publishing Inc., New York/London, 1980. Volume 13 includes 'Military Campaigns in China' and 'PLA Unit History'. Volume 14 includes 'Civil War in China'.

Dorn, Frank, *The Sino-Japanese War 1937–1941: From the Marco Polo Bridge to Pearl Harbor*, Macmillan Publishing Co. Inc., New York, 1974.

Eastman, Lloyd E., *Seeds of Destruction: Nationalist China in war and revolution 1937–1949*, Stanford University Press, Stanford, California, 1984.

Ezpeleta, Mariano, *Red Shadows Over Shanghai*, Zita Publishing Company, Quezon City, Philippines, 1972.

Fairbank, John K. and Feuerwerker, Albert, *The Cambridge History of China: Volume 13 – Republican China Part 2*, Cambridge University Press, Cambridge, 1986.

Feuerwerker, Albert, *Economic Trends in the Republic of China 1912–1949*, Center for Chinese Studies, University of Michigan, Ann Arbor, Michigan, 1977.

Field, James A. Jr, *History of United States Naval Operations – Korea*, US Government Printing Office, Washington DC, 1962.

Frank, Benis M. and Shaw, Henry I. Jr, *History of the US Marine Corps Operations in World War II – Volume V Victory and Occupation*, Historical Branch, Headquarters, US Marine Corps, 1968.

Furuya, Keiji (abridged English Edition: Chang Chun-ming), *Chiang Kai-shek: His life and times*, St John's University, New York, 1981.

Garthoff, Raymond L. (editor), *Sino-Soviet Military Relations*, Frederick A. Praeger Publishers, New York, 1966.

Gittings, John, *The Role of the Chinese Army*, Oxford University Press, London, 1967.

Gittings, John, *The World and China 1922–72*, Eyre Methuen, London, 1974.

Gras, General Yves, *Histoire de la guerre d'Indochine*, Librairie Plon, Paris, 1979.

Gray, Randal (editor), *Conway's All the World's Fighting Ships 1947–1982*, Part II, Conway Maritime Press, London, 1983.

Griffith, Samuel B., *The Chinese People's Liberation Army*, McGraw-Hill Book Company, New York, 1967.

Harrison, James Pinckney, *The Long March to Power: A history of the Chinese Communist Party 1921–71*, Praeger Publishers, New York, 1972.

Hinton, William, *Fanshen: A documentary of revolution in a Chinese village*, Penguin Books, London, 1972.

Hooper, Edwin B. and Dean, C. Allard and Oscar, P. Fitzgerald, *The United States Navy and the Vietnam Conflict: Volume 1 – The Setting of the Stage to 1959*, Naval History Division, Department of the Navy, Washington, DC, 1976.

Howe, Jonathan Trumbull, *Multicrises: Sea Power and Global Politics in the Missile Age*, The MIT Press, Cambridge, Massachusetts, 1971.

Huang, Philip, C. C., *The Peasant Economy and Social Change in North China*, Stanford University Press, Stanford, California, 1985.

Hsu, Immanuel C. Y., *The Rise of Modern China*, Oxford University Press, London, 1975.

Hsu Long-hsuen and Chang Ming-kai, *History of the Sino-Japanese War 1937–1945*, Chang Wu Publishing Company, Taipei, Taiwan, 1971.

Jordan, Donald A., *The Northern Expedition: China's National Revolution of 1926–1928*, The University Press of Hawaii, Honolulu, 1976.

Kalyagin, Aleksandr, *Along Alien Roads*, Columbia University Press, New York, 1983.

Kataoka, Tetsuya, *Resistance and Revolution in China: The Communists and the Second United Front*, University of California Press, Berkeley, 1974.

Leary, William M., *The Dragon's Wings: The China National Aviation Corporation and the development of commercial aviation in China*, The University of Georgia Press, Athens, Georgia, 1976.

Leary, William M., *Perilous Missions: Civil Air Transport and CIA covert operations in Asia*, The University of Alabama Press, Alabama, 1984.

Levine, Steven I., *Anvil of Victory: The Communist revolution in Manchuria 1945–1948*, Columbia University Press, New York, 1987.

Liaoshen Zhanyi Qin Liji, Peking, 1985.

Li Tsung-jen and Tong Te-kong, *The Memoirs of Li Tsung-jen*, Westview Press, Boulder, Colorado/William Dawson and Sons Ltd, Folkestone, England, 1979.

Liu, F. F., *A Military History of Modern China 1924–1949*, Princeton University Press, Princeton, New Jersey, 1956.

London, Kurt (editor), *The Soviet Union in World Politics*, Westview Press, Boulder, Colorado/Croom Helm, London, England, 1980. Articles: 'The Soviet Union and East Asia' by Harold C. Hinton pp. 146 *et. al.* 'The Soviet Union and the Rules of the International Game' by Adam B. Ulam pp. 37 *et. al.*

Lowe, Peter, *The Origins of the Korean War*, Longman, London, 1986.

Mao Tse-tung, *Selected Works*, Foreign Language Press, Peking, 1967.

Melby, John F., *The Mandate of Heaven: Record of a civil war*, Chatto & Windus, London, 1969 (University of Toronto Press, 1968).

Morwood, William, *Duel for the Middle Kingdom: The struggle between Chiang Kai-shek and Mao Tse-tung for control of China*, Everest House, New York, 1982.

Myers, Ramon H., *The Chinese peasant economy: Agricultural development of Hopeh and Shantung 1890–1949*, Harvard University Press, Cambridge, Massachusetts, 1970.

Office, Chief of Military History, (US), Department of the Army, *Civil War in China*, Library of Congress Photoduplication Service, (Microfilm 51461).

Peng, Dehuai (translated by Zheng Longpu), *Memoirs of a Chinese Marshal*, Foreign Languages Press, Beijing, 1984.

Pepper, Suzanne, *Civil War in China: The political struggle, 1945–1949*, University of California Press, Berkeley, Los Angeles, 1978.

Price, Jane L., *Cadres, Commanders and Commissars: The training of the Chinese Communist leadership 1920–1945*, Westview Press, Boulder, Colorado/William Dawson & Sons Ltd, Folkestone, England, 1976.

Rigg, Lieutenant-Colonel Robert B., *Red China's Fighting Hordes*, The Military Service Publishing Company, Harrisburg, Penn, 1951, Greenwood Press Publishers, Westport, Conn., 1971 (reprint).

Robinson, Thomas W., *A politico-military biography of Lin Piao Part 1 1907–1949*, US Air Force Project Rand, Santa Monica, California, 1971.

Rodzinski, Witold, *A History of China Volume 2*, Pergamon Press, Oxford, 1983.

Romanus, Charles F. and Sunderland, Riley, *Time Runs Out For CBI*, Office of the Chief of Military History, Department of the Army, Washington DC, 1959.

Salisbury, Harrison E., *The Long March: The untold story*, Pan Books, London, 1985.

Schmid, Alex P. and Berends, Ellen (editors), *Soviet Military Interventions since 1945*, Transaction Books, New Brunswick, New Jersey/Oxford, England, 1985.

Shaw Jr, Henry I., *The United States Marines in North China 1945–1949*, Historical Branch, G3 Division, Headquarters, US Marine Corps, Washington DC, 1968.

Short, Anthony, *The origins of the Vietnam War*, Longman, London, 1989.

Shtemenko, General S. M., *The Soviet General Staff at War*, Progress Publishers, Moscow, 1970.

Reading List

Spurr, Russell, *Enter the Dragon: China at War in Korea*, Sidgwick & Jackson, London, 1989.

Stueck, William Whitney Jr, *The Road to Confrontation: American policy toward China and Korea 1947–1950*, Chapel Hill, 1981.

Tang Tsou, *America's Failure in China 1941–50*, The University of Chicago Press, Chicago, 1963.

Thornton, Richard C., *China: A Political History*, Westview Press, Boulder, Colorado, 1982.

Topping, Seymour, *Journey between two Chinas*, New York, 1972.

Truman, Harry S., *Years of Trial and Hope*, Doubleday, Garden City, New York, 1956.

Tunner, Lieutenant-General William H., *Over The Hump*, Office of Air Force History, United States Air Force, Washington DC, 1985.

Tyushkevich, S. A. (chief author), *The Soviet Armed Forces: A history of their organisational development*, US Government Printing Office, Washington DC, 1978.

Ustinov, D. F. (head of editorial board), *Geschichte des Zweiten Weltkrieges*, Volume 11, Militarverlag der Deutschen Demokratischen Republik, Berlin, 1980.

Vladimirov, P. P., *China's Special Area 1942–1945*, Allied Publishers Private Ltd, Bombay, India, 1974.

Wedemeyer, General Albert C., *Wedemeyer Reports!*, Henry Holt and Company, New York, 1958.

Whiting, Theodore E. (*et. al.*), *US Army in World War II: Lend-Lease Statistics*, Office of Military History, Washington DC, 1952.

Whitson, William W. (with Huang Chen-hsia), *The Chinese High Command: A history of Communist military politics 1927–1971*, Praeger Publishers Inc., New York/The Macmillan Press Ltd., London, 1973.

Whitson, William W., Patrick Yang, Paul Lai (translators), *Military Campaigns in China 1924–1950*, Military History Office, MAAG, China, Taipei, Taiwan, 1966, (Library of Congress Microfilm 51417).

Wilkinson, David, *Revolutionary Civil War: the elements of victory and defeat*, Page-Ficklin Publications, Palo Alto, California, 1975.

Wilson, Dick, *Mao: The People's Emperor*, Future Publications Ltd, London, 1980.

Zaloga, Steven J., *Soviet Air Defence Missiles: Design, Development, Tactics*, Jane's Information Group, Coulsdon, 1989.

Zheng, Dongguo, *Du Yuming Jiangjun*, Peking, 1986.

Zhongguo Renmin Jiefang Zhanzheng Sinian Zhanji, *General Headquarters*, Peking, 1950.

Articles and Dissertations

Clubb, Edmund O., 'Manchuria in the Balance 1945–1946', *Pacific Historical Review* (November 1957), 26(4): pp. 377–389.

Clubb, Edmund O., 'Military Debacle in Manchuria', *Army Quarterly and Defence Journal* (January 1958), 75(2) pp. 221–232.

Pickler, Gordon K., 'United States Aid to the Chinese Nationalist Air Force 1931–1949', PhD dissertation, Florida State University, 1971. University Microfilms Ltd, High Wycombe, England, 1975.

Rigg, Robert B., *Campaign for the Northeast China Railway System*, Military Review (December 1947), 27(9): pp. 27–34.

Urken, Arnold B., PhD dissertation: 'Coalitions in the Chinese Civil War', New York University, 1973.

Wetzell, Caroll R. Jr, PhD dissertation: 'From the Jaws of defeat: Lin Piao and the Fourth Field Army in Manchuria', George Washington University, 1972.

Index

For convenience the words China, Communist and Nationalist have been excluded from this index as they appear throughout the book. Chinese place names are given with their province except for Manchuria where the confusion between Communist and Nationalist provincial boundaries and names makes this impractical. Personal names include original affiliation: Comm for Communist and Nat for Nationalist.

Index

Index

Index

Index